ALL THE DREAMS WE'VE DREAMED

A Story of Hoops and Handguns
on Chicago's West Side

RUS BRADBURD

Lawrence Hill Books

Chicago

Copyright © 2018 by Rus Bradburd
All rights reserved
First edition
Published by Lawrence Hill Books
An imprint of Chicago Review Press Incorporated
814 North Franklin Street
Chicago, Illinois 60610
ISBN 978-1-61373-931-0

Library of Congress Cataloging-in-Publication Data
Is available from the Library of Congress.

Typesetting: Nord Compo

Printed in the United States of America
5 4 3 2 1

for Frinda, Naja, and Malia Harrington

for Luther Bedford and Dorothy Gaters

... For all the dreams we've dreamed
And all the songs we've sung
And all the hopes we've held
And all the flags we've hung,
The millions who have nothing for our pay—
Except the dream that's almost dead today ...

—From "Let America Be America Again,"
Langston Hughes

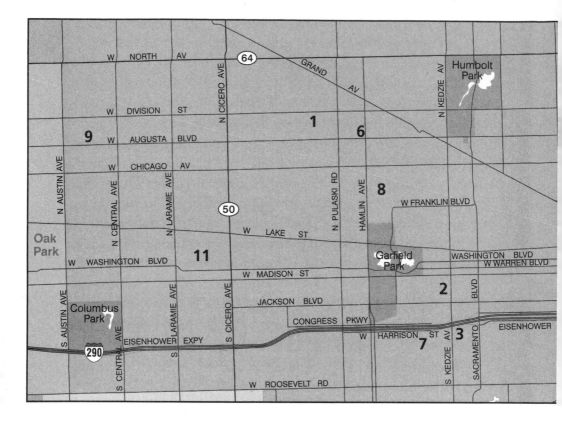

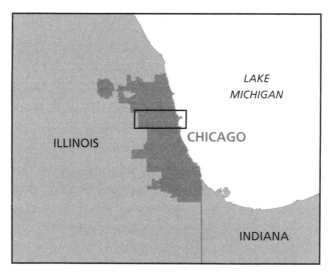

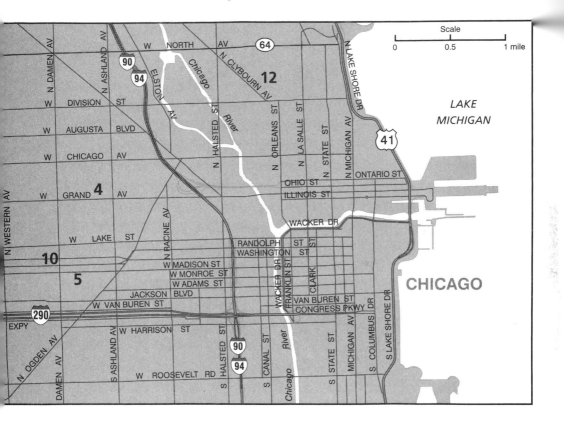

1. Shawn Harrington childhood home, 1135 N. Kedvale
2. Marshall High School, 3250 W. Adams (at Kedzie)
3. Chicago Police Deparment, 3151 W. Harrison
4. Chicago Public School Athletic Administration, 536 N. Hermitage
5. United Center (Chicago Bulls arena), 1901 W. Madison
6. Shawn Harrington shot, Augusta and Hamlin
7. Tim Triplett murder site, 3400 W. Flournoy
8. Martin Satterfield shot, Ohio & Ridgeway
9. Marcus Patrick murder site, 5800 W. Augusta
10. Shawn Holloway murder site, 2100 W. Warren
11. Keyon Boyd murder site, 100 N. LaPorte
12. Edward (and Edwin) Bryant murder site, 1300 N. Hudson

1

SHAWN HARRINGTON couldn't find his car.

After a decade at Marshall High School on Chicago's West Side—as a student, teacher's aide, and basketball coach—he had spent enough time in every corridor and classroom that his memory sometimes blurred. On the morning of January 14, 2014, he had hustled up three flights of stairs to keep from being late and tossed his coat onto the back of a chair in the special ed office. Now, after practice, he wondered if he misremembered parking behind the school.

Shawn was the varsity assistant under a man named Henry Cotton. Younger looking than his thirty-eight years, Shawn enjoyed an enviable level of trust and communication with students and players. He was open, friendly, and he knew when to joke and when to back off. He had overcome so much in his personal life that he was empathetic and compassionate about the struggles typical to Marshall kids.

Shawn checked on Adams Street, but his 2001 Expedition wasn't there, either. He cursed under his breath. The Eddie Bauer edition Ford SUV was his first decent car, a distinct two-toned job, light blue with a tan stripe. He had bought it used in 2012 for $3,500, a birthday present to himself. The car was functional, noticeable but not flashy, and he could fit seven Marshall players inside, eight in a pinch. It wasn't paid off yet, but it was insured. Or was it? An anxious moment passed as he tried to remember if his insurance was up to date.

Prior to the purchase, his travel routine was a taxi to Marshall, then the Green Line "L" train or CTA bus home. That simple travel schedule used to cost him about sixty dollars a week. He didn't relish even a temporary return to public transportation, although it was cheaper than the combination of car payments, insurance, city sticker, and gasoline.

The car, however modest, was a sign that this kid from the neighborhood had made good. Besides that, the car was crucial. It allowed him to drive his oldest daughter to school every day, and it served as a sort of rolling counselor's office for the players he drove home after practice each night.

Where had he left it? Rather than ponder his dilemma in the winter chill, he went back inside to the main office. Not until he jiggled his coat pocket did he connect the dots: his car was gone, and so was his second set of keys. On the coldest days, Shawn brought two sets. He would fire up his car after practice, lock up with the second set of keys, and run back inside to see which players needed a lift.

"Somebody stole my car," Shawn told security guard Tyrone Hayes outside the main office.

Hayes greeted kids coming into school, checked IDs as they marched through the metal detector, and made sure the students were in their required uniforms. He had held his job for thirteen years, spent time as a coach, and, like Shawn, been a terrific player for Marshall. On patrol in the hallways much of the day, he kept an ear to the ground. Sympathetic about the car, he figured Shawn didn't need him, so he punched out to go home.

In the main office, Shawn found himself on hold with the police department's nonemergency number. Somebody stole his car right off Marshall property? He couldn't believe his bad luck.

Minutes later his cell phone buzzed. It was Hayes. "What's your license plate number?" he asked.

Shawn hung up on the police and rattled the number off.

"I'm behind your car now," Hayes said. Driving north on Kedzie Avenue, he had noticed the Expedition parked facing south and swung a quick U-turn. In Shawn's car were two brothers known to school authorities as "the Twins." One sat behind the steering wheel, the other rode shotgun. The identical sixteen-year-old freshmen at Marshall already had a history of trouble and arrests.

The twins recognized Hayes and the Expedition bolted back onto Kedzie, heading south. After a few minutes on their tail, all the while giving Shawn the play-by-play, Hayes again pulled next to the car, honked, and rolled down his window. "Yup, it's the twins for sure," he yelled into his phone. "Two more knuckleheads are in back."

Hayes moved slowly alongside, nearing a stoplight, waving and pointing. Pull over! He didn't want an angry confrontation—who knew what the boys carried in the car with them?—although he figured it would not come to that. Hayes believed the twins understood he was a peacemaker, a compromiser, even if he ruined their joyride.

They took off again. Hayes continued to tail the SUV, winding down side streets. Soon the boys were sailing through stop signs and roaring through red lights. Hayes followed suit until they busted out of an alley onto a crowded street. He halted rather than risk an accident. He had kept Shawn on the phone the entire time. "I lost them," Hayes said.

"I'll just call the cops again," Shawn said. "At least we know who did it."

Hayes said, "We'll get the car back when we see the twins at school."

The next morning, Shawn shared a taxi with his eldest daughter, Naja, whom he dropped off at Westinghouse College Prep, less than a mile from Marshall. Naja aspired to have the highest grade point average in her sophomore class and she hated to be even one minute late.

Back at Marshall, Shawn waited, seething, by the metal detectors with Hayes until the late bell rang. No twins. He trudged upstairs.

Shawn worked as an ESP (educational support personnel) in special education. He had earned his college degree in communications, but he did not have a teaching certificate. ESP workers make about $32,000 a year and are not part of the powerful Chicago Teachers Union. It's not a bad job—the nine-month schedule gave him plenty of time in the summer to be with Naja and Malia, who was eight.

The Marshall building, well over a hundred years old, didn't have an elevator, but he liked the intense forty-second leg workout hoofing up to the third floor. He'd climb those stairs as many as a dozen times daily. On this day it seemed a long way to the top.

For three days Shawn took a taxi to work, with no clue as to his car's whereabouts. Finally, on Friday morning he got a call from the main office. Tyrone Hayes had nabbed one of the twins.

State Farm would reimburse Shawn the entire cost even if the vehicle were never recovered, so why was he so angry bouncing back down the stairs? He calmed himself as he approached the office. One deep breath, then another, the way he'd always done before sinking an important free throw. It was just a stolen car.

Hayes couldn't get over the theft, either. Ballers and coaches had often enjoyed a protected social status in the neighborhood. "I bet the good twin might show us where they dumped the car," he said quietly to Shawn before they went inside the office. Hayes thought of the pair as "good twin" and "bad twin." One instigated the trouble and the other would get dragged along. Hayes believed that was how the theft had gone down—and that dynamic would now help authorities recover Shawn's car. The good twin had already fathered a child and was a little less inclined toward mischief.

In the main office, a policeman, a detective, and two school administrators had the good twin cornered. Sure enough, the boy quickly came clean. Sure, he went along for the ride, but he denied stealing the car. "You're not talking about me," he said, "that's my brother, and I always get the blame. I wasn't the driver." He admitted they dumped the car very close to Westinghouse, less than a mile away.

Shawn's palms got sweaty at the mention of Westinghouse. He knew enough not to blurt out anything about driving Naja there every day. Protective of his children, the last thing Shawn wanted was this trouble-maker to know he had a daughter the same age.

An administrator, two policemen, and Shawn drove the good twin toward Westinghouse. It turned out the car hadn't exactly been "dumped." It was parked perfectly at the corner of Franklin and St. Louis, ready to be fired up for the next joyride. The twins had somehow disabled the theft prevention chip, so Shawn's set of keys no longer worked. Only the thieves could restart the vehicle. The good twin insisted he did not know who had kept Shawn's swiped set of keys. The police didn't buy the boy's story, or at least not his claims of innocence. They took him away in handcuffs.

Shawn called State Farm again, this time to get the Expedition towed. The agent reminded him that his policy included the use of a rental car from Hertz, so at least there was that good news. He could return to his routine of driving Naja to school and his players home after practice.

That afternoon, Shawn learned from his students how easily his keys had been lifted. Special ed shared an office with nursing and psychology, so a stream of foot traffic passed through. He remembered now: he had carelessly flipped his coat over an office chair, leaving it exposed to dozens of kids each time the bell rang.

The bad twin had even bragged about having a car to goof around in after school. He'd had the nerve to take Shawn's keys to the third floor window and hit the panic button. When he figured out which one had lights flashing below, he must have memorized the parking spot and quickly shut the alarm off. Although some students saw this happen from their seats, they assured Shawn they'd had no way of knowing it was his car down below.

A week after the theft, Shawn got a ride to the Hertz rental car office on Western Avenue, less than a mile from Marshall. He was disappointed to learn Hertz couldn't loan him an SUV, or anything else that might carry half the varsity basketball squad. Instead, the clerk walked him out to a white sedan. But then Shawn couldn't believe his luck—it hadn't occurred to him that he'd get a nearly new model. He would manage with the four-door SS Impala, a standard and nondescript car.

It had been a hard winter for Shawn. The combination of special ed duties and basketball practice often left him exhausted. The timing of the car theft was the worst part—in mid-January, when Marshall had lost three games in a row (not counting a forfeit win).

The Marshall team, a city powerhouse, was struggling uncharacteristically, with a record of 5-7 midway through the season. Shawn knew their fortunes were about to change, though, because three days earlier, Tim Triplett had finally been declared eligible. Triplett chipped in nine points his first game, a few days before the car was stolen, but that close loss was a small pothole. Shawn believed Triplett would get the team straightened out.

Their new senior guard was quick off the dribble, feisty, strong with the ball, and a natural leader—like Shawn had been in his playing days. Triplett wasn't Marshall's point guard in the sense that he always dribbled the ball up the court, but he was clearly in charge, and that began with him directing the team with his voice. Shawn had also been a fearless point guard, a crafty ball-handler, a leader—although not nearly as loud or brash. Triplett, Shawn figured, was precisely what the team needed, and although he stood just five foot nine, his swagger and confidence was highly valued in Marshall's rugged Red West conference.

Like any coach who'd played in college, Shawn was constantly analyzing their new star's potential. Triplett was small, but could he still play at the next level? No doubt. At a big state school? Maybe. Just maybe, after attending junior college, as Shawn himself had done when his ACT test score came up one point short.

Triplett was a double transfer: he left Crane High School near the end of his junior year, finished the semester at Farragut, then transferred again to Marshall to start his senior year. He told everyone he left Crane because his coach took another job. Besides, Crane had been designated as a failing "turnaround" school. He'd left Farragut, he said, because he had gotten in a fight.

Transfers are disturbingly common for players in Chicago's Public League, but Triplett's ineligible status for the first half of the season was a bit of a mystery with West Side coaches and players. He missed Marshall's first dozen games, while his new coaches had tried to keep him focused on bursting out of the gates when his eligibility was finally approved.

On the surface, sitting out the first half of the season barely deterred Triplett. With a charisma that even the Marshall seniors had to respect, he helped direct the team during timeouts and halftime still in his street clothes.

Gossip usually got back to Shawn, partly because Marshall was so small these days. Its enrollment had plummeted to just over four hundred total students. Lately he'd heard talk in the hallways and lunchroom where kids and teachers mixed freely that occasionally Triplett's boisterous personality rubbed people the wrong way. That was surprising.

Assistant coach Shawn Harrington (left) watches the Marshall Commandos with head coach Henry Cotton. *Worsom Robinson*

With the coaches, he was nothing but respectful, and he seemed to have always been a Marshall player.

A coach isn't supposed to have a favorite player, especially a first-year guy, yet it was nearly impossible not to be taken with Triplett. It was just a coincidence that Triplett wore number 23, as Shawn had worn at Marshall in the early 1990s. Shawn did not realize how much more history they had in common.

———————

In the fall of 2013, all predictors pointed to another typical Marshall team: small, quick, overachievers. The center for the Marshall Commandos would be the six foot four, lanky, dreadlocked James King. Their best returning player was six foot two Citron Miller.

Because the new kid, Tim Triplett, was practicing with them from day one, nobody realized what became obvious once the games began *without* their new transfer in uniform: the team lacked the heart and arrogance it took to win on Chicago's West Side. Shawn had been grooming Triplett to fit into the Marshall system, showing him the fine points of the offense, when to be careful of over dribbling, reminding him of the rotations on their presses. In some regards, this fine-tuning was secondary. "His point guard skills, we already had that," Shawn says. "What we were waiting on, what we needed, was Triplett's point guard *attitude,* his vocal leadership."

The Commandos, like anyone Triplett interacted with, became hyper aware of his voice. Because of this, Shawn worried Triplett might clash with Citron Miller, who was also a big talker. Miller was the team's most skilled and versatile player, and he began the season with major expectations—this was supposed to be his team, his year to shine. Nobody could deny that Triplett added something fresh, but the coaches were concerned that there might not be enough shots to keep everyone happy.

Having two different voices on the court and locker room, Miller admits, could have been touchy. "Tim had been such a strong leader at Crane," he says, "but we set all that aside. I still got my points, but Tim, he was all heart, the motor person. He brought fire to the game."

Splicing in a transfer can be problematic even for a quiet kid, particularly in a program with a complex defensive scheme. Marshall's gambling strategy usually meant pressing and harassing their opponent the entire length of the court, often doubling teaming, or "trapping" the ball. But Triplett's ability to switch allegiances and fit in quickly had more to do with his mindset than his skills.

"From the first day of practice in the fall," Shawn says, "I was thinking about Tim Triplett's future," meaning much further down the line than his high school or possible college basketball career. Past the inevitable end of Triplett's playing days. Past the all-too-common illusion of an NBA career. "I believed from the start that Triplett could be a coach someday," Shawn adds. "The kid was a pure leader with just the right amount of fearlessness."

Shawn preferred players who needed to be calmed down, not ratcheted up, and Triplett's engine ran in overdrive. Shawn might need to whisper to Triplett to relax, settle down, but that was preferable to having to motivate a timid kid. Triplett's hyperaggressive instincts made him a natural fit for Marshall's traps, but sometimes it could get him into

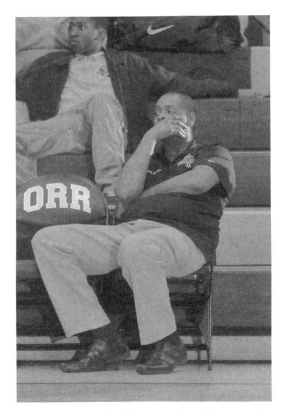

Tim Triplett, awaiting approval of his own eligibility, watches Marshall struggle while sitting behind head coach Henry Cotton. *Worsom Robinson*

trouble, leave him vulnerable. In some fundamental way the headstrong guard was already beyond the coaches' control.

This mentality would be on full display in the first conference matchup Triplett would play—or that's what the coaches hoped. Triplett had already sat out a total of eleven games when he took the court for the first time on January 11, 2014, a close nonconference loss to East Chicago High School of Indiana, but the score and Triplett's obvious impact was seen as a good sign.

Then Shawn's car was stolen on January 14, just a few days before their next game, against conference rival Farragut, the school Triplett had briefly attended, and everyone anticipated a rush of adrenalin on both sides with plenty to prove. The Commandos were now trying to turn around a three-game losing streak. Nobody at Marshall was concerned about getting their new player motivated, though, because Triplett took things to an extreme. "Triplett wore whatever uniform he wore with pride," Tyrone Hayes says. "It was as if he was claiming *This is my team!* And if Triplett played against you, he'd feel the same way once the game was over. *You don't play with me, ain't no love for you.* That's the way he would act."

Might this all mean there would be trouble with Farragut on the court? It could have. But Triplett did not compete: he had yet to be certified eligible for Public League play. An Indiana school had no idea about the Commando roster, but Farragut's coach certainly would. However, even with Triplett on the bench, Marshall won convincingly, 76–65. Despite Triplett being yo-yoed around, Shawn was in good spirits after that game and didn't even mind not having the Expedition for the players to pile into.

The good feeling carried over into the next matchup on January 18, as Marshall beat nonconference North Chicago in a close contest in the Martin Luther King Tournament. Triplett, who'd taken to wearing a conspicuous white headband, only had two points, but he quickly established himself as the best defender on the court, recording a half-dozen steals to go with as many assists. The locker room was abuzz after that one—they'd gotten the team turned around.

Two days later, the Commandos hammered Indiana school Gary Westside by twenty-five points, with Triplett scoring ten. They were ready to live up to the Marshall legacy. Coach Henry Cotton recalls the new Marshall guard was flying by this time. "We just had to put Triplett in the right spot, and he'd watch and learn fast. He knew what every guy was supposed to be doing." Naturally, Triplett didn't hesitate to share that knowledge.

It was freezing outside, but the team seemed immune, as if the exhilarating buzz from the modest three-game winning streak insulated them. Colder weather, an "arctic blast," had been forecast for the following week, which prompted Shawn to quit procrastinating. He got a lift the next day from Tyrone Hayes to the nearby Hertz dealership, and he drove off in the nondescript white Chevy Impala.

Tim Triplett leads the Commandos onto the court where Marshall built an impressive legacy. *Worsom Robinson*

Shawn and his fifteen-year-old daughter had plenty to talk about on their January 22 morning commute. Westinghouse High School, where Naja had earned a spot on the frosh-soph cheerleading squad, was Marshall's opponent that afternoon, and she'd be on the sideline for the rematch. Plenty of good-natured teasing went down between father and daughter. "We beat you last game," she reminded him for the fourth time before she jumped out.

Temperatures had indeed dropped, and Shawn didn't mind his daughter diverting his attention from the cold, even when she stood with the car door open and leaned her head in, bracing herself with her left hand against the headrest. Her tone changed this time: "See you after school, Daddy."

Yes, Westinghouse had won before Christmas, but Shawn figured it would be different this time, and he was correct: Marshall won, 64–58. But Westinghouse was a Red West conference opponent too, and certification from downtown concerning Triplett's eligibility was still not resolved. Westinghouse, like Farragut, would have been hyperaware of his issues and Triplett did not play. It was the thirteenth game he would miss as a senior.

The Commandos now had a four-game winning streak—nothing to brag about, but still a distinct turnaround. They had a chance to extend their winning streak to five when they faced private school Providence-St. Mel on January 26. Triplett's eligibility certification issue was finally resolved. He wouldn't miss another game.

The matchup would be intense partly because Triplett's pal from summer ball, Tevin King (no relation to Marshall's James King), was St. Mel's star guard. Tevin King, a bit over six feet tall, drew the assignment of guarding his friend. He was respectfully cautious, knowing his height advantage could be neutralized by Triplett's quickness. King had great affection for Triplett. "Tim could be really funny off the court," he says, but on the court that all fell away. "He had the little man syndrome," King says, something that manifested in Triplett's scrappy play and nonstop chatter.

With the score tied in the fourth quarter and emotions running high, Triplett stole the ball and had a breakaway layup. But King chased him down and soared to block Triplett's shot at the last instant. The play was a shocker—an easy basket denied and Marshall's good fortune dramatically erased. The crowd erupted, momentum shifted, and St. Mel won 64–61.

Despite his eligibility issues and the seemingly endless paperwork from downtown, the Marshall coaches were more than happy with their new player. Triplett never missed a practice, was never even late. This is unusual, considering most Chicago Public League teams practice or play six to seven days a week once the season is underway and many players have problematic home lives. "Triplett would have *kept* practicing, too," Cotton says, "until he was made to stop and we had to lock up."

One day at Marshall in the middle of a class period, while Cotton was just outside the main office on his security patrol, Triplett sprinted up. "Coach!" he gasped between breaths, "we've got a fight—broke out—in our classroom!"

Cotton and Triplett hustled upstairs, where the pugilists were separated. Triplett's actions impressed the coach. "Tim was often the peacemaker," Cotton says.

———————

Marshall played Whitney Young High School on January 29. A selective enrollment magnet school, Whitney Young is an academic bright spot for CPS and often gets held up as a model, as if every Chicago Public League team could produce both a great basketball team and the best ACT scores in the entire state.

This was the first Red West opponent that Tim Triplett faced, but Whitney Young was so loaded with talent that they were hardly bothered by the chattering little guard: their center, six foot eleven Jahlil Okafor, would be an NBA star within eighteen months. Triplett scored ten points, but Marshall was badly outsized. (In the first matchup, the Commandos had lost by twenty-seven without Triplett.) Losing 75–57 to a nationally ranked team was no disgrace, and Triplett had made a difference—just not enough.

Their next game at Orr High School was winnable. But Marshall had now lost two in a row.

———————

On January 30, 2014, head coach Henry Cotton arrived at Marshall early to get in his morning walk. It was twenty-three degrees outside, but the windchill made it feel like nine degrees—a day to get his exercise inside. Cotton called Shawn Harrington on his cell phone before the first period bell, as he often did. Shawn was in the rental car, waiting for Naja to come out and begin their morning commute.

Cotton and Shawn typically discussed what needed to be fine-tuned: zone offense, out-of-bounds plays, press breakers, or any problems within the Commandos team. Ten days ago it felt like the cloud hanging over their season had lifted, but last week the losses to St. Mel and Whitney Young set them back again. Shawn told Cotton,

"I'm heading your way now" as Naja appeared with her book bag and climbed in.

Later, after the first bell had rung, Cotton was back walking the hallways, his typical security patrol detail, when he saw the ROTC director weeping. She ran down the hallway and into the faculty washroom. Cotton thought it was odd, but before he could investigate, one of the players was at his side. "When was the last time you talked to Shawn Harrington?" the kid asked.

2

WHITE SEDANS ARE AMONG THE MOST COMMON IN THE CITY, and that was the car Shawn was driving when he picked up Naja from her mother's home on the morning of January 30, 2014. He drove southeast on Grand Avenue, an angle street that cuts off a bit of mileage but is filled with stoplights and is a popular truck route. When traffic bogged down, Shawn cut south down Hamlin, a side street, thinking he'd continue east at Augusta, a residential street at 1000 north. Augusta moves quickly, and this wasn't an unusual detour for Shawn—although he'd never taken this route in the white Impala.

The corner of Hamlin and Augusta has a stoplight, Chicago Police POD (Police Observation Device) cameras, and an unassuming little grocery store, Brothers Food Mart—which also has a security camera—on the northwest corner. Technically on the southwestern edge of Humboldt Park, it is also on the edge of East and West Garfield Park, as well as West Humboldt Park.

Humboldt Park is one of the city's larger neighborhoods, with a makeup of more than 50 percent Hispanic (mostly of Puerto Rican heritage) and 40 percent African American. The eastern side of Humboldt Park borders Wicker Park and Bucktown, two gentrified hipster areas. The western and southern borders of Humboldt Park are poorer, blacker, and more prone to violence.

Shawn and his daughter are both talkers, and they normally chatted away during the morning drive, Naja looking at her father while he kept his eyes on the road. But as they approached the corner of Augusta and Hamlin that morning, there was a long lull in the conversation and, deep in thought, she gazed out the window. That's when she noticed, as their car neared the stoplight, the two young men. One man hurried up ahead to the corner. The other was jogging alongside the car on Naja's side. "We stopped," she says, "they stopped. And I turned and looked at them. They were talking together at one point."

Shawn noticed the young men, too, as he stopped behind a van at the red light. He could see their faces, although both men had their hoodies up. He could not see the dreadlocks under one man's hoodie, or the multiple tattoos both men had on their necks. Any basketball coach can quickly discern height. The guy up ahead was about five foot eleven, and the man who was at the side of their car a bit shorter. The man up ahead looked east and west, up and down Augusta, as though searching for someone. He began pointing aggressively at the white Impala.

Naja turned over her right shoulder and got a quick look at the other young man, now slightly behind their car on her side. This guy, the shorter one, wore dark clothing, and he was pointing a gun at the car still twenty feet to the side and behind them. An instant later, the man in front of the car was pointing a gun as well.

Naja got the better look at the man behind them just before the back passenger side window shattered, and then the windshield. Shawn grabbed her by the shoulders and forced her toward the floor of the car, covering her with his torso.

He kept pushing his daughter down, forward, in her seat until she was contorted, her head toward the floor with Shawn sprawled on top of her. She screamed as another half-dozen shots rang out, smashing the other windows. Shawn felt a sharp, burning nip in his back, then one on his shoulder, but he continued to force Naja lower and lower. The shooting might have lasted ten seconds, although it felt much longer.

The roar of the bullets and flying glass finally subsided. Shawn felt his legs floating up to the roof of the car as they rolled through the stoplight, but Shawn was not sitting up at the steering wheel. The Impala jumped over a curb on the other side of Augusta, and Naja screamed again when they banged into a tree, coming to a halt directly in front of the apartment where Naja's mother had lived as a child. Shawn still wouldn't—or couldn't—sit up. Nor did he allow his daughter to raise her head. He finally lifted his eyes, twisting his head slightly.

The first thing Shawn saw was a bullet hole in Naja's headrest.

He ducked back down, kept pressure on her shoulders, and talked to her soothingly: *Calm down*, he kept saying. *We're all right*, waiting to be certain the shooters had finished and fled.

"I don't want to die!" Naja yelled. "Are we shot?"

Shawn continued to speak gently. Knowing something was not right, he said, "We're fine, we're okay. Do you have your cell phone? Let's call 911."

Naja first had to extricate herself from the car. Glass was everywhere—in her hair, on her coat, at her feet. She wiggled out from under her dad, wondering why he didn't sit up and get off her. She stepped out of the car feeling lightheaded.

Shawn tried to raise himself upright. He paused, resting, while tilted sideways on Naja's seat. "Call 911," he said again, "and then call your mom and let her know we're okay."

Naja did what her father asked, but like Shawn moments earlier, she feared that the shooters might return to their unfinished rampage. "I asked the operator on the 911 call to stay on the line with me," she says, "until the police got there." When the police arrived just minutes later, she thanked the dispatch and phoned her mother.

Naja had been bugging her mom that morning about wanting to go shopping after school. Kim was driving Malia, Naja's younger sister, to her school and she answered the call on speakerphone by saying, "Let's not talk about that now."

"My daddy's been shot," Naja wailed, "and I don't want him to die."

Malia, age eight, cried out from the backseat.

It wasn't until Naja turned back to the rental car, where her father was still tilted onto her seat, that she felt a wave of nausea. "I broke down," she says, "when I saw how many bullet holes were in the side of the car." Between the broken glass and the holes in the passenger side door, there had been at least ten shots.

The first officers at the scene must have assumed Shawn was connected to the recent gunplay, figured him to be a gangbanger. One cop reached into the Impala from the driver's side, grabbed Shawn by the collar of his leather coat, and jerked hard. "Let's go!" he said.

"Hold on, Officer," Shawn said, rattled for the first time that morning. "I can't feel my legs."

3

MY FIRST EXPERIENCE with Marshall High School came in 1981.

At the age of twenty-two, I was the youngest coach in the history of the storied Chicago Public League. My team, Von Steuben, finished with a winning record at 13-12, but only one contest from that season stuck with me over the next thirty years: our game against Marshall in the Mayor's Christmas Tournament.

Let me start by saying that we lost to Marshall by sixty-three points.

The Von Steuben team and their young coach were unable to solve Marshall's presses and traps. We rarely got the ball past mid court, and Marshall's interlocking web of defense had me so confused that at one point, I literally did not believe my eyes: I counted the maroon Marshall uniforms on the court. One, two, three, four, five, and . . . well, it *seemed* there must have been an illegal sixth player, such was their swarming coverage.

The loss rattled us. (After that day my assistant coach referred to a lopsided pounding as being "Marshalled." As in, "Did you see the Illinois game last night? They *Marshalled* Missouri!") Our competition on the North Side wasn't as fierce as the Red West conference that Marshall played in, and my team and I got the message: we weren't worthy.

Their coach, Luther Bedford, gave me a tepid handshake after the beating.

Within two years, I was an assistant coach and recruiter at the University of Texas–El Paso, and the trauma of the Marshall game was behind me. At UTEP, I made my mark by accidentally discovering Tim Hardaway in Chicago and signing him up. His game blossomed and he went on to become an NBA star, which had a Pied Piper effect on other high school prospects. I won't list them—it's a long list—but UTEP won with a bunch of Chicago guys, and in the 1980s, only the University of Illinois was as successful with kids from the area.

Although I never played a minute of varsity basketball in high school, I played on the frosh-soph team, and I knew even then what drew me to the game: it was a window into black culture. Besides the game—particularly the flair of the free-form playground game—the players' music, language, dress, attitudes, politics, history, and struggles were all compelling.

My high school, Von Steuben, might have been 10 percent African American kids who nearly all were "permissive transfers" from overcrowded West Side schools. Von's black basketball players were smart, loyal, funny, and interesting. Also, they had cool nicknames. Sugar Bear. Peanut. Sweetie Man. They turned me on to the music of the Chi-Lites, the Stylistics, the Spinners, and Curtis Mayfield. My Converse All Stars now needed colorful shoelaces. I could hardly imitate the confident-yet-casual swagger of Willie Williams walking the hallways (or his silky jumpshot) but I could read the essays of James Baldwin and see movies like *Shaft, Superfly,* and *Cooley High.*

My intense interest continued after I enrolled at North Park College, a small college two blocks away from my high school. Miraculously, I was picked for a spot on the varsity team one year, and, just as I had when I was younger, I made it a point to visit my black teammates at their homes and play pickup games at their local YMCA or playgrounds. Basketball would soon be a passport to see the world, but my visa began and ended in urban, black Chicago.

I never made much money at UTEP, but El Paso was a relatively comfortable town in which to be poor. I loved my work, and I learned the business of college basketball. I also learned about the mentality of administrators when I got unceremoniously dumped in 1991 for occasionally driving players to their summer jobs. (Unlike Shawn in his Expedition, I did not spend much time counseling players or worrying about their future.) The occasional shuttle service was not much of an offense, I still think, but it appeared at the time that my fast-lane career—seven NCAA tournaments by age thirty-one—had been ruined. Nonetheless, eight months later, UTEP and their pioneering coach Don Haskins qualified for the Sweet Sixteen with a mostly Chicago lineup.

My firing was how I landed back in Chicago in the summer of 1992, in time for Shawn Harrington's senior year at Marshall.

I came home to reinvent myself as a talent scout, figuring I could sell a monthly newsletter to colleges. The city had just one other scouting service in the days before the Internet, run by a talented guy named David Kaplan. But "Kap" was already rumored to be sliding over to the media side of sports, which he eventually did. I hoped there might be room for me, and there was. Within a few months I had more than a hundred colleges subscribing to the *Chicago Prep Magnet* newsletter—giant state schools, small colleges, and a few dozen junior colleges. I was still making paltry wages, but I earned a priceless education in Chicago basketball.

Like a lot of cities, Chicago was complicated when it came to basketball. The Public League had over sixty teams, and their games started at either 3:15 or 4:30 PM. Some Public League games were held on Wednesdays and Fridays, others Tuesdays and Thursdays, depending on the conference. Catholic schools and suburban schools usually started games at 7:30 PM, and often had Saturday games. From November of 1992 until the spring of 1994 I saw two, sometimes three, games a day.

I had attended Chicago Public Schools myself for eleven of my thirteen years, then attended college in the city. Toss in my coaching at Von Steuben, scouting the city for UTEP, and then running the *Chicago Prep Magnet*—it all meant that I knew Chicago so well that after a few years as a college recruiter, I had begun to decline the map the rental car clerk at O'Hare Airport offered, a quiet point of pride.

Despite my residual trauma from coaching against Luther Bedford over a decade earlier, I was anxious to scout his team—partly because I still wanted to figure out what made them so special.

Watching Marshall play was a very different experience than coaching against them. Instead of feeling like I was suffocating, I felt exhilarated. The Commandos—what a team name!—were always small, which gave them the reputation as perennial underdogs, and that was why Luther Bedford was considered by many to be the city's best coach. The Commandos were cohesive, but risk takers. Measured, but aggressive. Patient, yet intense. They still relied on their presses and traps that had annihilated my Von Steuben team back in 1981. At the most pressurized moments, when others panicked, they were calm and assured.

I became a regular at the Marshall games during the 1992–93 season. For one thing, Marshall was on Kedzie Avenue, a street I lived near—although my Albany Park neighborhood was seven miles to the north. I drove straight south, observing Chicago's distinct neighborhoods. In Albany Park, where Von Steuben High still stands, the blocks were mostly white, with a sprinkling of Korean, Middle Eastern, and Latino. Heading into Logan Square, I passed working-class whites and Latinos but no signs of the hipster mecca it has become today. Humboldt Park was a mix of African American and Latino, and then crossing Division Street, under a railroad track viaduct, I would find myself in almost entirely black East Garfield Park.

Marshall High School, at the corner of Kedzie and Adams, is a barometer for how the city of Chicago has changed over the decades. Until after World War II, the school was nearly all white, with a strong Jewish, Italian, and Irish population. After the war and the great migration from the South, particularly Mississippi, the student body quickly changed to mostly African American. At its height, Marshall boasted of three thousand students. The hundred-year-old building is grand, and the towering red brick structure with imposing parapets at the top has the look of a friendly fortress.

The school is also located three blocks from the Eisenhower Expressway, Interstate 290. The Eisenhower, which was built after World War II, runs east/west from downtown into the suburbs, and through the heart of Chicago's West Side.

There was hardly a sit-down restaurant to be found near Marshall. Most were takeout only, and bulletproof glass partitions often separated customers and workers. Liquor stores were easier to find, though, with the same security measures. The "L" trains so often depicted in Chicago films made far fewer stops in this part of town, and the areas outside those stations were often havens for trouble. Gangbangers roved in groups across empty lots and sidewalks strewn with broken glass, past boarded up two-flats and a proliferation of churches. Many hardworking families persevered in the impoverished neighborhood and still called it home, but that was not immediately apparent to a visitor like me.

If Luther Bedford remembered me from that Von Steuben game of 1981, he didn't let on. In fact, each time I showed up at Marshall with my shoulder bag, he seemed not to recall me from the previous game. He never warmed up, never offered his home phone number, never budged. He'd answer my questions about each player briefly, but that was it. I learned to leave him alone.

That year's Marshall team featured a highly coveted six foot three shooting guard named Courtney Hargrays. He was strong and could sink long three-pointers. Most of his teammates called him "Boo," but some called him "Slow Motion," because although he did not have great quickness, he could slowly take apart his opponent. As was too common in Chicago, Hargrays had gotten an inflated reputation by being an early developer—he was a starter by the time he was a sophomore. I'd learned over the years that guys like him, through no fault of their own, were often overrated. They'd get early notice in the *Tribune* or *Sun-Times,* yet were done developing as players.

Perhaps because I had been such a mediocre point guard myself, I knew what to admire in a prospect at that position. At Marshall, I immediately recognized that the brains and heart of the team was Shawn Harrington. Just five foot eight then, he was lithe, graceful, long-armed, and ambidextrous. Slithery-quick, he could dribble the ball deep into the defense, was unflappable against bigger players, and, most crucial, he made everyone around himself better. He carried the nickname "Shaky" due to his ability to shake defenders. He was a good shooter—not great, but plenty good. And when Luther Bedford barked, Shawn "Shaky" Harrington jumped.

Despite Bedford's demeanor, I grew comfortable and appreciated the standard his team set—it provided me a measure to accurately evaluate their opponents. I saw Marshall play a half dozen times, and I wrote about Shawn and his teammates in my *Chicago Prep Magnet*. As a scout and journalist you're not supposed to be partial to teams or players, but I was. Marshall's interconnected unselfishness was rare, and they'd usually beat much bigger teams with their quickness and smarts.

I mistakenly called him *Sean* Harrington in those original reports. I also called him "the city's smartest guard." That was not a mistake.

Marshall had one other player worth noting. Ontario Brown was bigger and stronger than Shawn, sure-handed, steady, and smart. Ontario was not quite the shooter his running mates were, but he was versatile and their best defender. Coach Bedford sometimes moved Ontario to the point guard spot to allow Shawn to score more.

Marshall had an amazing year, advancing deep into the 1993 city playoffs, and a showdown with King High School, a David versus Goliath affair, ensued. Ranked number one in the nation, King had a pair of seven-footers. Luther Bedford countered with a six foot three center and his vaunted presses and traps. Shawn scored a career-high twenty-seven points in one of the most dramatic games in Chicago history, but it ended in heartbreak. Marshall fell in triple overtime, and their season was over.

Near the end of Shawn's senior year of high school, Bedford helped him filter through the recruiting letters and phone calls and became the gatekeeper who asked the tough questions of visiting coaches. The process can be intimidating for a high school senior in the city, and unless you're a top prospect with a slew of choices, it's not an enjoyable time. Bedford knew that Mineral Area Junior College, although in a remote spot in Missouri, was a good fit. The school had done well with Arthur Agee, the Marshall graduate who became the star of the landmark documentary film *Hoop Dreams*. Agee had one bit of trouble there. The ballplayers were virtually the only black kids at the school, and one day a neighbor came to the isolated house they lived in and set their door on fire. Shawn had a few junior college options to consider, but he still chose Mineral Area.

A year later, I was considering my options, too. After two seasons writing the *Chicago Prep Magnet*, I knew I'd probably topped out my subscriptions. Business was fine for a second-year startup, but it wouldn't get more lucrative. I simply was never going to get every school to subscribe. Also, I took two impractical ethical stances. I declined to sell the newsletter to fans or parents because I feared that would taint its reputation for honest evaluations. Also, I didn't want to charge teenagers by setting up "exposure" tournaments or camps. Any time an adult used the word "exposure" in regards to young athletes it made me wary. Dave Kaplan hosted those kinds of camps briefly, and I don't think he was comfortable with them either. I considered myself to be on higher moral ground than other scouts.

By the spring of 1994, I was ready to get back into college coaching, and, three years out, but with a better feel now for the Chicago basketball scene than anyone, I learned of an enticing job opening for an assistant coach.

New Mexico State, just forty miles north of El Paso, hired me in June of 1994. My salary was twice as much as my best year at UTEP.

During my first month, I was perplexed to learn of NMSU's long history of signing up two-year junior college players and casting off the nonperformers after a single season. NMSU had, over the previous nine-year period, signed eighty-one junior college players in a row, an incredible total. There was not a single high school player in the mix.

I'll help you with the math. NMSU brought in an average of nine players a year. But each university team was allowed just thirteen scholarship players. That leaves some painful numbers to crunch. Four junior college players were deemed good enough (or able to remain eligible) after the season. The other five flunked out or transferred, sometimes against their will or best interests. After they packed up and left, nine more players were carted in.

It was a strange way to run a college team, but it was not against the rules. And NMSU had big success, with one of the best winning percentages in the nation in the 1990s. Just before I arrived, they had been in five NCAA tournaments in a row, quite a feat for a school in the Big West Conference.

It wasn't a shock to discover that my predecessor, Gar Forman, had gone six years without taking a single vacation day. Having only junior college players meant more work because the coaches had to replace two-year players twice as fast as they would have had to replace high school recruits, who would play for the full four years. A few years earlier I wouldn't have flinched, but getting fired at UTEP, where my life had been out of balance, had made me rethink my relationship to my job. In my three-year coaching hiatus, I read a lot more, went to films and plays, and even learned to play the fiddle. The idea of continuing NMSU's established grind of signing nine players a year was, in a word, unappealing. No more late nights in the office calling recruits, I decided.

It's true that I was not crazy about the ethics of a system in which teenagers were disposable, but mostly it was the workload that scared me. So I made up my mind from the start—I'd also recruit high school players who stayed for four years. I would stop the revolving door and we'd treat the players like people, not commodities. I went after only a select group of junior college players.

I began phoning Shawn at his junior college a few days after I started at New Mexico State.

"Thanks for calling, Coach Bradburd," he told me near the end of our first talk. Being thanked by a recruit was unusual, but I had an important point to make before we hung up.

"Call me Rus," I told him. That was something I told every recruit. My approach required the player to believe I was his friend. I was never, ever "*Coach* Bradburd." The "Coach" bit felt phony, and I believed that if I was to establish comradery with a kid, that honorific only got in the way, like a fancy oak desk between us. Rather than overselling players, always pushing, I had better results when we became friends.

Friendly relationships, like the one I was to cultivate with Shawn, happened easily with Chicago players. As the year progressed our talks went longer. We'd discuss anything but sales-pitch business stuff, and I fell into conversations with Shawn naturally.

"Which is a better conference, Shawn—the Red West or the Red South?" I asked once, knowing full well which he would choose, and I followed that up by teasing him about Simeon and King, two South Side teams. "Aw, come on, Marshall could never beat Simeon, could they?"

He laughed, but he was serious when he said, "Never underestimate the Commandos." He realized that I had done my homework on Luther Bedford, and I made it clear that I knew more about his high school and old coach than any other recruiter who might call.

"Did you appreciate Coach Bedford when you played for him?" I asked another time, "or did it take a few years to understand him?" Over the next few months I heard plenty of stories about his tough old coach.

Most people make important decisions based on friendships. When it came time for me to find a stockbroker in the Southwest, I went with a buddy because of my level of comfort and trust. If thirty-something men with disposable income are making decisions based on friendship, you can bet young basketball players do the same, and I understood that well. I hid the predatory nature of the recruiter/player dynamic, yet I honestly found Shawn charming, generous, quick to laugh, and, like me, intensely proud of his Chicago pedigree. Much of our bonding was genuine.

Shawn had played well as a junior college freshman at Mineral Area, averaging 16.5 points per game (along with 7 assists) on a team that finished 27-5. He'd grown a bit since I first saw him, all the way up to five foot eleven. I dug out my *Chicago Prep Magnet*'s final report on him, the one where I listed the top Chicago kids who were now away at junior colleges. Here's what I published in my newsletter of February 1994, a few months before I began working at New Mexico State:

> "Too small" was the label tagged on this kid last year at Marshall HS. My label was "the city's smartest guard." Fine quickness, great decisions, and toughness forged in the gritty Red-West. A good looking shooter in HS, he was more concerned with running the show. Now he's showing he can score too. . . . Flirting with big time status.

Classes were about to begin at both Mineral Area and at New Mexico State. Although I had seen him play so many times in high school,

I had not yet met him in person. "I'm coming to Mineral Area to meet you soon," I told Shawn in August of 1994, "but first I want to visit your high school coach and your mom."

"That would mean a lot to me," Shawn said. We were already becoming friends.

4

I STOOD AWKWARDLY at Luther Bedford's office door, feeling like a delivery boy who'd brought the wrong sandwich. The other Marshall phys ed teachers took one look at me, squeezed past in the doorway, and disappeared. I assumed that meant Bedford had plenty to say.

He didn't, although the first thing you noticed about Coach Bedford was, in fact, his voice. It was gravelly and gruff, somewhere between an ornery old cartoon watchdog and Otis Redding. No, Bedford didn't talk much, but the timbre of his words resonated.

I chatted up dozens of high school coaches every month, and I was accustomed to being the only white guy in the gym, but Bedford's manner bothered me. Rather, his lack of manner. College recruiters usually got a predictably warm, if vague, welcome: "How's your team going to be?" Maybe even, "Can I get you a cup of coffee?" Or, at the very least, "Take a seat." I got none of that from Luther Bedford, even after his colleagues vacated their chairs.

It was the first day of fall recruiting period, September of 1994, and I'd arrived as a courtesy, to show my respect, and to get the jump on signing Shawn Harrington. I didn't have to be at Marshall. Shawn was 350 miles away, but I was so intent on landing him that I wanted to cover my bases, outwork any competition. That meant honoring Luther Bedford first.

No, there was no cup of coffee. No warm greeting. No "We sure appreciate your interest in our kids." After my three-minute prattle, the Marshall coach, who had never gotten out of his seat, decided we were finished. He grunted, turned back to his desk, and left me standing. Despite my Public League background and my presence at several Marshall games Shawn's senior year, Luther Bedford and I would never be friends. Just before I left, Bedford turned back to grumble the only nearly full sentence he'd say to me that morning: "You going to support him and make sure he graduates?"

Could Bedford have known New Mexico State had a dodgy track record of graduating players in the 1990s?

I thought I handled Bedford's final question gracefully. I said the same thing recruiters have been saying to kids, their parents, and coaches since recruiting began. Yes, yes, we would surround him with tutors, make sure he was in class. Our staff planned to monitor his progress, not put him in phony courses. I had a background in the Chicago Public League, I reminded the coach, and I would take care of Shawn.

I had an appointment to visit Frinda Harrington, Shawn's mother, later that day. When I met him the next week in Missouri, I could use all this as leverage, emphasize that I was the first one principled enough to spend time with his mother and high school coach.

Frinda Harrington lived on the block of 1100 North Kedvale, in an area known unofficially as K-Town because of the street names: Kildare, Keeler, Karlov, Kilbourn. Technically, the block is now considered West Humboldt Park, but it sits near the border of three other neighborhoods: West Garfield Park, East Garfield Park, and Humboldt Park. Real estate agents rename neighborhoods for their own benefit, so parsing out the boundaries can be confusing. Shawn says nobody ever called it anything but Garfield Park or just the West Side. Much of the area is known for its poverty and violence (and exceptional basketball) but the Harrington's block was relatively stable.

Shawn was Frinda's only child. She was also a Marshall graduate, and his closest relatives had gone to Marshall as well, which still had around twenty-five hundred students when his mother graduated. So deep was Shawn's connection to the school that he had actually been there before he was born. Frinda was pregnant as a senior.

Frinda was petite, and she had a welcoming smile. In my experience, the majority of urban black recruits were raised by single moms, and this was true for Shawn. Frinda made no mention of Shawn's father, and I didn't ask. She offered a choice between strawberry and grape soda and set out a bowl of potato chips. A good sign, I thought, and a welcome surprise. What was unsurprising was Frinda's indifferent-yet-opinionated stance on her son's college recruitment. She seemed to be reading from the same script as nearly every other Chicago mother I'd meet over my fourteen years as a college coach.

"I don't care which school he goes to," she told me, "just as long as it's far away from Chicago." *Far away from Chicago*, she said over and over that day.

The visit with Shawn's mother left me feeling confident as long as I was able to tune out my memory of Luther Bedford's manner. As always, I'd brought along a souvenir media guide, which featured a map on the last page. I showed her the expansive distance between Las Cruces, New Mexico, and her town. She seemed disinterested in our winning team, overflow crowds, sunny weather, ESPN Big Monday TV contracts, or even our graduation rates and tutoring structure. What got her attention was that her son would be safe, a world away from Chicago's West Side.

5

SHAWN WAS BORN to Frinda Harrington on October 3, 1975, and he was a typical boy from Chicago's West Side in many ways.

Frinda bounced from apartment to apartment, so Shawn had attended Delano, Faraday, and Paderewski schools by the time he was eleven. "I got used to all the moving," Shawn says. "That was just part of life, part of growing up on the West Side." Friends and teachers dropped out of his life, never to be seen again.

Shawn's father, Charles Suggs, fancied himself a ladies' man and wasn't involved much in the family's life. With the father pretty much a no-show, Frinda needed plenty of help from her sisters. Shawn's aunts—Jaci, Vera, Lisa, and Renee—all pitched in, sometimes dispensing the discipline. "I was always at risk of getting my butt whipped," Shawn says. "Throughout my childhood I was spanked by five women."

On the verge of being the only seventh grader called up to play basketball for the eighth grade team, Shawn wanted to remain at Paderewski. But his mother said they had to make another move, to his fourth elementary school in six years, and this move hurt. "I had to start all over," he says. The switch, however, proved to be a positive one. At Calhoun Elementary, at the corner of Jackson and California, Shawn found a lifelong friend in his new classmate Ontario Brown.

Just a block away from Calhoun stood the Marillac House. Marillac is a community center/day care/social progress center run by the Catholic Daughters of Charity. Ontario and Shawn spent a lot of time hanging out at Marillac, where, in the winter months, the boys were drawn inside to the Ping-Pong and pool tables. The indoor gym was more an oversized classroom than a place to shoot baskets.

When the weather got warm, Marillac morphed into a mecca for playground basketball, and the cramped outside court was where Chicago's best black players convened. Shawn and Ontario would grab milk crates from the back of a grocery store to sit and watch all day. The games—some with referees, some just pickup ball—caused a buzz in the neighborhood. Overflow crowds gathered to watch future or current NBA stars like Isiah Thomas, Mark Aguirre, Hersey Hawkins, or Randy Brown. (Marillac loomed so large in the collective consciousness of the city that Bulls star Michael Jordan filmed a shoe commercial there.) The games had the effect on area kids that seeing Elvis on *The Ed Sullivan Show* did on a generation of white musicians: young men wanted in. Nobody felt that pull more than Shawn Harrington.

Shawn and Ontario soon turned their focus from table tennis to hoisting up shots at the wobbly rims between the men's games or after the neighborhood heroes had gone home. They'd imitate the crossover dribbles, reverse layups, head fakes, jukes, and spins of the older players.

The summer before eighth grade, Shawn suffered a stress fracture in his ankle. He was so filled with the spirit of Marillac that being incapacitated nearly drove him crazy. The cast was supposed to be on his ankle for eight weeks, but after a month of sitting on the sideline and exhorting Ontario, Shawn had his fill. He hobbled across the court during a time-out to ask his uncle if he could borrow one gym shoe. Shawn yanked the size-ten shoe over his cast. Then he pleaded with his summer league coach to let him play. He scored eight points in a cast.

Ontario grew to a thick and strong six foot one. Shawn was half a foot shorter and slight. After their eighth-grade season, the *Chicago Sun-Times*, in a dubious journalistic decision, published a list of the top twenty-five eighth-grade players in Chicago. Shawn and Ontario made the list. That spring, coaches made moves to entice Ontario to enroll at their high schools. For instance, the coaches from King brought him to visit their campus, took his shoe measurements, and even gave him a ball cap from a local university. But for Ontario, there was really no decision because his father had gone to Marshall. Shawn, at his size, did not generate much recruiting interest, but he concurred on the choice of schools. What remained unacknowledged between the two was that even after the exposure of the *Sun-Times* piece, neither young hotshot had heard a word from Marshall's coach. Luther Bedford was old-school, and he was not about to stoop to luring eighth graders.

Meanwhile, Frinda Harrington moved from job to job and was briefly on public assistance. She worked at a record store downtown for a stretch, but the position she held the longest was as a classroom assistant at a Catholic school near Marshall called Our Lady of Sorrows.

In June of Shawn's final year at Calhoun School, Frinda finally saved up enough to buy a house, a freestanding wood frame on the 1100 block of North Kedvale. It was the final move of Shawn's prep days, and although this was the first house he'd ever lived in, the move stung again—his new home sat twenty-four blocks from both Marillac and Marshall, too far to walk in the winters.

Ontario developed faster than Shawn, and he made the varsity squad as a sophomore. Shawn remained on frosh-soph until the varsity won the city championship in 1991—the focus year of the film *Hoop Dreams*. That's when, on the strength of his performance with the younger team, Shawn got the call-up to varsity just in time to make a brief cameo on the team bus destined downstate for the Elite 8 playoffs. After boarding the bus, he turns back to the camera, flashes a finger, and yells, "Number one, baby! Take State!" Marshall finished the year in third place out of over four hundred teams statewide.

Shawn grew to five foot eight that summer and was seen as Marshall's next starting point guard. That July, after a stellar summer league game, King High School came calling for Shawn, two years after their recruiting pitch for Ontario had fallen flat. This time, a King assistant coach bestowed on the impressionable sixteen-year-old all kinds of new gear, including a King jacket with *HARRINGTON* splashed across the back.

When Shawn remained steadfast, he felt his loyalty to Luther Bedford would be returned. But he missed practice one day in October, and Marshall was a hard place for a baller to keep a secret. Word got back to the coach that Shawn wasn't sick, he had attended classes that morning. Bedford cornered Shawn the next morning and told him he wouldn't be in the starting lineup the entire year.

"It was quite a difficult lesson," Shawn says, "but the lesson wasn't over."

Bedford believed in corporal punishment, and he used a long wooden paddle to emphasize a point, particularly when it came to discipline or attendance. An unexcused absence from practice meant six smacks.

With a missed practice to pay for, Shawn took his beating. True to his word, Bedford kept him out of the starting lineup all season.

It wasn't the first time Shawn was paddled.

Each grading period, the players were required to line up and show the coach their report cards. If you received an F in a class, you got three whacks, while a D meant a single blow. Once, as a sophomore, Shawn stood outside the coaches' office to await his turn, knowing he'd be punished for his lone D grade. In line just before Shawn that day was a varsity player nicknamed "Raisin," who had gotten six failing grades. Raisin had a total of eighteen whacks due.

"None of us could believe it," Shawn says. "*Six* Fs? That meant he wasn't even eligible to play anymore." Why wait around to get beaten before being permanently put off the team?

Behind closed doors in Bedford's office, Raisin must have stood his ground, put his hands on the desk, and gritted his teeth. His teammates could hear the *whap* of the paddle. "Outside, we were counting quietly," Shawn recalled, "and Raisin must have said something that touched a nerve with Bedford, because the total went way higher than eighteen. We all looked at each other, and we finally stopped counting."

Despite Raisin's trauma, Shawn was relaxed and moments later survived his own paddling without much anguish. "I prepared a little, I guess," he says. "I was wearing three pairs of gym shorts."

Of course, the threat of getting paddled could not compare to the perils on the streets of the West Side. Even daytime hours could be dangerous.

One afternoon, waiting at a crowded CTA bus stop after school, Shawn bumped into Westinghouse star Damion Dantzler. Both juniors in high school, they were friends from summer ball despite their schools' basketball rivalry. Being recognized as a ballplayer generally meant

Shawn got a pass, and he knew, like all young men in that part of town, how and where turf was divided. He could move about safely if he used common sense and kept his head down. He crossed the street if he saw trouble ahead and rarely traveled alone.

As Shawn and Dantzler traded stories and joked, an older man approached. "Hey," the man said, "you brothers play for Westinghouse?"

"I do," the six foot six Dantzler said. He pointed at Shawn and smiled. "He wasn't good enough though, he had to play for Marshall."

The man laughed, nodding as if impressed. He peppered the teens with a nonstop litany of questions about their teams, their coaches, and their prospects for a good season. Shawn glanced at his watch after a while. Either the CTA was slower than usual, or else this man was really annoying. As the bus finally approached in the distance, the crowd naturally shifted and lined up near the bus stop sign.

That's when the man pulled out a rusty gun.

"Both of you walk over this way and keep quiet," he said and turned to Shawn. "And give me that gold chain."

Shawn felt someone's hands around his neck, and he recoiled.

"Give us your jacket, too," the second man said as he helped shuttle the teens away from the line of commuters.

Shawn slowly took off his chain then surrendered his new Bulls jacket to the unseen stranger behind him. "Their timing was deliberate," Shawn says. "They understood everyone gravitated toward the bus stop, and that's when he put the gun in my face."

It was an unusual event, since basketball players were usually off limits, and it was an expensive day for Shawn. The chain and jacket had cost him nearly $300 combined. "And," he adds, "after all that, we missed our bus."

By age sixteen, Shawn's world was expanding to include more than Marshall High, the Marillac House, and making jump shots. He began to notice and keep tabs on a young lady two doors down from his house named Kim Jenkins.

Kim Jenkins was eight years old when her mother decided to buy a small home on Kedvale, not far from Division Street. Previously they had been renting an apartment at the corner of Augusta Boulevard and Hamlin Avenue. The move from their two-flat left Kim a little sad—the corner store across the street, with its ice cream and candy bars, was a haven that held a powerful allure to all the kids on the block.

Claretha Jenkins, Kim's mother, was frugal, determined, and protective. Her own family had moved to Chicago from Mississippi when she was a child in the 1950s, and she had attended Marshall.

Brilliant in the classroom, Kim was named valedictorian in eighth grade at Brian Piccolo School. Struggling boys sometimes targeted her, hoping to copy her homework or answers during tests, but she learned to stand tall and resist peer pressure, even with her quiet demeanor.

Kim was the same year in school as Shawn, but she didn't care to attend Marshall. Instead, she commuted an hour by bus to Mather, another public high school at the northern edge of the city. Mather was racially mixed, not a basketball power, and featured a respected licensed practitioner nursing program. She badly wanted to be an RN. Mather's diversity also appealed to her, and she thrived, nailing a 3.7 grade point average.

Unlike Shawn, Kim Jenkins was reticent but she was also decisive. One day Kim asked her cousin to approach the charismatic basketball player on the block to gauge his interest in being her boyfriend. Shawn graciously accepted her indirect advances and they started dating a few weeks later.

Shawn was proud to have his first real girlfriend, but they had not been officially dating when he agreed to go to the Marshall prom with a classmate, a platonic friend. By the time he and Kim were a couple, it was too late to back out of the prom. He knew he'd have to reveal these now-awkward plans.

"She was angry," Shawn says, "but in the end, she had to understand."

Kim did understand. Sort of. Shawn learned a few days later that she was going to her Mather prom—and he would not be Kim's date.

I loved that story about Kim—the headstrong woman who, despite her shyness, could be a force. I also recognized that she would have a strong influence on what Shawn did after junior college, although he had gone on to Mineral Area alone. I sometimes asked him during my recruiting calls, "What's the latest with Kim?" Shawn gave me Kim's phone number and I made sure to keep her on my radar. His girlfriend was shy but brilliant, and she laughed easily. Kim liked me, I could tell, and I hoped she'd communicate that to him.

Each phone call to Shawn, my policy was to be sure to limit myself to one—and only one—selling point. "We had an overflow crowd for the UTEP game," I might mention—then, quickly, "When do you guys play again?" By late October the talk would include, "It was so warm that I had lunch outside today" and we'd go on to the chatty stuff that friends talked about.

During one call, Shawn told me the latest with Ontario Brown. Ontario, Shawn, and Courtney Hargrays had been pushed by Luther Bedford to go away for school. Ontario had wound up at Westark, a junior college in Arkansas. He found two friendly faces waiting for him, a couple of players from the Marshall's girls team. He played well as a freshman, and in another year he'd have a great chance of landing a scholarship to a bigger school. But Ontario had a daughter who had been born in the midst of his junior year at Marshall. The girl's mother, Sabrina, was also a Marshall student. Pulled by his daughter, Ontario decided to come back to attend Kennedy-King junior college on the South Side, and his playing career ended soon after that.

Shawn was disappointed. He and Ontario had started playing ball seriously at age twelve, and this felt like an ending of sorts.

I stayed after Shawn with weekly calls. "Can the Bulls ever win it all again," I asked one day, "now that Michael Jordan is back from baseball?"

"Come on, Rus, man," he said, "you know they will."

Once Shawn asked me about who I was dating, and I knew then I had him in my pocket—he was ours, but that didn't mean I could let up. We talked dozens of times that season. The best Chicago pizza? What about favorite spots for a Polish sausage? Music, movies, his mom—Shawn and I covered it all. Before my first game coaching at New Mexico State, I had spent hours on the phone with Shawn.

6

WE ENJOYED A RIP-ROARING START in 1994, my first year at New Mexico State, winning three preseason tournament games, all on national television. I phoned Shawn from New York, the day before we were to appear again on ESPN in the championship, to remind him to tune in.

We had plenty to talk about besides the TV game. The previous evening I had taken a taxi with two of our players—both Chicago Public League guys—to see *Hoop Dreams* on its opening weekend. This was their first trip to New York, and some coaches might have used the time differently, perhaps pointed out the sights or city's history, initiated some kind of connection. But I was thirty-five, and our players, who had me sandwiched in the middle seat, seemed beyond my scope of influence as they yammered away over the top of my winter cap. I figured we could discuss the film on the way back to the hotel.

Hoop Dreams focused on two high school basketball players over a five-year period, and one, Arthur Agee, had transferred into Marshall. The hugely popular and critically acclaimed film gave a lot of screen time to Luther Bedford, and the school gained a sort of cult status. Seeing the coach and recalling the chilly reception in his office made me squirm a bit. The scenes where the predatory college recruiters appeared made me just as uncomfortable.

I still think *Hoop Dreams* is the best documentary film ever, and it is revered to this day in Chicago. Shawn had brief on-screen cameos, and he was now living in the same dreary brick building in rural Missouri seen at the conclusion of the movie. (Although they had played together at Marshall, Shawn and Arthur Agee did not overlap at the junior college.)

In the taxi back to the hotel, the NMSU players and I didn't talk much, as if we had been swept into different corners by the power of the storytelling. The film seemed to isolate rather than connect us. We had a curfew to make and I was a coach, so it's not like we could have gone out for a drink to discuss the movie. In retrospect, I know it was a missed opportunity to really bond with the young men, to get them to consider and discuss their own journeys from rough Chicago neighborhoods to the sunshine of New Mexico. Instead, as the lights of New York flashed by, I thought about what Frinda Harrington had said to me, and I believed that I was doing a good thing in trying to recruit Shawn to move away from Chicago. From New Mexico, I knew, I could more directly and honestly answer Luther Bedford's challenge to take care of Shawn.

When the team returned to campus, I learned that NMSU had had an elaborate scheme going for years. Many of the junior college players they were signing were not academically eligible, so our coaches enrolled the recruits in "correspondence classes" at an obscure Florida college in summer before they arrived in New Mexico. In this way, the Aggies could attract top players that other top teams would not bite on. (This was years before web classes became popular. Today, online courses offered on nearly every college campus have simplified the problem of getting athletes eligible.)

I'm sure NMSU's system started innocently enough. A coach might have sat the first struggling player down with the correspondence paperwork, envelopes, and stamps, in the film room. He likely prodded him to do his homework all summer. That must have gradually evolved into correcting their work, and finally into completing the entire class for the kid. And if it worked well for one player, why not try a few more? Coaches are great copycats, and any success can get copied ad infinitum. After a few summers of this, NMSU began winning big in the early 1990s with barely eligible athletes, and the school got a reputation as a place where dodgy students could get certified to play. During my first months at NMSU, a junior college coach from South Carolina phoned to gauge my interest in one of his best players. Although I'd never heard of the young man, he sounded like a heck of a prospect. When I asked about grades, the coach admitted his guy wasn't anywhere near graduating or qualifying for a scholarship yet.

"I heard you guys know how to get him eligible," he told me.

Our head coach in those days was the rough-around-the-edges Neil McCarthy, and he molded those juco players into a tenacious and furious bunch. His matchup zone was a puzzle that stumped opponents in the West for years, and I figured a Marshall player would pick up the nuances quickly.

NMSU's wide-net recruiting philosophy relied on volume, not efficiency. It was an unusual way to run a program, but it was feasible for a few reasons. First, Las Cruces is remote, with a negligible media presence. If a player at, say, UCLA flunked out, that got blasted across the sports page of a nationally recognized newspaper, and the story could damage the team's recruiting in Los Angeles and elsewhere. But NMSU was flying under the radar and our recruits were strangers from hundreds of miles away. Nobody at the town's tiny newspaper wrote about the revolving door the coaches spun. Also, the school's administration turned a blind eye—or, rather, kept a closer watch on game attendance and winning percentage than class attendance and graduation rates.

Basketball was all business to McCarthy. If a young man was not playing well, he'd soon be packing for another school. McCarthy drove his luxury car through the parking lot, over the curb, across the grass, and parked illegally in front of the door to the basketball office. Once inside he chain-smoked behind his desk. Nobody questioned a thing. Approval from the school was given in the form of raises, contract extensions, and rollovers.

That fall, only New Mexico State and the University of Illinois at Chicago were pursuing Shawn. I didn't worry about UIC, although it was a winning program with a highly respected coach. We had UIC beat by fifteen hundred miles.

Shawn was probably under-recruited because of his size: five foot eleven, and maybe 150 pounds after a couple of Italian beef sandwiches. I didn't care. I knew what I'd seen in a dozen high school games against the quickest teams in the country. I'd made my living, built my reputation, on uncovering Chicago gems. Shawn was next.

Shawn had a good "official visit" to New Mexico State that fall. The weather was perfect and the football team lost again in front of a sparse crowd (always a point of emphasis to recruits: "We're not a football school"). But a week later, Shawn threw a wrench in my plans, saying he would not be signing with us, or any school, in the early signing period. National Signing Date came and went.

That was not good news. I feared the visit was a waste, that the glow might wear off by the April signing date. We could beat UIC in a head-to-head competition because Shawn's mother would veto a Chicago school, but other colleges could come calling after they'd seen Shawn play. Mineral Area was a perennial winner and *Hoop Dreams* had put the school in the national spotlight, just like Marshall.

We did not sign another point guard that fall, although most of the nation's top junior college point guard prospects signed early. Confident we'd get Shawn, I had no solid backup plan. I had little choice but to go after some high school kids and pin my hopes on the April signing date. That would give me time to become even better friends with him, make it harder for him to tell me no when it was time to make the biggest decision of his life.

As it turned out, I was the only recruiter to meet with Shawn's mother and Luther Bedford all year. Naturally, he had great respect for Bedford, and, more important, Shawn was deeply attached to his mother. I occasionally dangled the "I was the only one to meet Frinda" over him that winter, to appeal to his obvious sense of loyalty.

In January of that 1994–95 season, the bubble burst and my workload tripled. New Mexico State was accused, first in the media and then by the NCAA, of academic fraud.

The correspondence class scandal kept growing, and by February, with a few games to go, our program began to implode. One assistant lost his job immediately after breaking down and admitting he'd done much of the homework himself. Another assistant coach, who came out untainted, left after our last game to take a small-college job in Ohio.

That left me as the lone assistant coach, with a whole lot of recruiting to do.

By season's end, a handful of players were declared ineligible. A couple of others flunked out. And just like that, I had to replace all thirteen players for the following year. By myself.

Assistant coaches at NMSU, it turned out, were as disposable as the players, and expectations were high. I was earning a larger salary than any full professor in the English department—a shocker at the time, although that's the national standard today. Even though I was alone in the office that spring, I knew I wasn't going to get sympathy or patience from the head coach, fans, media, or administration. The pressure was on to replicate the wins, and replicate them immediately. I needed players.

And, as any recruiter will tell you, I needed a point guard first.

My anxiety about getting Shawn mounted. Coach McCarthy reminded me incessantly how much we needed new talent, and he didn't understand why the national disgrace of an academic scandal might damage recruiting and undo all our good ESPN exposure. After all, he reasoned, we still finished the season at 25-10 (although we didn't qualify for the NCAA tournament).

The pressure increased as other point guards lower on my list, back-burner guys I had kept warm, committed to other schools. With nobody else within my recruiting reach, I had nothing but a couple of average high school kids left. I needed options and didn't have any.

Still, since I'd never been better friends with a recruit than I was with Shawn, I remained guardedly confident. On April 9, 1995, a day before national signing date, I phoned, ready to hear him commit.

"I think I need more time," Shawn said. "Oklahoma and Arizona called, and they might offer me a visit." Shawn had never mentioned either school before. I was surprised, exhausted, and more than a little bit irritated. New schools suggesting visits were not substantial offers, not like a solid scholarship—as I'd been offering Shawn since September. They hadn't taken the time to meet Luther Bedford or Frinda Harrington. But Arizona and Oklahoma were big-time, a cut above NMSU. They must have missed out on the point guards they really wanted.

My recruiting philosophy had always been to tell a prospect, "Take your time, I'm going to be here for you, you'll always have a home at our school"—all part of putting on the appearance of being a caring friend.

But that day, for the first time, something snapped in me.

"Look, Shawn," I said, not even trying to hide my exasperation, "if you want to wait around, see if those schools truly have a full ride, that's your business. Have they taken the time to meet your mom? Or visit Luther Bedford?"

Shawn was quiet.

"I've got to sign a point guard here," I went on. "If it's not going to be you, I'll sign another guard and you'll get left behind. I'm going to give you until noon tomorrow afternoon, and then I'm moving on."

Shawn said he understood. He'd let me know before my deadline the next day.

I surprised myself making that ultimatum. For one thing, it wasn't true. I had nobody else of Shawn's caliber to turn to. I felt bad because I had never spoken harshly to a recruit. I held no cards to play except this dishonest bluff.

My ultimatum to him was a con, a head fake done out of frustration and fatigue. I tossed my telephone headset onto the desk, pivoted from my chair, got on tiptoes, and looked out the long thin strip of window behind me. The odd design meant I had to stretch to see outside. I figured I had a sleepless night ahead, worrying if Shawn would bite.

Within the hour, Shawn phoned to say he was ready to sign at New Mexico State.

7

THE CORRESPONDENCE CLASS SCANDAL WRECKED our chances to have a good team in 1995–96, Shawn's first season. Not a single player returned for New Mexico State's Aggies, meaning all thirteen were new, and we took the court for our first game with nobody who'd ever scored a basket in Division I, including the first two freshmen NMSU had signed in a decade. The looming NCAA sanctions that stalled my recruiting also wrecked our team morale. Just before our first game, the school announced it was self-imposing a ban on participating in the NCAA tournament. Bitter and wounded, we had nothing to play for.

Shawn nailed down the starting point guard job early on, but with two freshmen forwards in the lineup, we spun our wheels in the desert sand and got off to a poor start.

"I need to talk to you," Shawn said one day early in the season.

I immediately hung up the phone and closed the office door behind him.

"I've never been on a losing team before," he said, like a kid who had been passed over by Santa Claus.

I tried to buck him up. After all, he was leading us in just about every statistical category. "You're playing great," I said. "You're doing all you can. We just have to be patient and we'll get this turned around." I asked how his classes were going. When was the last time he had spoken with his mother? Wasn't this a lot better than a Midwest winter?

"Hey, Randy Brown is getting to play quite a bit," I said. The Bulls had signed the former New Mexico State star and Chicago native just before the season. One of our biggest selling points with players and recruits in those days was the Randy Brown story. He was a Chicago West Side native who'd also graduated from Collins before starring at NMSU. By the mid-1990s, Randy was well into a long and productive

NBA career. His story had great appeal—he was unselfish, a sturdy war-rior of a guard, and he'd grown up in housing projects under the guid-ance of a great mother and strong-willed brothers.

"I'd rather be doing what Randy is doing," Shawn said, but he didn't mean playing in the NBA. He meant being a role player on a great team, rather than being the star of a struggling squad. Soon, we were on to other topics again. Except now our lives were intertwined. His success or failure would contribute to mine.

Interacting with him in person every day, I began to notice some-thing in Shawn's personality that marked him as different from other Chicago players. On the court, sure, he was similar—persevering, aggres-sive, quick-witted, battle-hardened. But once practice ended he was oddly affectionate and genial. Instead of fist bumps to say good-bye,

Shawn "Shaky" Harrington salutes a sell-out crowd as the clock winds down. The author, hand on his chin, looks on from the bench. *NMSU/ Dennis Daily*

the casual nod, or mumbling "Later," he'd hand out hugs as if they were Halloween candy. He might call out, "I love you, man," to a teammate leaving the locker room.

Once, I was surprised to find him leading the cheers at a New Mexico State women's game. Shawn was on his feet, stomping and waving, trying to ignite the sparse crowd. Unlike nearly everyone else associated with the men's program, he was genuinely interested in the success of our women's team, and he didn't view their players as potential bedmates. He had an aura of warmth, a feeling of family about him. I don't think anyone made fun of him for this. Maybe nobody else even noticed, but I did: Shawn was unusual, a genuinely warm, decent, and welcoming guy.

The NMSU season is focused on four rivalry games before conference play, the home-and-home series with UTEP and the University of New Mexico.

Before we made the trip to Albuquerque to play the UNM Lobos, Coach McCarthy came down with a mysterious nosebleed. With our head coach hospitalized, we went up to play in the Pit in front of eighteen thousand fans. UNM featured Kenny Thomas, a savvy six foot nine strongman who'd go on to play thirteen seasons in the NBA.

We lost by sixteen points, but the final score doesn't indicate how they'd dominated us until the very last minutes, when we scored a string of meaningless baskets.

Before the return game in Las Cruces, McCarthy recovered from his nosebleed and we practiced with a frenzied purpose. In Albuquerque, for some reason, we'd tried to slow the pace, a dumb idea. For the rematch we went back to the scrambling and trapping style we normally used.

In that game, Shawn Harrington dominated. He poured in eighteen points to lead all scorers, and he dished out a team-high four assists. We had the game won with a two-point lead and just a few seconds on the clock. Then one of our freshmen missed the free throws that would have sealed the victory, and a University of New Mexico player grabbed the ball and launched a seventy-foot heave.

The prayer shot went in and counted as a three-pointer. We lost, 69-68.

The sense of doom in the locker room was palpable. The outcome seemed an awful omen.

The NMSU Aggies won their first conference game in early January of 1996, making us 4-5 overall before we left for San Jose State. Shawn Harrington, despite our mediocre record, had been terrific in those first nine games, leading the team in scoring, steals, and assists.

Early in the action at San Jose, Shawn scooped up a loose ball and pivoted to protect it. Their best player, Olivier Saint-Jean (who later changed

Shawn Harrington appears to be floating as he directs the New Mexico State offense. Before a knee injury ended his season in 1996, he led the New Mexico State Aggies in scoring, steals, and assists. *NMSU/Dennis Daily*

his name to Tariq Abdul-Wahad and played in the NBA), made a desperate move—he dove for the ball anyway. He missed the ball but shouldered into Shawn's knee. Our point guard buckled and hit the floor hard.

Shawn got up after a brief conference with the trainer and played the rest of the game, but he was ineffective. The next morning, he awoke with a knee the size of a volleyball. He'd miss the rest of the season with a torn medial meniscus.

We promptly lost five games in a row. The Aggies finished 8-10 in Big West play, and 11-15 overall, their worst season in over a decade.

Our coaches had a decision to make, a calculated move, and we had three options to choose from. Did we give Shawn—and his knee—the benefit of the doubt and hope he could regain his pre-injury form? We could count on him to fully recover and allow him to keep his full-ride scholarship.

Or we could dump him.

The third option was somewhere in between. We could sign a junior college player at Shawn's point guard position for insurance. That would allow Shawn to stick around, give rehab his best effort.

We chose this last option, and for spring signing date in April 1996, we corralled another junior college point guard. Shawn could either earn back his spot or, the more likely scenario, be a substitute if his knee wasn't totally recovered.

With Shawn now slated as a backup, and our staff shorthanded again (our newest assistant had quickly grown discouraged with McCarthy and our correspondence class scandal), I had to hustle again to find players. I didn't have the time—or feel the urgency—to check on Shawn's academic progress every week. So I left him alone. I didn't grill him about classes or upcoming tests. We no longer discussed the Chicago Bulls. I didn't phone Frinda anymore to give her progress reports. Then, after grades were calculated in May, we learned that Shawn's only F (in Spanish, often a stumbling block for a nonnative speaker surrounded by fluent in-state residents) made him ineligible until the end of the next semester, in early December. He would miss the crucial four games against bitter rivals UTEP and New Mexico. With the bad knee *and* the failing grade in Spanish, Shawn's value was fading. McCarthy and I met, and he said it would be in the best interest of the team if Shawn and the Aggies parted ways.

We decided to dump Shawn Harrington and take his scholarship.

Naturally, we didn't involve Shawn in our discussions about the direction of his life. I had a chance to object, disagree, or plead Shawn's cause, stick up for him. I might have been overruled—it was ultimately the head coach's decision—but in any case, I kept quiet, knowing Shawn was likely not coming back, the basketball version of a dead man walking. Our meetings in my office ceased and I made myself less available. Most of this happened naturally because I was still pushing to finalize our roster, often out of town on recruiting trips. We signed yet another junior college point guard.

Shawn was never outright told he wasn't getting his scholarship renewed. But he could read the newspapers and he knew that us signing high school players at his position would have been a vote of confidence—the youngsters organically slated as his understudies. The two junior college players we'd inked at his position sent a very different message.

When the Aggies took a trip to play in Australia that summer, Shawn came along and did reasonably well. (Due to our ever-changing roster we feared we wouldn't have enough players to put a team on the court. Shawn was one of eight on the trip.) In Australia, Shawn cornered me before our last game. "Rus, have you got a minute?" he asked. "I've decided to transfer." He said he thought he would be happier where he knew he would be assured of playing time.

"You sure?" I asked. I wished him good luck and said we'd stay in touch.

That was August 1996. I didn't see Shawn again for nearly twenty years.

8

SHAWN HARRINGTON TRANSFERRED to Northwest Missouri, a Division II school. Missouri borders Illinois, but Maryville is nearly five hundred miles from Chicago. That was a distance Frinda Harrington could make peace with—she feared that after New Mexico State evaporated, Shawn might return to attend UIC. He tried to stay true to her wishes, only coming home for holidays and a few brief weeks at the end of the summer. He'd check in on Kim Jenkins, who was studying for a nursing degree while working part time at Sears & Roebuck.

His new coach, Steve Tappmeyer, was delighted to get a big-school transfer. Shawn sat out the first year as a "red shirt," meaning he could practice but not play. In his final year of eligibility, his knee totally healed, he had an impressive impact. Northwest Missouri State qualified for the Division II tournament in 1998 and finished 23-7, the best record for the school in a decade. It was Tappmeyer's tenth season, and the first of several subsequent NCAA postseason bids.

On the surface, Shawn appeared to have nothing but fun that last year. He was named conference MVP and third-team All American for Division II. He had a mind-boggling eight steals in a single game. He was a campus hero (although he'd fade from memory when Northwest won their first of a slew of Division II NCAA football titles the following fall).

In spite of his success it was a stressful year for Shawn. In October 1997, Kim Jenkins called to say she was pregnant. Shawn played the entire schedule knowing that she'd be having a baby that spring. He told his mother the news right away, and Frinda became a constant source of support for Kim and her family.

On April 21, 1998, two weeks before Shawn walked across the stage to accept his degree in communications, Kim gave birth to Naja Harrington.

Shawn and Kim had agreed that winter that he would not hold Naja in his arms until after he earned his diploma. It was Frinda who was there for the birthing, who looked in on Kim every afternoon. Checking on neighbors and family came naturally to Frinda.

Like so many players, Shawn had dreamed of playing professionally—sure, the NBA was remote, but there was Europe, South America, and Australia.

Not now. He was coming home to Chicago's West Side.

Kim Jenkins understood all along that it was difficult for girls dating basketball stars when the common advice to players was "get out of Chicago." There was no chance an outstanding student would tag along with Shawn to a junior college in rural Missouri. Instead, Kim accepted an academic scholarship to Fisk University in Nashville.

Fisk looms large in the legacy of African American academics, but Kim returned to Chicago after a single year. "Campus life wasn't what I expected," she says, and after a pause adds, "plus, I got homesick." This is a common story for even the best students from inner-city Chicago—intellectually, they are anxious to get away from the city, but home is still home, even for an A student. Kim enrolled at Malcolm X College, which, like her high school, features a highly regarded nursing program.

Kim was still studying nursing when she took a job as a teacher's aide at a preschool in the now-razed LeClaire Courts housing project on the Southwest Side, where airplanes from nearby Midway Airport rattled the windows every few minutes. The brief experience discouraged her from switching from nursing to a teaching career. "There was a lack of respect with the kids that was surprising," she recalls. "The kids had extremely young parents who didn't care what was going to happen in the future. And they'd say *I get free money for my kids, and my mom never worked, so why should I?*"

Kim graduated and landed a job at Trinity Hospital on the far South Side. Shawn was back on Kedvale Avenue, but not with his mother, taking a room with his aunt Vera. Shawn saw Kim regularly, but the on-again-off-again nature of their relationship troubled him, and the picture was further complicated by the baby. He still saw Kim and played with Naja nearly every day. Though he wasn't chasing new girlfriends, marrying Kim never seemed to be in the cards.

Shawn worked for a time at the Menomonee Club for Boys & Girls in Chicago's trendy Old Town neighborhood. Soon he got the urge to play ball again, hoping to make a run at the career that might have been. In November 1999, he signed on with a minor league IBA team called the Des Moines Dragons. (The IBA is long defunct.) He hoped that the experience and limited exposure might lead to a job offer overseas. His career rebirth was short—he was home before Christmas, which, surprisingly, was a relief: missing a few weeks of Naja's first year tugged at him. When it became clear that even a low level pro career was unrealistic, he vowed to be an even bigger part of Naja's life.

In the late 1990s, the talk on the West Side was that Luther Bedford would retire soon. Shawn wondered for the first time if a return to Marshall as a coach could be something to consider. He knew he didn't want to replace Bedford—it would be too much pressure to follow a coach with such a long history of winning. Shawn didn't have a teaching certificate but with a college degree he might be able to get on with the public schools in some capacity.

Instead, in 2000 he began working for the aptly named scouting service guru Rick Ball, and they formed the Chicagoland Hoops Scouting Network. While Rick Ball had specialized in junior college coverage for the benefit of four-year schools, his new foray into Chicago, with Shawn's support, was a natural move. Many of the Public League players didn't qualify academically for Division I basketball, so Ball decided to expand scouting coverage to kids who would soon be playing at junior colleges. Shawn helped open up the high-school-to-junior-college market for Rick Ball in the city.

The subscription-only newsletter—like my own *Chicago Prep Magnet*—put Shawn back in touch with college coaches, and his contacts mushroomed. For a short time, he partnered with a friend to do his own scouting service, just as I had done, which he called No Books, No Ball.

He canvassed the summer tournaments and events and helped place dozens of local players in colleges, advised them on their options, and got them out of Chicago.

Frinda Harrington was still living on Kedvale in the winter of 2003. The neighbors on one side were an older couple whose live-in grandkids were a source of great joy to her, and Shawn's mother was back and forth constantly between the homes.

These neighbors had a low-profile business selling candy and single cigarettes, more a community service or hobby than a lucrative black market enterprise. Kids pooled their nickels and dimes to knock on the door for Milky Ways or M&Ms on a Saturday afternoon. Adults might pop in for a chat, a can of Coke, or a single loose Marlboro.

Andrew James and Cory Lloyd were half brothers who lived just a few streets away on Keystone. They had never met Frinda or her neighbors, but they'd heard talk about the cash-only business. Andrew James, nearly thirty years of age, was a huge man, at six foot two and three hundred pounds. On one arm, he had a tattoo that read "Mafia Insane." Another tattoo, a top hat and cane, indicated that James was a member of the Vice Lords street gang. The other arm read "Thug" and "R.I.P. Squirt."

Cory Lloyd was older but much smaller, and his face seemed locked in a permanent sneer. His arms were covered with tattoos that also signaled his gang affiliation, including the five-pointed star and "V.L." for Vice Lords.

James and Lloyd came to scout out the home early one evening in February 2003. Later that night, they borrowed a gun from a friend before returning to pound on the door.

"Chicago Police!" James yelled.

When the grandfather unlocked the door, Lloyd, brandishing the gun, barged in. He and James ordered the two children, ages six and ten, into the bathroom. "This will all be over soon," he told the kids. "Don't worry."

James and Lloyd demanded all the money in the house, which was immediately handed over. The older kid kept trying to escape from the bathroom, which distracted the duo, but James finally bound and gagged the owners, along with another man who was visiting, then slit their throats.

Right around this time, Frinda Harrington heard the shouting and walked in. When she realized what she'd stumbled upon, she ran out the back door. Cory Lloyd chased her. Before she could get out of the yard, Lloyd shot her twice in the head at close range.

Miraculously, the homeowners and their visitor lived. Frinda Harrington did not.

Andrew James and Cory Lloyd were convicted for the murder. James was sentenced to thirty-five years in prison. Lloyd got a life sentence and is ineligible for parole. The men, who had served time previously for armed robberies, testified that after the home invasion they split the take of forty dollars.

Minutes before Frinda Harrington was pronounced deceased, Shawn was approached by a representative of Gift of Hope, the state's procurer of organ donations. The rep asked a difficult question at an impossible time. Was Shawn willing to allow Frinda's organs to be harvested to help others stay alive?

"The question really caught me off guard, but it didn't take me long to decide," Shawn says. Frinda's lungs, kidneys, and liver were all donated, saving three lives.

The name of the organization, the easy way it rolled off his tongue, stayed with Shawn. *Gift of Hope, Gift of Hope.* Soon after Frinda's death, he was approached by Illinois's secretary of state, Jesse White, who had gotten wind of the story. White, a longtime advocate of organ donations, approached Shawn to invite him to appear in a televised public service announcement in support of the program.

Like most black Chicagoans, Shawn knew the Jesse White story: White was himself a standout athlete in Chicago who later starred at Alabama State University. A war hero and teacher, he could claim years of humanitarian involvement at the Cabrini-Green housing projects. His most visible community involvement was the Jesse White Tumblers gymnastics show team, but his hands-on philanthropy with the poor made him a hero in the black community.

Shawn agreed to do the commercial, which aired statewide. After the filming, the secretary of state cornered him. "Shawn, if you ever need anything," White told him, "a job, help, whatever, be sure to give me a call." When Shawn admitted to being ready for a career change, White suggested that since he had earned his college degree, he should come downtown and apply for work at the secretary of state's office. Shawn applied, and while he never heard back, he figured if there was ever an emergency he could count on Jesse White.

Shawn often talks about how basketball saved him as a boy, and the sport was again his salvation in the year after Frinda's murder. This time he was not vying for a scholarship or leading his college team to the playoffs. Rather, it was simply pickup basketball at a local XSport Fitness facility. Not yet thirty years old, his only concession to aging was his preference for a wooden gym floor rather than outdoor asphalt. Playing more basketball than at any time since his college days, he'd get lost in the competition, the joy of the fast break, the no-look pass for an easy bucket, and it helped him hold things together emotionally. The fact that it was usually anonymous competition—not friends who knew the details of the tragedy—made him more comfortable.

"I'll admit I was a momma's boy to the fullest," Shawn says, "and I was trying not to be bitter about what had happened. I had to swallow a hard pill."

Three years had passed since I had walked away from college coaching. I traded phone messages with Shawn that spring offering my condolences, and I kept his number.

Back in Chicago without a four-year college degree, Ontario Brown worked odd jobs with his uncle until 2004, when he hooked on with food distributor European Imports, filling orders in their warehouse. The new job included a simple commute and a steady paycheck that was a substantial raise. He had a good future ahead—European Imports was a respected company that dealt in fancy cheeses, meats, and seafood. The potential to move up the ladder was strong and the timing was good. He'd been unsatisfied with previous positions, and besides, he and Sabrina also had a young son to look out for—Ontario Brown Junior.

It wasn't just the older generation of parents who wanted their kids out of Chicago. Sabrina, the boy's mother, felt that the city was too dangerous and rents were too high, and she started looking around for a town not so far away where housing was affordable. Her search eventually led her to Elkhart, Indiana, and she moved there with Lykeisha and Ontario Jr. This decision bothered Ontario Sr.—he did not see what was so great about Elkhart, but he kept quiet about it, and drove the eighty-seven miles to see his kids whenever he had a free weekend.

Shawn still had an army of aunties who would do anything for him, and a biological father somewhere, but Frinda's murder forced him to look inward—he was an orphan now—and at his own history. He needed to examine his own path, and with no home or parent to cling to, he began thinking more about Luther Bedford and the coach's influence on his life.

Bedford was a native of Rockford, a town about a hundred miles west of Chicago. After graduating from high school in 1955, he enrolled at Illinois Wesleyan, a small college two hours south of his hometown, intending to play football and basketball. He was one of the two first black athletes in the history of the college. (Another black athlete had already attended briefly, but he left under pressure after trying to date a white student.)

Football teammate Dennis Bridges, who went on to coach basketball at the college for thirty-five seasons, says Bedford was not sensitive about being a minority, and he came off as unconcerned about people's prejudices. "Luther might have been burning inside," Bridges says, "but had a way of laughing off slights."

There were limits, however, and proper respect was important to Bedford. As a freshman, he learned that Wesleyan often scheduled basketball road trips to Mississippi, where segregation laws meant he wouldn't be allowed to play. Rather than deal with the indignity of being left behind, he quit after half a season to concentrate on football and run track. Bedford's time at Wesleyan was mostly without incident and he fit in reasonably well. He could often be found at the center of nickel poker games on the team bus, and he established a reputation on the field for being audacious and focused enough to catch passes amid a swarm of defenders.

During his senior year, Bedford was at the heart of a postgame fight. Illinois State had Wesleyan beat, but rather than run out the clock on the last play, the Illinois State quarterback tried to toss one more long pass to run up the score. Bedford, who played both offense and defense, took exception to this insult and mauled the quarterback, tackling him hard as the final whistle blew.

Bedford was the last one out of the pile after referees and coaches broke up the brawl. A photo of the fight wound up on the cover of the *Chicago Sun-Times* the next day. Nobody ever ascribed racial tension as the cause—the schools were less than two miles apart and heated rivals.

After a short stint in the army, Bedford began working at Marshall as a teacher in 1963. He spent four decades there, twenty-six as the boys' basketball coach, and even after retiring from coaching in 1999, he still taught. Bedford's win total was impressive: 450 wins against 267 losses. He never won a state championship (four hundred other schools competed in Marshall's AA division), but he'd qualified for Illinois's final four on three occasions—which he'd advanced to after winning Chicago's ultracompetitive Public League title (involving roughly sixty other teams).

Bedford could never quite give up football, serving as an assistant coach for years, usually working with the receivers. His best football player was Darryl Stingley, whose NFL career got cut short when he was paralyzed from the neck down after an on-field head-on collision. Bedford remained close to Stingley, serving on the board of his youth organization. (Stingley died in 2007 at the age of fifty-five.)

Bedford had a long partnership with Al Williams, his frosh-soph coach. Williams was more of an "X & O" coach than Bedford, who was more likely to use his instincts than his notebook with the game on the line. And Bedford's instincts often led him to seek advice from Al Williams.

"For being so strict," Ontario Brown says, "Bedford was very receptive to suggestions. In a crucial timeout, he would openly ask Williams *What should we do here?*"

The players didn't often appreciate Bedford's strong-handed discipline. "He was always telling them what was right from wrong," iconic Marshall girls basketball coach Dorothy Gaters was quoted once as saying, "instead of trying to be their friend."

Hoop Dreams star Arthur Agee says Bedford made the rules and divisions between the street and basketball clear. "He'd say *You want to be a gangbanger? Don't be part of my team. We ain't having none of that bullshit.* He understood there'd be gang members that the players knew, but there was nobody on his court throwing up gang signs. If Bedford knew you were affiliated, he didn't even let you try out for the team."

The coach's door was open, but a kid needed a legitimate reason to bother him. Players could joke with Bedford, but not too often.

Bedford was impossible to deceive, and because he taught within the building (as nearly every Public League coach did at that time) word of anyone screwing around filtered back to him quickly. And, of course, that meant a paddling, which could have unanticipated consequences. Once, a player named Magellan Fitzgerald got a D on his report card. The next day, the whack of Luther Bedford's paddle startled Fitzgerald so much that he leapt forward and banged his head, resulting in a gash.

"Bedford was grumpy, plain and simple," says Tyrone Hayes, the security guard who helped recover Shawn's stolen car. "We really needed structure. We weren't bad kids, but we were desperate for father figures. We weren't scared to be taught or coached, but with Bedford there was a kind of fear involved."

Hayes, who served as team captain in the late 1980s, was not immune to Bedford's wrath, and after a pause, he mentions the Bedford staple that even the players' parents condoned. "Of course I got paddled," he says, "and I wish the paddling had never happened, but I also think it

Luther Bedford had an old-school view of the world and ran his Marshall basketball team accordingly. Magellan Fitzgerald, bandage still on his forehead, stands behind his coach. *Chicago Sun-Times*

made us become good citizens. I'll admit I didn't even begin to understand him until I was older. In my era, even a white coach paddling a player wouldn't have been a problem."

Like all great coaches, Bedford evolved. "In the 1980s," Hayes says, "and even up to when Shawn was the point guard, he wasn't quite ready to really let us loose to play." After decades, the coach made concessions on the offensive end, but Bedford refused to budge on altering his daunting presses and traps.

A few months after Frinda Harrington was killed in 2003, Luther Bedford, who'd already given up coaching, retired from teaching as well.

Other major changes were on the way. By this time, Kim Jenkins was working at Saints Mary and Elizabeth Hospital in Humboldt Park. Shawn and Kim's second daughter, Malia Harrington, was born in 2005, and Naja quickly took to her new baby sister.

A year after Malia was born, Luther Bedford died of cardiac arrest. He was sixty-seven.

Chicago Tribune columnist Barry Temkin wrote about Bedford after attending his funeral, an overflow event in Marshall's spacious old auditorium. "He was old school in the best way, living by a code of integrity and morality in which you talked straight, played by the rules and put kids first. Later in his career, when too many coaches were practically general managers piecing together all-star teams, Bedford still took what came through the door and turned out responsible adults. Winning was a happy byproduct."

Bedford's death hit Shawn hard. Although he didn't spend a huge amount of time with his coach after Frinda's murder—an extended audience with Bedford was rare—he thought about the man constantly. Like so many Marshall players, he viewed his former coach with enormous respect, as a great source of wisdom.

With Bedford and Frinda gone, Shawn was adrift. Naja was eight. Soon he would have to explain to her that her grandmother had been murdered. He had decisions to make about what to do with Frinda's house and whether to continue to live on Kedvale. Life on their block had been disrupted, and Kim began considering a move to get her kids out of the neighborhood. Where might Shawn find a home now? He'd rarely been without a job, yet he didn't have much to show for his time out of college in terms of a career. He needed a new direction, and he wondered about working at Marshall. Former basketball stars without college degrees were finding work within the school system. Coach Bedford was gone, but Shawn was on good terms with girls' coach Dorothy Gaters. In the midst of this uncertainty, Shawn put in an application with the Chicago Public Schools. A return to Marshall to help carry on Luther Bedford's legacy now seemed to be where his heart was taking him.

9

CHICAGO RUNS ON CLOUT, and if Shawn was going to get hired at Marshall, he would need Dorothy Gaters's help.

Like so many others, Gaters's family migrated to Chicago's West Side from Mississippi in 1950, when she was seven years old. She attended Marshall at a time when no girls' basketball team existed, although their boys were a perennial city power. Gaters earned her degree from DePaul University, but she didn't begin playing basketball seriously until after college, at a park in the historic Bronzeville neighborhood on the near South Side. Televised pro and college games were scarce in the 1960s, so she was influenced more by the Chicago Park District games and local high school teams.

In 1969, Gaters began teaching at Marshall, but she had few inclinations to coach. In the fall of 1974, at a faculty meeting the day before classes commenced, the room fell silent when the principal asked for a volunteer to be the girls' basketball coach.

Gaters raised her hand.

At that time, the girls weren't a "team" so much as a "club," with just four games on the schedule. "We had a very long road ahead," Gaters says in her typical understated fashion. Girls' sports had always been given short shrift, especially in the days before President Nixon pushed through Title IX. Then, fewer than 4 percent of high school girls played any sport at all.

At Gaters's first practice that fall, Luther Bedford walked into the tiny girls' gym unannounced. She looked at her watch. Her team had another hour left. She had heard that at other schools, workout times, use of the big gym, uniforms, practice gear, or respect of any kind were hard to come by. She feared Bedford would attempt to order her girls out of their own barebones gym, and that might lead to a verbal confrontation.

"He said he'd just come to observe us and help out," Gaters says. "I was very surprised."

Bedford continued to attend her practices when his schedule permitted, often in half-hour blocks. He'd sit on the girls' bench during games. They even scouted upcoming opponents for each other. Bedford required his boys to attend the Lady Commando contests if they didn't have a game themselves. Sometimes they'd view the first half, then slip off into one of the smaller practice gyms and go on about their business. The girls returned the favor by backing the boys.

Gaters studied Bedford and became a regular at his training sessions and games. Bedford took the time to share his philosophy, the defensive schemes, the presses and traps. "You could say I *borrowed* from Luther," she says, "and I can't emphasize enough about how that affected my career. I watched real close to learn his system." For decades now, both boys and girls have tagged defensive sets and plays with the same names. "From those early days," she recalls, "it was as though Marshall had one program. Not a boys' team and girls' team, but simply a *Basketball Program*. We weren't getting the respect as young women that we deserved, yet we always got it from Luther and within the building at Marshall."

This peculiar idea had a profound effect on the mindset of Bedford's boys. If the gruff old-fashioned coach treated the girls as equals—a freakishly unusual concept even today—women must be equal to men. "It was just understood," Ontario Brown says, "that supporting the girls was expected of the boys. They were our equals and we were taught to respect women." It was a simple but extraordinary fact.

Often the frosh-soph boys were used as fodder to scrimmage the varsity girls. When that happened, the concept of equality played out in terms the young boys could understand.

Tyrese Williford, a boys' team star who graduated in 2016, still recalls what Shawn told him when the freshmen marched to the girls' practice gym for the first time: "Those girls are going to kill you guys."

"We thought it was all talk," Williford admits, "but they beat us by six. Looking back, sometimes I wish I could have played for Ms. Gaters.

Anyway, scrimmaging the varsity girls was something us boys did a lot when I was a freshman, and you'd never talk smack to them."

Bedford's legacy was less about his impressive win totals and more about the way he honored the Marshall girls' teams and interacted with Dorothy Gaters. "[Bedford] savored rather than resented Gaters's gigantic success," the *Tribune*'s Barry Temkin wrote in his homage to the coach.

Chanel Khammarath, the girls' best player in the 2013–14 season, says, "It didn't have to be explained to us. We just had a different understanding and it affected the students as a whole, growing up and respecting each other." This became more apparent to her when she went away to junior college in Kansas. "There, the boys would come in to interrupt our practice, we'd have to ask them to be quiet, or send for our coach. That never went down at Marshall." Despite Gaters's maternal nature, Khammarath says her coach had an edge: "She doesn't like weakness or anybody going through the motions. And she does not like losing."

Gaters did not shy away from the paddling.

"She lit us up, too! And I thank her for it," says Jennifer Jones, who went on to star at Kansas State, and later served as Dorothy Gaters's assistant coach. Gaters and Bedford were in lockstep on nearly everything, but Gaters gave up the paddling policy in the late 1980s.

Even as Gaters approached her one thousandth win at Marshall, she remained a study in humility and grace, although she exudes an air of royalty. "I don't think winning a thousand games has much relevance outside of Marshall High School," she was quoted in *SLAM* magazine as saying. "Nobody has had more help than me. I've had five WNBA players, including Cappie Pondexter and Kimberly Williams. This neighborhood has always been a hotbed for talent, and I think the credit for my wins should go to my players." When asked about her biggest influences, Gaters is hardly a name dropper. Everyone she credits is either a Marshall coach or a dear friend.

A decade after Luther Bedford's passing, the boys and girls still feature many of his plays and presses. Gaters's record is unparalleled: twenty-six Chicago Public League titles, eight Illinois state championships. The one visible concession to her success is that she buys a new Cadillac every year.

Nearly every one of Gaters's players has gone on to college, and most get a scholarship of some kind, an astonishing fact. What's just as impressive is that when things go badly—turnover, missed shot, defensive mistake—her girls never hang their heads, pout, or scowl at the referee. "If a coach loses her cool, the players will see that and follow suit," says Jennifer Jones. "You're not going to see Dorothy lose her cool." This seems an invaluable mindset for a West Side kid, and Gaters herself is the model Commando in chief, unflappable at every turn.

Gaters never considered taking a college coaching job. "It was a different world when I first started having success," she says. "And honestly, it would have been difficult because I'm somewhat of a homebody and I couldn't leave the Marshall family. That's what I feel we are at Marshall, a family."

When I pressed Dorothy Gaters about Shawn's respect for the girls, she insisted that in his case it was something he was born with. "I don't think we can take credit for the way Shawn thinks," she says, "that's just his character." She still recalls meeting him for the first time in the late 1970s. "Frinda first brought him up to Marshall," she says, "and he was very small, he couldn't have even been three years old." One of the teachers asked him, "What are you going to be when you grow up?"

Young Shawn didn't hesitate, and his answer has remained in Gaters's mind for decades. "I'm going to buy my momma a house," Shawn declared.

Shawn began as an assistant basketball coach at Marshall for the 2007–08 season under his former teammate, Courtney Hargrays. He reported to the school in time for practice, but was not working full time in the building yet.

That Courtney Hargrays was named the head coach might have raised eyebrows anywhere besides Marshall—he had been Dorothy Gaters's assistant the previous year. This was another sign of the bridge between the boys' and girls' teams at Marshall. Promoting a girls' assistant into the head boys' coach position is unheard of in high school sports. Shawn had briefly held hope that he might get named head coach, but he could not be upset. Hargrays was one of his oldest friends.

The transition into his new career was smooth because Shawn was easygoing with the players. The fact that "Coach Shaky" had been a star player as well gave him even more cachet.

A decade after his college days, Shawn still jumped in to demonstrate on a drill, and he played in the open gym pickup games in the off-season. He quickly became known as a motivator, a coach who lifted his players and asked them to push themselves. "He still had that jump-shot," 2014 team captain Citron Miller says. "He'd tell us to never give up, to be the one to put up extra shots after practice. He was outspoken in a good way, and we all respected him."

Hargrays, with Shawn as his assistant, had extraordinary success in his rookie season of 2008, winning the Public League's city title and the Illinois state championship, something that even Luther Bedford had never done.

Hargrays must have been stunned by the controversy that followed that championship season: a student accused the coach of paddling him. While corporal punishment was a given under Luther Bedford, nobody had ever complained. Administrators had either condoned or ignored Bedford's policy, but what was once considered necessary a decade earlier was now being called archaic, even brutal.

Like all Marshall players from the 1970s through the 1990s, Hargrays had experienced Bedford's corporal punishment, so it's easy to imagine him thinking that paddling was not only an acceptable policy, but an important one. (In this case, Hargrays's accuser made the accusation during a television interview, though he was not even on the basketball team. The entire episode suggested a setup, and Marshall insiders believe Hargrays's ousted predecessor was behind it.) Although Hargrays denied paddling kids, he was fired, never resurfacing at another school or coaching another game.

In the summer of 2008, on the heels of the state championship, with the program unstable, another Marshall boys' assistant—not Shawn—was the surprise pick as new coach.

Henry Cotton hadn't attended Marshall. He graduated from Austin High School in 1985. While hiring a girls' team assistant coach had surprised outsiders, hiring Cotton as the next head coach surprised Marshall *insiders*—not only was he not a Marshall grad, he'd been a longtime Westinghouse assistant coach. Former Commando players (a proudly loyal insular group) were dismayed, not because they had anything against Henry Cotton—rather, they remembered the fever-pitched Westinghouse v. Marshall rivalry.

Dorothy Gaters was the athletics director and instrumental in hiring the new basketball coach. "I had asked Henry Cotton to come over to Marshall in the first place," she says. "He'd been around for years and he'd worked at Austin YMCA and knew a lot of the young kids. I thought he would be a stabilizing influence."

Not being offered the job again was difficult news for Shawn, but he liked Cotton. The two had worked well together as assistants on the state championship team. Cotton was well regarded in Chicago basketball circles and had apprenticed under Chris Head, a rabid disciplinarian who won a lot of games at Westinghouse. Unlike the alumni, the current Commando players cared less about tradition and pedigree and quickly adapted. The new coach implemented Head's regimented program, but with a more caring touch. Cotton does not have a teaching certificate, but like Tyrone Hayes he works in the building as security.

Shawn, loyal to a fault, never considered leaving Marshall.

———

"Shaky was the *cool* coach," says Tyrese Williford, who would rise to stardom in 2016. "He could be strict like all of them, but he also had a phenomenal presence on the court. We all knew he'd been a college star, and he was the reason I wanted to stay late in the gym and keep working on my game."

Part of Shawn's charisma, Williford says, emanated from his sense of humor. "Shaky talked a little trash, but he'd do it to get you to laugh, get you motivated."

"We could all connect with him," says Citron Miller. "He seemed young like us, and he was usually our motivator, getting us fired up."

And, of course, the big Ford Expedition helped. No Marshall player had a car, and securing a lift home after practice or games was always an issue. The players understood that getting in the big car with Shawn meant a significant conversation was about to unfold.

One player who always climbed in Shawn's vehicle after practice was Martin Satterfield, a typical Commando in many ways. Satterfield was six foot two, too small to dominate rival big men, but he toiled away. Lean, hungry, tough, and unskilled, he was a key player on the 2011 team that finished with a sparkling 27-7 record. He was a classic "tweener," not a college prospect because he was too small to play inside and not an accomplished enough shooter or ball-handler to convert to playing guard.

Satterfield lived just ten blocks from school, an easy walk if not for the bitter cold and the threat of the streets. He recalls a powerful level of intimacy on those car rides. The coach would stop outside his apartment and let the engine idle. "Shawn was like one of us," he says, "and the kind of coach every kid in Chicago would want. He treated me so well, and because we lived in the same area, he made sure I got home safe."

Henry Cotton, like Shawn, drove the players home from practice and games, a typical move for Public League coaches, particularly in the winter. Most Marshall players came from the West Side, and Cotton had his own routine, a policy, as they approached a player's apartment. "Get your keys out of your pocket," he'd tell the player, or else, "Call your mom and make sure she's unlocked the door."

Once the basketball season was over, Satterfield and Shawn began to talk about Richard J. Daley College, nine miles south of his home, as an option. Maybe Satterfield could try out for their team. Although only a small percentage of players from the two-year city colleges go on to make rosters at four-year schools, Satterfield still wanted to keep his playing career alive, and Shawn wanted him in school. The city colleges don't have full scholarships for basketball or dorms, but occasionally they offer tuition and book waivers.

"Shawn respected all of us young men, not just because of basketball," Satterfield says today. "We could go to him with our problems, and we had some very serious talks about life in the Expedition." He says the coach warned him constantly about the dangers of the street.

"We had a lot of one-on-one time," he continues, "and he was very much like a father figure. We could tell jokes and crack on each other. I could tell him everything I was going through."

Satterfield was going through plenty: his oldest brother was incarcerated, and both coach and player knew the trouble and temptations that waited outside the Expedition, and what was at stake.

"He was my coach," Satterfield says, then adds the footnote that every Commando tacks on: "He was my friend, too."

Shawn understood the dangers and temptations West Side kids like Martin Satterfield faced. He also knew that arrests for minor infractions could be typical, that good kids could be popped by the police for possession of weed, loitering, or fighting. Run-ins with the police were common, and Shawn, despite his basketball star/model citizen status had his own stories to tell, although he had never been arrested.

Home from junior college for a few weeks in the summer of 1997, Shawn and a handful of young men were gathered on the corner one afternoon, the men poking fun at Shawn's rundown brown car with Missouri plates that read SHAKY 20. Shawn's block on Kedvale was fairly close-knit and relatively trouble free, and that afternoon, he was with three old friends.

Out of nowhere, a police cruiser bounced aggressively over the curb and two cops leaped out. The officers ordered Shawn and his friends to put their hands onto the side of their squad car and spread their legs while they frisked them for weapons and drugs. One cop, a young African American man, began to taunt the boys. "You guys think you're gangbangers? Think you're tough? We're the biggest gang in Chicago, and I'm licensed to carry a gun!"

Some of the young men started to yelp in protest until Shawn cut them off. "Let them do their job," he said. "Let's get this over with."

The police had likely noticed his Missouri license plates. The racial makeup of the young men was likely a factor, although Shawn knew that his neighbors Manuel and Peter were Puerto Rican. The police began to search the car and even go through his Nike gym bags. "After a while," he says, "we were all sitting on the curb waiting for them to finish." They weren't done, though. The officers questioned him about the car and his residency status. Shawn was perplexed. A 1987 Chevy Celebrity was not a car a drug dealer might be sporting, wasn't exactly "probable cause." But Shawn figured if being respectful was going to get him on his way sooner, so be it. Eventually the police left without charging anyone with a crime.

There were other instances when Shawn was stopped for no apparent reason, but he negotiated his way through with dignity and composure. Once, while in a car borrowed from a friend, he was pulled over by Chicago police. An empty sandwich baggie in the backseat prompted the officers to handcuff Shawn—the implication was that he was some sort of drug dealer, or why else would he have a baggie. Shawn pleaded with them: check out his gym bag, his sweaty T-shirt and wet towel. He was just coming back from playing basketball.

The cops shoved him into the back of their squad car anyway, and Shawn kept quiet, trying to calm himself to keep from lashing out. He figured they couldn't charge him with possession of a sandwich bag. When the two officers began to argue about what was wrong with the Bulls in the post–Michael Jordan era, Shawn saw an opening. "The Bulls need to abandon the triangle offense they've been using," he said. "Without Jordan, it won't be as effective." Shawn spoke with such calm authority that one officer twisted around in his seat and gave Shawn a look.

"What the hell do you know?" the cop said.

"I played at New Mexico State," Shawn offered. That began a conversation about the local high school basketball scene. Who were the best players to come out of the city? What was the best Public League team ever? The conversation continued as the squad car drove right past the police station at Grand and Central Avenue. Shawn, still in handcuffs, figured he might be okay at that point. When an emergency call came over the radio, the cops pulled over.

"If we let you out here, can you get back to your car on your own?" one cop asked.

"Let me out on the moon," Shawn said, "and I can get home."

Most male coaches would balk at Marshall's built-in gender equality, but Henry Cotton, who can seem aloof at first, has a deep respect for Dorothy Gaters. Cotton is not only a shrewd head coach, he's also deeply involved with his players' lives. A steady stream of ballplayers flow in and out of his office, even during the off-season, and often for no explicit reason. Although he's six foot three and sturdy, he's not an intimidator, and he communicates freely with his players.

Cotton is comfortable delegating decisions to empower his assistants. For instance, it was one of Shawn's many duties to decide on the matching outfits the staff wore to their upcoming games. *Black pants, white shirt, maroon sweater* Shawn might text to the other coaches.

This open line of communication also included a systematic "texting tree" to implement an in-season curfew for the varsity, sophomore, and freshman teams, over thirty players. Not a cell phone junkie or lover of the Internet, Cotton didn't want to get overwhelmed, so he utilized his assistant coaches in this plan. Each night, players were required to text or call their assigned coach from their *mother's* cell phone to announce that they were home for the night.

Tyrese Williford confirms the tight control the coaches had on the players during his time at Marshall. "After every game, whether it's for the regular season, summer league, or spring, you have to let the coach know you got home," he says. But the policy stemmed more from safety concerns than heavy-handedness. "Once you get in the house," he adds, "you don't want to go back outside anyway."

Part of this all-encompassing structure for the program included assigning a senior to mentor a freshman basketball player. The nightly texting and calls went from player to player as well, the elaborate checks-and-balances designed so no Commando fell through the cracks.

The appointments of Courtney Hargrays and Henry Cotton at Marshall represented a significant break from tradition—but also a city-wide trend. Previously, all coaches had to be certified teachers. When that requirement was tossed out, the change destabilized the Chicago Public League.

Until the 1980s, *every* coach taught in the public schools, and most in the high school building where they coached. Occasionally a teacher came over at the end of the school day from a local grammar school. When I was the coach at Von Steuben for the 1981–82 season, I did not teach in the CPS system, but I had a college diploma and teaching certificate.

Over a decade ago, the CPS dropped the requirement that all students pass four years of physical education—and dropped many teachers along with it. Since many of the varsity basketball coaches taught P.E., this reduction cut deeply into the potential pool of coaches.

Dorothy Gaters says the challenge of finding coaches with college degrees who teach is compounded by another obvious problem—declining enrollments. She blames what she calls "the so-called charter school movement." Some Chicago high schools now have as few as two hundred students; Marshall has just four hundred enrolled. "We're all trying to offer a dozen sports, so where are the coaches going to come from?" she says. "There isn't enough faculty to cover every sport."

The stipend that the head basketball coaches get—about $6,000—is woefully weak. Most suburban schools offer twice that amount. "You can feel underappreciated," Gaters says, "and some people would rather go home at the end of the teaching day." Gaters at one time served as a one-woman girls' athletic department, coaching tennis, track, softball, and volleyball too. She wouldn't have time now, with summer basketball leagues and spring tournaments.

Chicago Public School teachers make a decent salary, starting at just under $50,000 annually. While many experienced teachers don't feel that the coaching stipend is worth it, a security guard or educational support personnel worker like Shawn often needs the bonus.

Between the cutting of physical education teachers, declining faculty numbers because of the expansion of charter schools, and substandard compensation for coaches, most CPS head basketball coaches don't have teaching certificates, and many do not have college degrees. Gaters is not a proponent of this trend, but she says, "As long as the coach works in the building, it shouldn't be a problem." Basketball isn't physics, after all.

However, critics suggest that there's a very specific time when having a degree is helpful: "Chicago kids need help finding a college that is out of town," one veteran coach insists. "If the coach has a degree and has been through the process of hunting for schools, that really helps players who need to get away." While you don't need a college degree to understand the game, getting to college is a difficult process—applying, getting SAT or ACT training, gathering official transcripts, negotiating financial aid, connecting to college coaches, selecting a school—and an experienced hand helps a high school player navigate the system.

At Marshall, this was part of the reason Shawn was such a good complement to Cotton. He had played basketball in junior college, Division I, and Division II, and even directed his own scouting service briefly. Shawn had his communications degree and was usually the bridge between out-of-town schools and under-recruited players.

Marshall coach Henry Cotton is by all measures a respected leader. Citron Miller says Cotton stressed to the boys that once they graduated from Marshall, they would not have the same circle of friends as a safety net. "He said that after high school we were going to be on our own," Miller recalls. "Everything he said was true and we respected him for that." Cotton is strict, but reasonable. However, like the vast majority of the city's coaches, Cotton doesn't have a degree, which sends a mixed message to the players. *If education is so important, how come our coach didn't graduate from college?* Critics say that the coaches-without-degree trend means the schools are prioritizing winning over academics. The trend has evolved even though boys' basketball is the most prestigious sport at nearly every Chicago public high school. It was always nearly impossible to locate a qualified public school swimming or wrestling coach. Today it has become difficult for school principals to find a qualified, certified teacher willing to take on the challenge of basketball.

In 2010, Kim Jenkins's nursing job allowed her to save enough to make a down payment on a home in a mixed neighborhood just north of where Shawn was living. Kim's mother, Claretha Jenkins, moved into the newer housing development as well, which had basic security measures. Residents punched in a code at the gate to drive into the enclave. Kim's move from Kedvale was prompted by her belief that the neighborhood had gotten too violent. She'd seen the block deteriorate, and the brutality of the neighborhood was numbing. And sometimes it could be just plain bizarre.

After Frinda's house was sold, Shawn had moved in with his grandmother on west Wabansia, a thirty-minute walk northwest. But in the summer of 2012, Shawn was back on his Kedvale block for a social visit. Before he could knock on a friend's door, he bumped into Hawk, a longtime resident. After handshakes and hugs they chatted away until an argument broke out between a few men across the street. One teenager yelled something about killing somebody.

Hawk, a man in his fifties, left Shawn on the doorstep and approached the group as the calming voice of reason. "All of you stop all this," he pleaded. "Let's quiet down. Ain't nobody killing nobody."

Shawn, curious, slowly moved down the steps.

Suddenly, one of the men in the argument, whose arm appeared to be injured, pulled a gun from his sling. "Who's talking about killing somebody?" the man yelled, and fired at Hawk from just a few feet away. The bullet hit Hawk in the face.

Everyone scattered, and the shooter opened fire on them as well, spraying shots all around Kedvale Avenue. "I was taught that if somebody's shooting," Shawn says, "it's best to run zigzag." Since most of the fleeing men ran headed south, Shawn ran north until the shooting stopped and the gunman took off in a car.

Shawn cautiously walked back to Hawk, where a half dozen people, mostly women, gathered around his body. There were gunpowder burns around Hawk's neck. The shooter had been that close. "I took one look and went up to sit on the front steps of my old porch," he says, "and I just sat there thinking about Hawk. He'd tried to be the peacemaker, and look what happened."

One of the women began to pray loudly over Hawk's body. Others shouted *amen* and *hallelujah,* while some just shook their heads or wept. It was then Shawn noticed Hawk's teenage son pacing in front of his father. The boy soon drowned out the prayers by hollering over and over, "They killed my daddy!"

The howl of ambulances and police cars sounded from the east. Shawn sat with his elbows on his knees, chin in his hands, and tried to keep from crying. Hawk had lived on the block as far back as Shawn could remember.

"Just then," Shawn says, "Hawk sat up! I mean, *straight* up! It was freaky."

The women screamed and, as the men had done minutes before, took off at a sprint in both directions.

Hawk's survival was a miracle. "The bullet had gone through his cheeks," Shawn says, "and knocked out a couple of teeth, but Hawk walked into the ambulance on his own."

Shawn was relieved to have his daughters move a few miles north, and it was not much of an inconvenience for him. When Malia became old enough to attend elementary school, she didn't get admitted to the same one as her older sister. (The splitting of families is another indicator of the unraveling of Chicago's public education system.) When Naja finished eighth grade in 2012, her outstanding grades got her into Westinghouse College Prep. Shawn and Kim opted to send Malia to a charter school in the trendy Bucktown neighborhood, a long way from Naja's new high school but not far from Kim's job. Shawn took on the daily task of delivering Naja to Westinghouse each morning before heading to work.

One day in May 2011, a Chicago Police Department sergeant showed up at Marshall and insisted on a face-to-face meeting with the principal. The cop, who was a regular at Commando basketball games, claimed he'd seen a basketball player hanging out by the curb on the corner of Homan and Ohio, a known hotspot for drug dealing.

The cop was talking about Martin Satterfield—the kid Shawn Harrington had driven home so many times.

The principal asked the policeman to stick around to help intervene with Satterfield, and he agreed. But first, the principal did what every Marshall administrator did when a crucial meeting took place or decision was to be made. She asked Dorothy Gaters to attend.

"It was very emotional for me," Gaters says. "We challenged Martin right there."

The principal said, "I'll take those Air Force Ones right off your feet. That's the only reason you're out there, to get yourself a new pair of Nikes."

"She knew if I was barefoot," Satterfield says, "I wouldn't be on the corner." He once held a part-time job at a convenience store, but the lure of bigger money was irresistible. That day, however, Satterfield didn't admit that he had been selling drugs.

"But he didn't deny it, either," Gaters says.

Shawn warned him, too, but Satterfield kept his street life a secret. By the time Satterfield was twelve years old, he says today, he was running packets of cocaine and heroin to cars that pulled up to the corner near his home. He thinks that many of the buyers came from the suburbs, and occasionally the buyers were white. He'd make anywhere between $100 and $500 for a long day of work. "I can't even lie," Satterfield now says, "no sir. The recession had hit and I had to work the streets. It was strictly a money issue."

Shawn began working full time at Marshall as educational support personnel in the fall of 2011, four years after he took on his after-school coaching duties. His focus was on special education, where the case manager was a charming woman named Liz Chambers.

Chambers was raised in Englewood, now one of the city's most dangerous neighborhoods. She recalls longing for Shawn—or someone remotely like him—before he was hired. The school had only one paraprofessional and desperately needed a male role model for the boys to look up to. "He carried himself with such dignity," Chambers says. "He was immaculately dressed, and that's how he grabbed the boys at first, by how he presented himself. When he started talking they could right away see that he knew the school, knew the neighborhood. Shawn immediately connected with our students."

Perhaps most impressive, Chambers claims, was the way Shawn could code switch. "While he was very professional with the teachers," she says, "he talked to the boys just like he was one of them. I can't stress enough how much we needed Shawn."

Soon after Shawn started, Chambers told him that his first big challenge in special education was a kid named Anthony Hunter who had autism. Afraid of loud noises, Anthony rarely went to eat with the other kids, and "Turn It Up Thursday," a thunderous DJ-infused tradition in the Marshall cafeteria, wrecked him. He couldn't make conversation or eye contact, and simple social cues were hard for him to understand. Most times he appeared slow, unresponsive. No teacher at Marshall had been able to break through and connect with him. "Anthony had been missing so much of the world," Chambers says.

In Shawn, Anthony Hunter found a mentor who was patient and gentle enough to explain the world to him. Anthony sometimes stuttered and always avoided connecting, so Shawn sat next to him whenever he could. He whispered, soothed, joked. Because of the boy's fear of crowds—he was skinny and short, which compounded the problems—Shawn suggested the school dismiss him ten minutes early so he was not rattled by the swarming hallways or the crowded CTA bus home.

Although Shawn had never been trained to work with kids with autism, he was able to gradually peel back layers. A talented artist, Anthony began to blossom, drawing all the time. He feared sharing his original work with anyone, letting it out of his own hands, but he eventually allowed it to be Xeroxed.

In October of Anthony Hunter's senior year, Shawn approached him with a wild idea. "I think you should run for homecoming king," Shawn said.

Anthony was perplexed. Homecoming king?

Most Marshall students referred to Shawn as "Coach Shaky," but not Anthony Hunter. "At first, when Mister Harrington told me about homecoming," he recalls, "I had my doubts, but I gave it a try. Because he was a nice chill-out person and he helped me out with a lot because I wasn't very social."

"I wanted Anthony to get the respect that I got at Marshall," Shawn says, "like all the players got." Like any good coach, Shawn came up with a game plan. First, he had a few hundred lollipops made with *Anthony Hunter for Homecoming King* printed on them. The duo tied ribbons and a card to the candy, and Hunter sketched something original on each one.

Shawn figured the girls might be more sympathetic to this quest than the boys, so their first campaign stops were lunchroom tables where the girls clustered. Shawn and Anthony approached side-by-side at first. "I knew if anyone made a mean or rude comment," Shawn said, "even if they were joking, he might go back into his shell."

Just as Shawn had hoped, the girls gushed after Anthony's awkward campaign pitch and candy giveaway. Anthony grinned, and on they went with their bag of lollipops to the next table. That's where Shawn got another idea. As the boy gained confidence, Shawn began to prep the clusters of kids, moving to the next group ahead to forewarn the girls. "I'm sending Anthony Hunter over," he'd say, "and I need every one of you to be nice to him." Then the coach would return to Anthony, point at a new table. "Try that group now."

Gradually, over a few days nearly all the girls became receptive. But the boys' voting bloc might not be as sympathetic. Shawn had another idea.

That year's homecoming race offered stiff competition. Dorothy Gaters's nephew, Korbin McClain, was the most popular boy at the school. Not only was McClain the best player on the basketball team, he was handsome, generous, and brilliant. McClain was seen as the easy winner before the voting even commenced. A week into the campaign, Shawn went directly to the popular senior and made his pitch.

"If you win homecoming king," Shawn told him, "your life won't be any different. You're going to get a full ride to college, graduate, and be happy. But if Anthony Hunter wins, can you imagine how it would change his life?"

McClain got quiet for a minute, then offered up his own strategy. He would instruct his friends not to vote for him—vote, instead, for Anthony Hunter. The hoops star practically became Hunter's assistant campaign manager.

On election day's final class period, the principal and assistant principal appeared at Shawn's special ed class. They wanted to talk to Shawn and Anthony in the hallway to give them the news: Anthony Hunter had won by forty votes. The administrators and Shawn laughed and hugged. Nobody thought the kid had a hope of winning. Someone took out a phone and suggested a group photo. That's when Shawn realized that Anthony Hunter was gone.

"Anthony was so excited," Shawn says, "that he just took off running! He was ecstatic, and he literally ran up and down the hallways for ten minutes." (Hunter has no recollection of his hallway sprints.)

Hunter was just as thrilled when he got the traditional kiss from the homecoming queen.

"After that," Shawn says, "everyone just called him *King*. They would call out to Anthony, *What's up, King?* He just lit up at that, and people called him King for the rest of his time at Marshall."

In January of his final year, Anthony began to sit in front of the music speakers for the cafeteria's "Turn It Up Thursday," bobbing in time to the music, grooving. The King, holding court. He was drawing prolifically now, spending all of his free time with his art. Any image or photo could be reproduced with just a pencil. That spring, he was awarded admission at the prestigious Art Institute of Chicago.

Anthony, for financial reasons, did not plan on attending the senior prom—until Shawn heard about the situation. Shawn feared it might not be the kind of event for which Anthony could land a serious date, so he suggested the boy's sister be his chaperone. A teacher named Mrs. Marsh arranged for a nearby Men's Wearhouse to donate a tuxedo. Shawn rented a fancy sedan—his Expedition wouldn't do for prom—and his own tuxedo. He found a chauffer's hat and served as the driver.

"The fact that Mister Harrington actually believed that he could help me," Hunter says, "that's why I was willing to give everything a try."

Anthony Hunter's experience is not uncommon among former Marshall students or athletes. Upbeat, emotionally available, and caring, Shawn had an indelible impact on students and coworkers alike. Although he only taught or coached a small percentage of the student body, he knew virtually every student by name.

Korbin McClain, who went on to play college basketball and earn his degree, more-or-less declined the homecoming crown for a reason—respect for the coach who could switch codes. "Shaky was different," he says. "A lot coaches *say* they care but don't put much effort into it."

"After Anthony Hunter," Liz Chambers recalls, "Shawn became known as the go-to person in the entire school for students with any difficulties."

10

Minutes after Shawn Harrington was shot, Chicago police officer Eric Von Kondrat arrived at the corner of Augusta and Hamlin. Von Kondrat knew the area was a hotspot for shootings and drug deals and that police were already canvassing the area that morning. The scene, even to a battle-hardened veteran, was ominous. "There was shattered glass," he says, "and casings everywhere."

A Chicago cop for over twenty years, Von Kondrat was trim, fit, and looked much like the star football player and wrestler he'd been in the northwest suburbs. He was also very different from the white Chicago cops who make up 60 percent of the city's force in part because he was one of the very few white homeowners in East Garfield Park. Deeply involved in the neighborhood, he had even spent a few years as a football coach in the Chicago Public Schools—by chance, at Westinghouse High School.

When Von Kondrat saw Naja Harrington weeping next to the car, he went straight to her. First he had to get her to calm down and talk, so he asked where she went to school. "Let me call Ms. Jackson at Westinghouse," he said, "and tell her what happened."

Von Kondrat's training in emergency medical care often required him to be in the emergency room. He and Naja could both ride with her father in the ambulance, but he felt that was a bad idea. He continued chatting with Naja about Westinghouse to gain her trust before he convinced her to get in his squad car to follow the ambulance. "She was tripping out pretty good," he says, "and she was obviously in shock. She kept asking if her dad was going to be okay."

Von Kondrat felt a sense of relief wash over him on their drive behind the ambulance. Nobody had been killed, although the extent of

Shawn's injuries was unknown. "I kept thinking," he says, "How the heck did she keep from getting shot? *Somebody* should have gotten killed. I mean, there were bullet holes everywhere and they were shooting from six feet away."

Back at the crime scene, a search of the car led to recovered bullets and the hole in Naja's headrest. Naja survived because Shawn had pushed her down, risking his life to save hers.

"I still couldn't raise my body up," Shawn says of the ambulance ride, "couldn't sit up straight." He wasn't in terrible pain. Not yet.

Shawn, who never lost consciousness, fished out his cell phone and called Marshall to say he was running late and would not be coming to work.

The police officer in the ambulance must have assumed Shawn was a gangbanger, because he kept circling around, asking the same thing from different angles—"Why would somebody want to shoot you? Who are you affiliated with? Who do you run with?" And finally, "What gang are you in?"

"I teach at Marshall," Shawn kept saying. "I was on my way to work, Officer. I don't know why they were shooting at me."

Soon he began to ignore the cop's repetitive questions, and he started in with a question of his own, one that echoed all the way to the hospital: "Where's my daughter?"

Meanwhile, EMT workers went to work on Shawn, cutting his clothes off while the ambulance was still in route to Stroger Hospital. A bullet clanked to the floor when they removed Shawn's shirt.

Stroger, on the Near West Side of downtown, used to be known as Cook County Hospital. It's close to UIC, twenty-four blocks from the shooting site. Stroger serves the indigent community, but it is also one of the nation's elite hospitals for gunshot victims, where Shawn's mother, Frinda, was brought in 2003.

Since the 1984 murder of nationally lauded high school star Ben Wilson—and the resulting lawsuit—Chicago's trauma units have experienced a dramatic upgrade, and there are far more hospitals that can treat victims of gun violence. Wilson, ranked as the number one senior in the nation, waited forty minutes for an ambulance after the initial 911 phone call, and nearly three hours before a doctor finally tended to him because there was not a trauma surgeon on staff at St. Bernard's Hospital in the Englewood neighborhood. The repercussions and changes after the lawsuit have saved countless gunshot victims. While reported shootings in Chicago have escalated in the last decade, murders are actually down because of the subsequent availability of state-of-the-art trauma units. Each year, Stroger Hospital's emergency room is one of the busiest and largest in the nation. Their "Red Team" cares for about seven thousand trauma victims annually.

———————

Dorothy Gaters and principal Angel Johnson agreed that the coach should represent the school at the hospital while Johnson addressed both the boys' and girls' teams. Minutes later an announcement came over the school PA system: "All basketball players please report to the library."

Tyrese Williford says, "I knew something was wrong because when I saw Henry Cotton coming in, he was crying. Whatever it was would hurt all of us if it hurt Coach Cotton like that."

Angel Johnson's announcement to the teams squashed some rumors. Shawn Harrington was alive but he was in critical condition. Nobody could make sense of the incident. *Why did this happen to Shaky?* players kept asking each other. Cotton knew that Tim Triplett was his most emotional player, and it didn't surprise him that the little guard cornered him immediately. What Triplett said next did surprise Cotton: "Coach, are you okay?"

The girls identified their coaches as a single unit. "Shaky was *our* coach, too," girls star Chanel Khammarath insists. She became more upset when she noticed Triplett, who minutes earlier had seemed so controlled and measured with Henry Cotton. She went to him, out of view from the rest of the team. "I'd never seen him cry before," she says. That nearly set her off again too, and she struggled to regain control. "I knew Shaky would want us to be strong," she says. "He wouldn't want to see any of us down."

Shawn's shooting was the only topic of conversation in the Marshall lunchroom, hallways, and classrooms. Nobody had a definitive answer on the extent of Shawn's injuries. Marshall's administration considered canceling the game scheduled for the next day against Orr High School. With only a month remaining, canceling the season seemed a possibility, too.

Later that day, Marshall coaches elected to play. Orr, by chance, is located four blocks from the corner of Augusta and Hamlin. Naturally, the Orr players would learn the basics about Shawn because the story was all over the news in Chicago, and Orr's best guard was Issaiah Hayes, Triplett's best friend from his Crane days.

Practice that afternoon was dry. Shawn, as an assistant, had been the vocal leader, the motivator. Even Tim Triplett was quiet. Coach Henry Cotton knew that the emotional balance of the team would be unpredictable, but he figured if the Orr game was canceled, players would go home and brood, possibly skip school entirely. Cotton believed they needed to play the game far more than they needed a day off. Neither option was great. "Shawn would have wanted us to play," Cotton says. The fact that the game site was just a few blocks from the shooting made their appearance important symbolically. Canceling the game, Cotton believed, would upset the team even more.

As might be expected, the Marshall family had to filter through misinformation and rumor. Shawn's immediate supervisor, Liz Chambers, was typing away in her office when a coworker ran in and told her Shawn had been shot.

"At first," Chambers recalls, "I thought she was talking about a student named Shawn Holloway."

By chance, this other Shawn played basketball for a couple of years at Marshall and had been in and out of trouble. Chambers wasn't totally shocked by this news, and when she said as much, her coworker, said, "No, not Shawn *Holloway*. I mean *your* Shawn."

Officer Von Kondrat only needed to be in uniform to gain access into the emergency room alongside Shawn's gurney. Chicago police require an immediate assessment from the medical team after a shooting, a transcription of the doctor's initial analysis. "We have to know if the victim has passed away or what his status is," Von Kondrat says. "It was quite a scene, but I had to stay."

Nurses hustled to cut off the rest of Shawn's clothes. He was quickly listed as being in critical condition. Doctors discerned that his lung had been punctured, so they inserted a tube to drain the blood, while a nurse searched for spots where he had feeling in his legs. The area was jammed with a dozen medical professionals, along with Von Kondrat, who noticed one doctor whispering to a nurse in her hospital-issued scrubs. The lady collapsed into a chair and wept. Von Kondrat had been in hundreds of ERs before under the ugliest of circumstances, but he had never seen this kind of behavior. These were supposed to be veterans at Stroger, yet here was someone on the front lines having an emotional meltdown. He wondered if this was Shawn's wife. Von Kondrat couldn't have known that this nurse was Shawn's aunt Vera—a sister of Frinda's—who happened to work at Stroger.

Shawn, who'd initially been relieved that Vera was on duty, picked up on the exchange, although he also couldn't hear the conversation. "I could tell that something was seriously wrong," he says, "by Vera's reactions."

One shot had grazed Shawn's shoulder, but the serious damage was done by the bullet he took at the T4 vertebrae, the fourth uppermost of the twelve thoracic vertebrae at the center of the spinal column. His spinal cord had not been severed, but it was unclear still as to how much damage was done by the bullet, or by being jerked at the collar by an impatient cop. Nobody knew what might heal in the crucial hours, days, and weeks after the injury.

Pressure was building in Shawn's lung and he was in pain now but until doctors were certain of the damage done to his internal organs, they couldn't risk administering pain killers. One doctor used the bullet's exit wound in Shawn's side to insert his finger into the body cavity, hoping to make an incision, open up the muscle tissue that encased his lungs. This caused Shawn excruciating pain. He let out a howl that continued as the doctor used a scalpel to open a two-inch gap to insert a tube to drain excess blood.

This invasive procedure was also done so that doctors could stop the bleeding while nurses checked Shawn for difficulty in breathing or obvious discoloration. The lungs, which have no muscles and function under negative pressure, will collapse if a hole allows in outside air. Pressure inside the pleural cavity would be problematic and sealing off any holes was critical. Doctors realized Shawn had one collapsed lung.

Though Shawn was conscious and lucid, that meant little at this point. The most important determining factor in his survival, Von Kondrat knew, was simple, blind luck. How much damage had the bullet done? Bullets wreak havoc after the initial penetration. They can cut through arteries and veins without any visible signs. Bullets can deflect, recoil, ricochet, and change angles and vectors, especially after they hit bone. Blood loss is the number one preventable cause of death on the battlefield—and on the West Side of Chicago. Until doctors accurately identify and sort out the damage, nothing can be certain with a gunshot wound. Any ruptures to the body's main arterial thoroughfares could mean massive hemorrhaging and could cause irreparable harm within a matter of minutes.

"It was different doctors coming and going," Shawn says. "It was kind of gloomy."

Out in the waiting room, Kim Jenkins arrived and sat with Naja, comforting her daughter. The other women in Shawn's life began to appear one after the other. Soon, Shawn's aunt Jaci arrived. A working nurse at another facility, Jaci ran to her sister Vera, who'd been advised by doctors to leave the ER and compose herself. Jaci began praying loudly, until she was reproached by a nurse. "This is the only thing I know to do!" Jaci cried.

Naja calmly intervened, took her by the elbow, and led her outside.

Tyrone Hayes spent the day working at Marshall. He says, "I was stunned. I just couldn't believe it. Pretty soon anger set in because I knew it was because of Shawn's stolen vehicle."

It was a dismal day at Marshall. "Everyone could tell the difference," Hayes adds. "Kids didn't even know how to handle it. Some of them were very close to Shawn, and to see them you would have thought their own father had gotten shot."

While the teams met in the library, Dorothy Gaters drove straight to Stroger Hospital. From her car she called a friend who also knew Shawn.

"You sound like you're crying," her friend said.

"I can still picture Shawn," Gaters recalls, "leaving Marshall the night before. He had on gray sweatpants and a maroon top. We had all been practicing late, and he called out to me, *See you tomorrow, Coach G!*"

Only immediate family was being let in past the waiting room at Stroger, but Shawn wanted to see Dorothy Gaters. There wasn't much for her to say when she finally got through. "I just wanted him to know I had to come by," she says, "to check on him, that I was there for him."

Shawn told her, "I'm doing good, but I can't feel my legs or move my feet."

Henry Cotton collected details through phone calls, Facebook, and texts over the next few days. The shooting unnerved Marshall's head coach, partly because he knew it could have just as easily been him.

Cotton hadn't ever told his team—or Shawn—about what had happened to him when he was twenty-nine. He'd never shown the Commandos the scar on his leg.

In 1994, a few months before Westinghouse won the city championship, Cotton, then a Westinghouse assistant, walked with his cousins out of their home near Parkside and Central Avenue on the West Side. They intended to drive to the Brickyard Mall. While he noticed four young teens on the sidewalk, he was unconcerned when the group split. Two boys walked on ahead, the other two lagged behind. The delay was deliberate, and when Cotton and his cousins got to the sidewalk, they were surrounded.

"Give us what you got," one of the teens said, while two others waved guns. This was in the days before cell phones were prevalent, and Cotton's crew pulled out beepers, wallets, and cash as they were shuttled into the gangway between buildings. Cotton figured the ordeal was over until one of the teens barked out an order: "Everybody get facedown on the ground!"

Cotton feared they were about to be executed gangland style, a gunshot to the back of the head. The cousins complied, but he rebelled just before he got on his knees and saw the teens scurry out into the back alley. The ploy must have been done to ensure their getaway, and he sighed a breath of relief until one teen turned and shot. Cotton and his cousins scrambled back into the house. That's when someone noticed the coach was bleeding.

By the time Cotton was released from West Suburban Hospital that same day, Chicago police had nabbed the teenagers, catching them with guns in their pockets. The teens were members of the P-Stone Nation street gang.

Coach Henry Cotton (right) joins hands with both teams in a postgame prayer for Shawn Harrington following the loss at Orr High School the day after the shooting. Keyon Boyd, far left, looks on. *Worsom Robinson*

Months later when Cotton appeared at the courthouse to testify he was approached by another young man he immediately recognized, a former player. The young man apologized at length for his brother, the shooter. The coach was surprised and then incredulous when he remembered how he used to goof with the younger brother when he was little, how he had been brought to the gym because the family couldn't get a babysitter to coincide with the required Saturday practices. Cotton had even bounced the boy on his knee. Now he had grown into a pistol-wielding teen.

Although he never felt compelled to talk to his Marshall team about the incident, Cotton says, "I'd often stress to them *Y'all need to be careful.*"

"I thought they would cancel the Orr game," says guard Tyrese Williford, who was hardly in the mood to play basketball. The team had dedicated the game to Shawn, but what good did that do? Williford found himself keeping a close eye on the older Tim Triplett, who was taking the news hardest.

Some teams are inspired by tragedy, but Marshall came out lethargic and lost, 63-51. Triplett had just four points. When the final horn blew, Orr coach Lou Adams suggested that both teams gather at midcourt in a circle, and he led everyone in prayer. The *end*-of-game prayer was a highly unusual move. Orr's coach said something about "rest in peace," and that set something off in Triplett. Shawn wasn't dead, was he? No, he couldn't be. But then what was the R.I.P. bit about? "Man, fuck them," Triplett said quietly to Tyrese Williford. "They don't even know, and they don't care for real. Why do you think he said *rest in peace?*"

The *Sun-Times* ran a photo of that moment. An agonized Triplett is surrounded by teammates. Triplett looks a decade older than the other Commandos, and he has a weary, almost Renaissance look of suffering, his white headband the halo.

Shawn's shooting got plenty of media attention compared to the other half-dozen daily shootings in the city. Over the next few weeks, the *Tribune* and *Sun-Times* wrote about him on a couple of occasions, and local television newscasts carried the story. Shawn was decidedly optimistic in his comments to journalists, tagging the tragedy "a minor

After the postgame prayer and the loss to Orr, an anguished Tim Triplett (in white headband) is comforted by Commandos Tyrese Williford, Citron Miller, and Orr assistant Lauren "Magic" Foster. Sophomore Terrell Allen (winter coat) passes by. *Worsom Robinson*

setback before a major comeback." He predicted he'd recover and be back playing basketball within a year.

Like the best point guards, Shawn focused on everyone but himself. He was most concerned about the stress on his grandmother, Lily Harrington. Now in her mid-seventies, Lily had never stopped grieving over the murder of her daughter Frinda. "We often keep things from her," Shawn says. His call to reassure his grandmother was the first he made from Stroger.

Girls' team star Chanel Khammarath waited a few weeks to phone the coach who served as her alarm clock in Marshall's main office so many mornings. "I had been distraught" she says, "it hurt me so bad. If Shawn ever saw me down, he'd make me smile, he'd make me forget about what had been bothering me."

It wasn't an easy phone call for her to place. "I've been crying about this," she admitted to him straight away.

Triplett burst into tears moments later. *Worsom Robinson*

"You shouldn't be," Shawn told her. "I'm alive, I'm still here."

When Shawn's condition stabilized, he was placed in a room at sidewalk level, where below the window curtain he could see foot traffic, legs and shoes walking by. Doctors decided to take his cell phone away so he could get some rest, but this had the opposite effect—being cut off from contact with his daughters unnerved him. "After I spoke to my grandma," he says, "I guess I started to really think about my daughters and how this would all affect their lives."

Get well cards stacked up, and Shawn noticed an impressive amount of outreach from a surprising group. "The problematic, most hard-hearted teens at Marshall sent me the warmest cards," he says. "I would have never expected that."

The waiting room was filled with friends, ex-players, coaches, and general well-wishers who lingered patiently in hopes of visiting Shawn. "I was getting a lot of love from around the city," Shawn says, and naturally the common denominator was basketball. On several occasions parents he barely remembered came to say, "Thank you for helping my son get into college."

Shawn was especially happy to see Anthony Hunter, who visited three times. "You've helped me more than I helped you," Shawn told him at the conclusion of Hunter's third visit.

When Kim Jenkins came, Shawn always used her phone to speak to his youngest daughter. Malia, eight years old, wasn't allowed past the waiting room, so the calls were his only contact with his younger daughter in the first week after the shooting.

Shawn came up with an innovative idea after a few days. "Malia stood outside my window with Naja, and we lifted the curtain a bit inside. I talked to Malia on the phone. She'd duck down below the curtains, peek in, wave at me through the window," he says. It was better than nothing but a poor substitute.

After ten days, just before he was moved to the Rehabilitation Institute of Chicago, Shawn finally couldn't stand it anymore. He pleaded his case to a Stroger nurse, who snuck Malia into his room. The nurse closed the curtains so Shawn and his youngest daughter wouldn't be disturbed.

"That marked the beginning of the healing process for me," he recalls, "finally seeing Malia for the first time."

Chicago Police believed the POD cameras on the corner of Augusta and Hamlin would help them quickly identify the gunmen, especially the man who had approached Shawn's rental car from the side. When police examined the recording, though, they realized the camera wasn't working. It was quite possible that this would be yet another Chicago shooting to go unsolved.

Since 2010, according to the University of Chicago's Urban Crime Lab report, more than 90 percent of Chicago's shootings have gone unsolved, and the staggering total in Chicago (roughly three thousand reported shootings in 2015, for example) is a huge factor in why more crimes do not get solved. A higher profile case is far more likely to be resolved, and Shawn's situation was unusual because of his modest reputation, his tie to *Hoop Dreams*, and the media's subsequent coverage.

Cops would have to overcome the often-cited "code of silence" in the law-abiding community to crack this attempted murder case, even though it had unfolded during a busy morning commute.

One policeman from the West Side says that the code of silence among a different group, the city's young gang members, is overrated. "Somebody is going to flip under pressure and talk," he says. "What everyone forgets is that selling drugs is, first and foremost, a business." When business is significantly interrupted, gangs make a significant change. "They're going to give up the shooter," the cop says. "In Harrington's case, it was a bad shoot, an incredibly stupid move. And these guys will flip on you and talk in a heartbeat."

———————

I thought a magazine piece on Shawn might help bring attention to his situation, so I began writing about his story. I requested reports from the Chicago Police Department and used the Freedom of Information Act (FOIA), hoping to learn as much as I could about the hunt for the two gunmen. Finally, my FOIA demands got a response: dozens of documents, all redacted beyond recognition. They seemed of little value with all the black streaks, and the fact that there were a dozen separate documents made it even more of a mess. I figured I'd comb through it anyway. Maybe there'd be something I could use. An address. A date. The name of a cop I could talk to. But before I started to wade through the attachments, I decided to copy and paste everything onto one single new document. At least that way I could more easily refer to the information.

A funny thing happened then. When I pasted the copied documents onto my new page, all the redacted parts fell away. Largely through those unredacted police reports, I was able to piece together this part of the story:

In the hours after Shawn was shot the street was buzzing with rumors, as is often the situation in cases of mistaken identity. By late afternoon, a man whose nickname was Bang Bang showed up at Chicago's Eleventh District police station, three blocks from Marshall. He had told a policeman canvasing the neighborhood earlier that he had information on who shot the basketball coach.

According to police, Bang Bang was an admitted "Traveler," or Traveling Vice Lord, an offshoot of the Vice Lords. He said the drug dealers from the Augusta and Hamlin area had been feuding with the dealers from a block away. By eavesdropping on his sister's phone call, he'd learned that two men had shot the coach by mistake. One man was called Lil' Ced. The other was known as Stay High. This was of intense interest to Bang Bang for a couple reasons. First, because his sister was close friends with Lil' Ced.

Detectives wondered why Bang Bang would out somebody so close to his own sister.

Bang Bang said it was because his friend had been shot by the same guys and he'd witnessed that shooting two days previous to Shawn Harrington's. That shooting took place at the corner of Thomas and Lawndale, just a few blocks away, also before 8:00 AM. He had seen a vehicle screech to a halt. A man in a full ski mask and handgun jumped out to confront a young man—his name was Darren Deer—on the sidewalk. When Deer turned to run, the ski-masked man opened fire. Deer was hit several times.

Police already knew much of that story. Deer was still able to flee and he lived to describe the masked man, the van, the chrome handgun. Deer wasn't able to identify the exact make or color of the vehicle or who shot him, but police reports say he did admit to being a member of the Four Corner Hustlers, a gang in the area. During the ambulance ride, a bullet fell out of Deer's clothes, just as with Shawn Harrington a few days later. Police easily matched that bullet to casings found at the scene. Their hunch was that the bullets and casings could someday lead to a gun—and the shooter.

Bang Bang corroborated the detail that the cops already knew. The victim had both arms broken by bullets and he took a couple more shots, but he was able to run away. Bang Bang could better describe the car that the shooter had jumped out of—a maroon Pontiac minivan. He added that Stay High had been driving and Lil' Ced was in the passenger's seat, but it was Stay High who'd jumped out of the car and fired shots that day. How he could identify Stay High, who'd been wearing a mask, is unclear.

Detectives rifled through photos until Bang Bang identified both young men. He was able to do the same thing two days later, picking out the shooters again from dozens of photos.

Their names were Cedryck Davis and Deandre Thompson.

Soon detectives tracked down the man who phoned Bang Bang's sister to tell her about the shooting. This man didn't step up and volunteer but he was easy to find. "Hollywood," by chance, had been arrested in an unrelated case the same day Shawn was shot. Police reports emphasized that Hollywood hadn't witnessed Shawn's shooting either, he was just relating the word on the street. He also quickly picked out the photos of the young men.

The hunt was on for Stay High and Lil' Ced.

11

IN TELEVISION INTERVIEWS and follow-up newspaper pieces updating the public on the tragedy, Shawn Harrington always vowed to walk again. However, in the crucial days and weeks after the shooting, as doctors waited for the swelling to go down, there was little to be optimistic about. For spinal cord injuries this is the make-or-break window where every improvement or change is studied intensely. Occasionally a miraculous healing unfolds, but if months go by without improvement, hope can slip away.

For Shawn, it was more than the days after the shooting that should have come under scrutiny. What happened in the rental car at Augusta and Hamlin minutes after the gunfire subsided might have destroyed his chance at any substantial recovery.

Hold on, Officer, I can't feel my legs.

Every coach in America understands that a seriously injured player should never be moved. First responders know that unless the intent is to clear an injured man from a burning building, fast-moving traffic, or an ongoing shootout, you allow the injured to remain still and wait for the ambulance. In Shawn's case, the shooting was over, the rental car was bumpered halfway up the curb against a tree, and his daughter was weeping on the phone to her mother.

The police must have assumed that this was another gangbanger to be hauled off. Hands around Shawn's collar, no questions asked, the sudden jerk—it was possible that whatever damage the bullet had done had been exacerbated by the quick and forceful motion from an irritated police officer.

For battle-weary cops, as well as the media and the public at large, any victim can appear to be a deserving gangbanger. In this case, in a hot area on the border of four distinct neighborhoods, with cops constantly combing the alleys and one-way streets, the shooters were not the only ones who misidentified Shawn.

This was the first of dozens of instances where my advocating for Shawn fell flat. I realized eighteen months after the shooting that he had a damn good case for a lawsuit. I began to contact Chicago attorneys on his behalf, but by then the statute of limitations for claims against the police had long expired. Shawn, for his part, never once expressed an interest in suing the city or the police. He was to have a dozen interactions with the police after his shooting and he believed they had done a good job. He would continue to have that opinion during the ongoing hunt for his shooters.

On February 1, Chicago detectives returned to Stroger Hospital to interview Shawn again. First, they wanted to know if he remembered talking to them two days earlier, the day he was shot. Shawn reminded them that he'd never lost consciousness, even in the immediate aftermath. He remembered everything.

The police told Shawn that the POD cameras on the corner of Augusta and Hamlin had not captured the shooting. They had made no arrests as yet, but they were close. Could the coach and Naja be certain who the trigger men were? Shawn said he believed that he and his daughter could identify the shooters.

A few days after Shawn was shot, according to police reports, Deandre Thompson was observed by surveillance crews walking buyers to a place where he'd buried baggies of heroin in the snow. The sales were going on less than four blocks from where Shawn was shot and within a thousand feet of Exelon Charter School. Thompson was arrested that day, and he knew the seriousness of selling heroin near Exelon could mean a lengthy sentence. According to police documents he said to the police, "Please don't put that school [charge] on me, officer, I can't take no delivery [charge]."

The cops say that under questioning Thompson admitted he was a Four Corner Hustler. He had nearly a dozen arrests on his record. His trouble with the police began when he was nineteen, and the arrests were usually near the same corner as Shawn's shooting. First it was gambling, then soliciting unlawful business, disorderly conduct, possession of a controlled substance, possession of cocaine, another soliciting charge, selling heroin near a different school, and a couple more possession charges.

According to police reports, when asked if he knew anything about the Shawn Harrington shooting on the morning of January 30, Thompson said he'd been home asleep at that time. He also said he'd heard talk about some guy who had been shot at the corner of Lawndale Avenue and Thomas Street two days earlier.

The oddity of Thompson volunteering even scant knowledge about the other attempted murder made the detectives sit up. The police did not know that detectives were just twenty-four hours away from putting a case together, waiting on test results from the several expended .40 caliber shell casings from both shootings. Detectives had Thompson's name already from Bang Bang. When police pressed forward with more questions, Thompson suddenly clammed up, refused to say any more. That ended the interview, but it planted a seed. Everyone in the area knew about the January 28 shooting, but why would Thompson bring it up when he hadn't been asked about it?

Thompson bonded out and was back on the street.

Two days later, detectives had put enough information together to put out an alert and a warrant for the arrest of Deandre Thompson for the shooting of Shawn Harrington.

One Chicago policeman on the lookout was Jason Edwards. In the late 1990s, the six foot three Edwards was a high school basketball star for suburban Schaumburg. The *Tribune* called his 1997–98 team "the darlings" of the prestigious Proviso West Christmas tournament after a run of shocking upsets got them to the championship game. Racially mixed Schaumburg lost to Farragut, but Edwards was named to the All-Tournament team. That spring Edwards was selected for Chicago All

Area honors, a list that included four players who would go onto the NBA as well as Farragut's strongman, Michael Wright. (Wright had a stellar career at the University of Arizona, earned six-figure salaries playing overseas, but was found murdered in his SUV in New York in 2015.)

Edwards never played college ball although he surely could have. His heart was set on going to Northwestern University, whose African American coach, Ricky Byrdsong, had been in constant contact during Edwards's junior season. But Northwestern fired Byrdsong, mucking up Edwards's plans. (Two years later, Byrdsong was dead, a victim of a white supremacist's statewide shooting spree.)

A Chicago cop now for over a decade, Edwards served as a tactical officer and he cultivated a long list of contacts, friends, and informants on the West Side. He became keenly interested in the case when he learned that Shawn Harrington was a basketball coach. Everyone in the area was talking about the mistaken identity shooting, and Edwards kept hearing the same names that Bang Bang had mentioned: Stay High and Lil' Ced.

The common response when people heard about Shawn's shooting was one of awe at a father's breathtaking courage. The second reaction was often incredulity about men wielding pistols at that hour of the morning. Nobody is safe if we have to worry about our morning commutes, the reasoning went. Perhaps it is unwise to be out after midnight, but there seemed to be no logic as to why kids with pistols would be roaming side streets before 8:00 AM.

Jason Edwards knew the answer. "It's the heroin trade," he says. "If a guy wants to buy weed, he can wait until dark or whenever. But when a junkie wakes up, he needs his fix now. The early morning hours are the busiest and the sellers are often done for the day by 9:00 AM."

By late morning on the day Shawn was shot, Edwards engaged in a common practice used by Chicago police officers. He'd collar a young man for selling weed or another minor infraction then dangle a carrot in front of the offender: give up some information on Stay High or Lil' Ced and we will let you get back to the street.

Soon, using the same catch-and-release strategy, he uncovered a cell phone number for Deandre Thompson.

Edwards's department sent an affidavit to the phone company along with that number. For the next week, Edwards and his partner would "ping" Thompson's phone and receive a live report that provided the phone's longitude and latitude. Still, Edwards kept coming up short, until February 5, 2014. That day the pings came back at an unusually rapid rate. It appeared Thompson was on the 4100 block of Madison Street, a major West Side thoroughfare. "I could tell we were really close," Edwards says, "so we kept circling the area."

The electronic pinging is not always accurate, but Edwards trusted his hunches. They parked their unmarked car on Madison and walked around. A beauty shop. Nah. Maybe the furniture store. The Foot Locker might be a good bet.

Before they went in the shoe store, Edwards noticed a small barbershop at 4131 W. Madison called This Is It. He decided to pop in. As usual, he was in plain clothes with a bullet-proof vest. He did not have his gun drawn but his partner was close behind.

"Just as I walked inside," Edwards recalls, "here comes Deandre Thompson from the back of the barbershop, walking right at me. I completely caught him by surprise."

Thompson froze, which gave the policeman a moment to lunge and grab him in a bear hug. "For me, that usually works," Edwards says. "I can feel around quickly to find out if the suspect has a gun."

Deandre Thompson was not armed. The police read him the Miranda warning and cuffed him. Edwards noticed that the back door to the barbershop had been barricaded, as if Stay High had been expecting the police to come barging in through the back.

Deandre Thompson was charged with attempted first degree murder, aggravated battery, and discharge of a firearm in the shooting of Shawn Harrington and detained without bail. Less than a week had elapsed since the shooting.

Naja Harrington, teary-eyed and trembling, picked out Deandre Thompson from a police lineup as the young man who was running alongside the rental car. And she confirmed that it was Thompson who she had witnessed pointing the pistol in the instant before she heard the gunshots from his direction.

Police had also interviewed a forty-something man who said he'd seen the shooting at the corner of Augusta and Hamlin, but this man was unable to ID Thompson in the lineup.

Shawn was less certain than Naja, so he did not attempt the lineup identification with Thompson. The prosecution might have to rely on Naja's testimony, but maybe that would prove to be enough. Soon, though, cops learned that the security cameras at Brothers Food Mart—where Naja's mother had shopped for candy as a kid—had recorded the entire incident.

The cops had collared Stay High. Now they needed Lil' Ced.

I had not spoken to Shawn for two decades until the afternoon he answered his phone at the county hospital.

"You know Ms. Gaters is putting on a benefit for me," he said soon after we began talking. Marshall alums would play other former players from the West Side to help defray Shawn's medical expenses. I had not given any thought to coming up to Chicago from NMSU, where I was teaching in the English department. This felt like an invitation, so I blurted out, "I'll be at the game."

Shawn said his exercise times were the best part of the day. He had the goal of getting approval from his doctors to travel to Marshall for the afternoon game in his honor. We spoke only a few more minutes. I started pricing plane tickets. A few days later, he checked out of Stroger Hospital and moved into the Rehabilitation Institute of Chicago (RIC) where he would live for the next two months.

The benefit game was set for March 1, 2014, at Marshall, just a few days before the Illinois state playoffs. I flew up to see Shawn, to be part of the crowd and the recovery effort. I dug out two old media guides to trigger my memory because it had been years since I thought about him. Sure, I knew his year was a failure of a season, but I wanted to remember the details before I saw him. By looking through newspaper clippings, box scores, and photos I was able to piece together specific memories.

In Chicago media reports, Shawn continued to refer to the tragedy as "a minor setback before a major comeback," a catchphrase he'd repeat for the next two years. He talked about playing basketball again one day and that he was too active and young to be kept in a chair for long. Spinal cord injuries can surprise both doctors and patients and there is a small element of mystery—and sometimes miracle—to the healing process. Shawn had bought into that line of thinking.

The RIC is located downtown on Superior Street, where the high-rise glitz contrasts sharply with Shawn's West Side. Nationally recognized as a leader in spinal cord injuries, the RIC provided him a glimmer of hope. The nurses and workers at the RIC often surprise visitors by dancing on the countertops and tables, leading a crew of wheelchair-bound patients in a series of aerobic exercises. Shawn had full use of his arms and hands, and there'd be a chance he could walk with braces even if he never walked on his own. He could drive a modified car. But he didn't have feeling in his legs, which had already begun to atrophy in the weeks since January 30.

The first time I saw Shawn in nearly two decades, we talked mostly about his time in New Mexico, focusing on NMSU's loss to the Lobos on that eighty-foot throw, the sheer luck that had gone against us. "Man, it still hurts me when I think about that," Shawn said, then wondered aloud if anyone had a video of the game. Our team of newbies had been destined to struggle, he said, especially with two freshmen playing all year. He could still name the entire team—Chewy, Jamal, Keith, Spelling, Bostjan, Marquis, Mush, Aaron, Chris, and his roommates, Tobias and Enoch. We talked about each one, although I did not have a clue what most of them were up to.

Shawn spent ten months in New Mexico and it was the only big-time basketball he played. Playing major college ball is a coveted status symbol, especially on Chicago's West Side. He said he still analyzed his playing days, just ten games, and he pondered his departure.

I started to apologize for the way things had ended at NMSU.

But his take on his transferring was very different. "*I decided to leave Las Cruces,*" Shawn told me that day at the RIC. "Sometimes I wonder if I should have stayed," he added. That he did not feel he'd been run off was how it was supposed to go down, because a player who felt unfairly treated could make waves—in the media, with his former teammates, or with his old high school coach. He believed that leaving was his choice, but I still think it was done, like a lot of moves in college sports, through innuendo, attitude, delay, and silence.

Twenty-four hours before the benefit game tipped off, Shawn's doctor had not cleared him to attend.

Perhaps because the game was on a Saturday or because of the circumstances of the tragedy, the metal detectors Marshall had used since the 1990s were pushed off to the side. Nobody would dare bring a weapon to Shawn Harrington's event. The hallways, stairs, and entrance to the gym were shiny and spotless, and the school appeared to be doing well despite their shrinking enrollment.

A giant mural of a helmeted Commando on the run remained on the gym wall, just as I remembered. The seats were already filled thirty minutes before tipoff—five hundred people had paid twenty dollars each.

Some players and friends of Shawn avoided the event because they could not digest the fact that the popular coach was now in a wheelchair. "I couldn't face it," Martin Satterfield says. "I just couldn't go. Shawn was a father to me. I was heartbroken and I couldn't see him like that."

The game pitted Marshall alums against graduates of rivals like Westinghouse, Crane, Whitney Young, and Manley. As warmups commenced, the music blared. Dorothy Gaters welcomed fans. Chicago Bulls general manager Gar Forman and his wife, Leslie, had taken an interest in Shawn's plight and made sure that Randy Brown attended. Brown was now working for the Bulls, and although he hadn't played with Shawn at New Mexico State they knew each other because Shawn had watched him play at Marillac House.

The Chicago Public Schools sent a giant bouquet. Nobody suspected that this was a gesture for the cameras and that nearly three years would

Commando in Chief: legendary Marshall girls' coach Dorothy Gaters was the first speaker at the benefit game she organized for Shawn.
Michael James

pass before the CPS administration did anything more to help Shawn than drop off some flowers.

The game started on time, a rare occurrence anywhere in the Chicago Public League. Shawn had still not shown up. As expected, the play was terrible. You can't grab a bunch of thirty- and forty-somethings and expect them to be competitive even in a hotbed of basketball.

When halftime began, a singer cued up her boombox and cut loose. Still no Shawn. It seemed he hadn't got the doctor's approval. But in the midst of the song, Shawn came rolling into the gym in a wheelchair. With no natural way to greet the fans (and the soprano still wailing away) Shawn took a lap around the perimeter of the court. Naturally it was slow going, which whipped the crowd into a frenzy of anticipation. By the time he'd pushed his wheelchair around the gym, the second half commenced. After the game, Dorothy Gaters, Alderman Bob Fioretti, Randy Brown, and finally Shawn all made brief speeches.

Shawn Harrington, surrounded by members of the Marshall family, implores the crowd members to do their part in ending gun violence in Chicago. *Michael James*

Shawn appeared relaxed and comfortable when he thanked everyone for the overwhelming flood of love and support. He spoke optimistically about returning to Marshall, walking again, even playing ball. In the history of the school just a handful of people had spent more hours there than Shawn. He posed patiently for photos, signed everything thrust in front of him, and finally holed up in the corner surrounded by the women he had worked alongside. He was surprisingly positive. Nobody could predict what would happen with his job. Shawn could not follow his special ed kids from class to class, as he had previously, without an elevator. He'd been carried up the stairs like a sultan to the second-floor gym by an army of Commandos, but that could not happen every morning.

The hero's welcome that afternoon glossed over some hard realities. His contract as a Chicago Public School employee entitled him to get 80 percent of his salary, but ninety days after the shooting his pay would be terminated if he couldn't physically return to work. As an educational support personnel worker, he wasn't under the same contract as the Chicago Teachers Union. Although Shawn would soon have no income, he still believed his health care would be taken care of since he'd been paying into Blue Cross/Blue Shield for years.

Before the shooting, Shawn might as well have been the poster boy for Chicago Public School athletes. That poster might read: *Go away and earn a degree. Come home and try to make the city a better place. Never forget your roots. Give back to your school. Take special care of your children no matter what the sacrifice. Remain cool under pressure, stay optimistic in the face of disaster.*

Shawn needed the Chicago Public Schools to return the love and dedication he had shown to Marshall. He'd never applied for another job once he began working there. Home was home, and a better-paying job offered little temptation. The work was exhausting, especially during the basketball season, but he was not at all burned out. The benefit game was an unprecedented outpouring of love and concern, but what would happen to Shawn when the ovations ended and the bleachers got pushed back into place?

12

Tim Triplett rededicated himself to basketball that winter. Up until Shawn got shot, Triplett had been a better leader than a scorer, but now he caught fire on the court, scoring baskets as well as directing his team. He dropped in ten points in Marshall's next game, a one-point loss to Kenwood. Against league rival North Lawndale he scored thirteen, his highest total of the season in an important victory before the city playoffs. That may seem like a modest scoring output, but college coaches know that Chicago, like most cities, requires a sliding scale. Double figures in the Red West usually indicates a kid is good enough for a scholarship.

Although he played just half a season, a chorus of coaches and players believed that Triplett could soon be good enough to play Division I basketball. Nobody, however, ever commented on Triplett's basketball ability without also mentioning his mouth. One player from Triplett's basketball and social network was Providence St. Mel guard Tevin King. King insists Triplett had enough game and guts despite his size to play college ball. "Tim was tough," King says, "outgoing, and he always said what he had to say. He wasn't a great shooter but he could penetrate, get to the basket. He talked a lot of trash but he backed it up."

Triplett's first coach at Crane, Tim Anderson, became an assistant at the University of Texas–Pan American after Triplett's sophomore year. Anderson phoned his former player from afar because he felt that in two years Triplett might be good enough to play for his college team. "Triplett exemplified Chicago high school basketball," Anderson says. "His teammates loved him, his opponents hated him, but he embraced that leadership role."

Tim wasn't the only vocal guy on the court. Plenty of players spew trash talk during the game. However, another friend says, Triplett was very different in one important respect. "Most people can turn that on and off. After the final buzzer, they can say that was the game and now we leave it alone. But Tim couldn't control it like we did."

In the Commandos' opening game of the city playoffs, Triplett upped his scoring output again with fifteen points in a victory over Foreman. The team's despondency just after the shooting might have been expected, but now Marshall had won two out of three games.

More important was Triplett's change off the court, where he focused intensely on school. Rattled by the shooting of the coach he most identified with, he was spending more time with his girlfriend and books. By all accounts, Triplett was a good student at Marshall and was on schedule to finish his high school career with a grade point average above a 3.0, a solid B. The disastrous spring grades after his brief stint at Farragut High School were in the past.

The rest of the Marshall boys' team could never quite get on track. The boost from finally getting Triplett in uniform was negated by the loss of Shawn Harrington. After beating Foreman, they lost to Hyde Park. In the lull before the Illinois state playoffs, nearly a month, the team had a chance to consider all that had happened. When the games resumed, Marshall beat Triplett's old school, Crane, then Westinghouse again to win the first round of the playoffs, the regional championship. But on March 11, nemesis Orr High ousted the Commandos in the first game of the sectional playoffs.

The Marshall boys' season was over. "We tried," Citron Miller insists. "We wanted to use Shawn's shooting as a motivation thing. We talked about it as a team, how we had to cherish this time, and we dedicated the rest of the season to him."

Marshall finished 13-13, the four-game winning streak in late January and their regional victory the only real bright spots. Their record indicated a modest improvement with Triplett in uniform, but his seemingly eternal wait for eligibility, then playing, then waiting again meant that the Commandos' transfer from Crane—whose fifty-point outburst as a junior should have been a harbinger of what was ahead—was not the hero everyone had hoped for, although he had done fine in his classes. "Basketball was the reason he made it," Jutuan Brown says. By "made it," his mother means that Triplett would earn a high school diploma in four years.

After the 2013–14 season, the coaches presented Tim Triplett with a plaque that read "Outstanding Leadership Award" for "exhibiting great qualities throughout the season."

Although Triplett's grade point average was good enough to qualify for a four-year NCAA college, he never bothered to take the ACT test, not an uncommon omission for Chicago high school kids. After the season, the kid who'd only been around for nine months began to slip off the radar of his coaches and counselors. That spring as graduation approached, Triplett began to consider his options for two-year junior colleges where he could play basketball.

This, of course, was the same strategy Shawn had used twenty years earlier when he followed the path of *Hoop Dreams* star Arthur Agee. Playing well at Mineral Area Junior College had opened plenty of doors, and while Shawn didn't believe Triplett was quite seasoned enough to play immediately at a big school, a junior college was a natural next step.

Placing Triplett at a two-year college outside of Chicago was a project Shawn normally would have taken on. Shawn had extensive ties to two-year schools from his time as a player and as a scout. But Shawn was in no position now to help Triplett.

———————

As the weeks passed at the Rehab Institute of Chicago, Shawn made small progress and continued to hope for the best. He gradually gained sporadic feeling below his waist, revealed by the nurses' pin pricks on his bare legs. Improved use of his stomach muscles meant he could sit up on his own. Hunger-generated rumblings in his gut proved to be more good news. He'd lost weight just sitting in his wheelchair but his appetite was returning.

This wasn't enough to stir real hope among his nurses and doctors at the Chicago Rehab Institute. They seemed to be preparing him for the inevitable, that with a T-4 spinal cord injury, he'd be in a wheelchair the rest of his life.

Chicago Rehab Institute therapist Kate Scanlon searches for new feeling in Shawn's legs. *Michael James*

A year before I considered writing this book, I began to advocate for Shawn. I was obsessed with two things. First, getting his story publicized would help raise money for his medical expenses. Second, Shawn needed a new career. I had my own vision about the direction he should now take in his life, as if he were a chess piece I could move around.

I've been interested in the intersection of sports and politics since I read *Out of Their League*, David Meggyesy's classic memoir about walking away from a professional football career. Although not yet a teenager when the 1960s concluded, I admired athletes like Muhammad Ali, Bill Russell, Tommie Smith, and John Carlos, who'd all come on the heels of Jackie Robinson. I knew the stories of trailblazers like Billie Jean King and Curt Flood.

After years of coaching I was beginning to connect the dots, identify trends, and analyze the history of sports as a vehicle for social justice, particularly along racial lines. I worked for Don Haskins at UTEP, who opened the door for African American kids to get basketball scholarships in the 1960s. Twenty years later I wrote the biography of trailblazing coach Nolan Richardson, *Forty Minutes of Hell*. I was undergoing an awakening. Where once I might have seen Dorothy Gaters as the greatest high school coach the game had ever known, now I also saw her as a powerful advocate for gender equity.

I couldn't stop myself from pointing my new sport/social justice goggles at Shawn Harrington, and I began to push him to think about his life in a different way. Shawn, nearly forty, was older than, say, Muhammad Ali when he reinvented his career. I wanted Shawn to believe in a new quest—as the face of a nonviolence movement through basketball in Chicago—that would invigorate him, repurpose his life. Shawn was vulnerable in so many ways, but especially to this kind of talk. Besides, he literally could not do his old job because Marshall was not wheelchair accessible, other than the single ramp that would allow him to get to the first floor of a three-story building.

Much of this—my presumptive reimagining of Shawn Harrington's life—had to do with my own politics. I worried that Shawn and I were now caught in a relationship, a power dynamic, similar to when I recruited him two decades earlier. While I admired, say, Arthur Ashe, I am inclined to find outspoken sports heroes like Nolan Richardson or Muhammad Ali more compelling. Shawn loved Michael Jordan and Derrick Rose. He had volunteered not a single word about being on a new career trajectory or repurposing his life. Still, he listened, and I hoped that he'd bite.

"Jackie Robinson didn't wake up one day in 1947 and think *I guess I'll desegregate America's most popular sport*," I told Shawn one day. "This is your new path."

"What path?" Shawn wanted to know.

"As a spokesman for the antigun and nonviolence movement in Chicago."

Shawn was bogged down with rehab. He worried about the delivery delay for his new wheelchair. His checks from the Chicago Public Schools had ended ninety days after the shooting. Naja was having nightmares and he feared her grades might dip. He was skittish about his younger daughters being raised on the West Side. And with all this weighing on him, I was bugging him about taking a progressive political stance.

"Let me think about it," he said.

He had his mantra: "A minor setback before a major comeback."

I had mine: "You already saved one kid's life, Shawn. Go save a few more."

I called or texted him every few days. I realized I was recruiting Shawn Harrington again.

13

Lɪʟ' Cᴇᴅ ᴡᴀꜱ ᴀʀʀᴇꜱᴛᴇᴅ by the Chicago Fugitive Apprehension Unit on April 8, 2014.

Cedryck Davis had shorn the dreadlocks he had hidden under his hoodie, but detectives knew who they were looking for. He was charged with attempted murder, aggravated battery, and the unlawful discharge of a firearm. As with Deandre Thompson, Davis was held without bail at the Cook County Jail.

Cedryck Davis's previous arrest record was astounding. By the age of twenty-three, he had been arrested thirty-six times. The first arrest was for possession of cocaine when Davis was fourteen years old. He had subsequent arrests for possession and sale of cocaine, heroin, and marijuana, soliciting unlawful business, battery, gambling, possession of a controlled substance, a few minor traffic violations, aggravated assault, use of a deadly weapon, aggravated kidnapping, and obstruction of a police officer.

Police often identify a shooter (or victim) to the media as a "known gang member" or "reputed gang member." In Davis's situation it would be a challenge to interpret his record as anything other than that of a habitual criminal. Cops had him pegged as affiliated with the Conservative Vice Lords, Four Corner Hustlers, Gangster Disciples, and Brickyard Fours. One longtime police officer says nobody belongs to that many gangs, but that Davis was likely selling drugs in different territories. Police might have assumed that his soliciting on certain corners meant he might be affiliated with the local gang in control of that area, though the boundaries kept shifting.

There's no application process for selling drugs. Although location is critical—and open to dispute now more than ever—one cop says that it's easy for a newbie to get approval from gang leaders. "Pretty much anyone who wants to sell drugs is allowed to sell," he says.

Cedryck Davis was hauled down to Chicago's Area North Detective Division. He'd already been arrested twice that same January on two aggravated battery charges and once for aggravated assault. Police noticed from his long arrest record that Davis couldn't seem to expand his criminal horizons beyond a few blocks from his residence, as if he were a misbehaving child who needed to be able to hurry home. He was arrested—where else?—at his home. When a detective finished reading the Miranda rights and began the questioning at the police station, Davis refused to talk. Except, police reports say, he kept repeating, "I want my attorney and my mama." Forty minutes later, Cedryck Davis got what he wanted, or half, when his attorney arrived.

Shawn, Naja, and the forty-something man who was involved in trying to identify Deandre Thompson were all called back in to see if they could pick Davis from a lineup. Police don't want a quorum or discussion, so their first move was to separate the victims. Shawn and Naja both were able to quickly point out Cedryck Davis as the young man who had shot at them. Even the forty-something guy (who couldn't positively identify Deandre Thompson earlier) could identify Davis as the man he saw running with a pistol the instant gunshots sounded.

———

Ontario Brown worried more than ever about his two children. His trepidation had been growing long before Shawn got shot. Since his teenaged years he had begun to accumulate experiences with guns. He was robbed three times at gunpoint and the narrow escapes stayed with him, adding to his worry. The first time, he was held up by a man wielding a pistol who demanded his Los Angeles Raiders Starter jacket.

The second time, Ontario happened to be shirtless at a gas station, airing out a new tattoo of the cartoon character Yosemite Sam. Ontario offered to fill the tank while his friend went inside with his kids to pay and buy candy. He was cleaning the windshield when he noticed a trio of young men walking past the parked cars toward the pumps. He thought nothing of it until one pulled a handgun and demanded his gold chain and pocket money. It was just before noon.

The third incident happened at Ontario's mother's home. The family was relaxing, watching sports on television when friends who had just arrived were brought into the house at gunpoint by two unknown men. The armed robbers proceeded to empty the house of valuables.

Ontario was still doing the regular commute to Elkhart to see his son when he didn't have to work weekends stocking artisan cheeses at European Imports. Back in Indiana, Ontario Junior was doing well. The boy liked basketball, but the game was only about fun and he never really played competitively. Besides, unlike his father, he could be accident prone and clumsy until it came time to show off his dance moves, when he morphed into a light-on-his-feet and graceful athlete. Ontario Junior was also very fashion conscious. The combination of being a fluid dancer and stylish dresser made him popular with the girls, although he would change girlfriends nearly as often as he changed clothing styles. Whenever he made the trip home to Chicago, he came back to Elkhart with some new accessory, a shirt, pants, hat, or belt. At age sixteen he got a large tattoo across his chest. It said *Truly Blessed.*

Lykeisha Brown says, "The girls flocked to my brother, even though he was quiet and shy like our dad." The shyness might have manifested into a distinct verbal tic. Ontario Junior ended every sentence with "boy," even when talking to a girl.

His father was more worried about Lykeisha, who had moved back to Chicago and graduated from Marshall in 2010. Conditions had deteriorated on the West Side from the days when he and Shawn practically lived at Marillac. "A lot of the social centers are gone," Ontario says, "less stuff for kids after school." Some of his worry was probably typical parental concern over a young lady, but he felt that with his boy safe, productive, and away from the city, he could focus on her.

Ontario's nagging anxiety seemed to pay off. By 2012, Lykeisha finished school at local Malcolm X junior college and earned her certification to be a pharmacist technician. She landed a good job with the CVS drugstore chain in Chicago.

One evening, after a quick visit to her workplace, a sense of calm descended on Ontario as he drove out of the parking lot. He knew Lykeisha would be just fine. She was smart, self-assured, polite, focused, and she had launched herself into a good career.

———————

Tim Triplett wanted to continue his education and he had an important choice to make—would he leave Chicago to play basketball? Or stay at home, commute to a local city college? Fewer than 40 percent of his senior classmates in 2014 continued their education, and teachers at the school speculate that most of them would have gone on to local colleges.

Triplett had three toddlers to consider, fathered before he ever enrolled at Marshall. His children lived with their mothers in Chicago. He also had a girlfriend who figured strongly in the decision. Torn about what to do next, occasionally he'd get excited about the chance to get away.

In May 2014, Dorothy Gaters saw her best senior, Chanel Khammarath, sign to go away to Coffeyville, Kansas, for junior college. Khammarath knew she needed to leave for a remote junior college anywhere outside Chicago if she wanted to someday land a Division I scholarship. She says a chorus of friends and coaches advised Triplett to leave town, too, and he seemed responsive at first. "Tim always talked about getting his mother out of the 'hood," she says.

Triplett's senior-year sweetheart Kashanna Haggard says, "Tim *did* consider leaving Chicago for junior college, and I know there were two schools he considered. One was in Iowa." She says another bureaucratic blip stalled him again. "Marshall didn't send all his paperwork," she says, "or maybe didn't have all his transcripts over at the school."

Triplett's mother Jutuan Brown says, "Marshall had them [the transcripts] but they didn't send them over in time for him to make the schools' deadlines in order to attend." While most community colleges will accept students as last-minute walk-ins, often as late as a week after the first day of class, it's possible that an out-of-town basketball scholarship hinged on timely proof of grades and graduation. And with three high schools on his resume, it's possible that depending on three transcripts might have stalled Triplett. Like so many mothers in Chicago, Jutuan wanted her son to go away, and the lure of the streets was only part of the problem. "As soon as he started at Marshall," she says, "he had multiple girlfriends," she says, naming a handful but confirming he was especially fond of Kashanna.

Getting the proper paperwork together and into the right hands is a common hurdle for Chicago Public League players who want to play ball at a higher level. A prospect might be the first person in his family to attend college. His high school coach, focused on upcoming summer leagues and camps, could be looking to the future and thus forget to follow through with a former player.

The search for a good fit in college is often made without appropriate guidance because, again, in today's Chicago Public League most basketball coaches are not teachers. Many either don't work in the building or never graduated from college—or both.

Two of Marshall's senior boys from 2014 chose out of town schools.

Citron Miller, who led the team in scoring, was the only Commando to earn postseason honors, named 4th Team All City. That got him a spot in an all-star game, where he was noticed by the coach from Highland Community College, three hours away in Freeport, Illinois.

Miller says that leaving town had been his number-one goal going into his final season, and today he'd suggest that as sound strategy to any senior player from the West Side. "Everybody from Chicago should leave," he says, "and not just Tim Triplett, that's how I felt."

Perry Willis, the team's second-leading scorer, signed at Mineral Area. Shawn had notified the coaches at his old school the previous summer to keep an eye on Willis.

Marshall seniors had leaned on Shawn and his scouting service for help in finding the right college even before he began coaching at his alma mater in 2008. Countless Marshall players and other West Side kids had gotten basketball scholarships through Shawn. Now Tim Triplett, the first in his family to attend college, had to negotiate the search blindly.

As the summer of 2014 progressed, Triplett's chance to leave town faded. He briefly considered the commuter school Malcolm X College, on the West Side, where Kashanna planned to study nursing. By the end of the summer, though, he decided to enroll at Wilbur Wright junior college, located in a mixed neighborhood on Chicago's Northwest Side. In the 1970s, the school was a national power and their coach, Ed Badger, parlayed that success into a job with the Chicago Bulls. Wright's glory days were long gone, but they still had a team.

Wright sat nine miles from Triplett's home, which seemed to be some kind of compromise. It wasn't the *closest* community college. He was awarded a basketball scholarship that included tuition, books, and fees. Wright had no dormitories or meal plan but their players were invariably local, lived at home, and pocketed the full Pell Grant of $5,500.

Triplett was tethered by some of the same factors that brought Shawn Harrington back to the West Side in 1998—family complications, a newborn child, the comfort of home. Yet when Shawn felt the pull of home and Chicago, he was twenty-three years old with a communications degree in hand.

Kashanna says she was disappointed by Triplett's decision. "I told him he should try a lot harder to go away from Chicago because of the violence. It would be a fresh start for him."

Martin Satterfield, who declined to attend Shawn's benefit game, still lived on the West Side. Satterfield struggled after redshirting (taking classes and practicing, but not playing in the games) at Daley College on the South Side. He planned on enrolling at Malcolm X in the fall of 2014—a sometimes empty plan which never materializes that West Side kids cling to as an imaginary safety net.

On July 3, five months after Shawn was paralyzed, Satterfield was outside shooting dice near the corner of Ohio and Ridgeway, not far from his home. "Just kicking it," he says, "doing typical things we do."

Satterfield had taken a break from the dice game to chat up a young lady when gunshots were fired from behind a tree. In an instant, a gunman was upon him. Satterfield was hit six times at close range—twice in the face, twice in the gut, and, after he spun from the gunfire, twice in the back.

Miraculously, Satterfield lived, but the T-9 spinal cord injury left him paralyzed from the chest down, and in a wheelchair like Shawn—although without the same network of sympathetic support, and without the media attention.

Now living near Hyde Park on the South Side, Satterfield says he is not totally certain what prompted the attack. "It was jealousy about a female, I believe. I actually don't really know. I was standing at the gate talking to a young lady." Predictably, he adds, "I was at the wrong place at the wrong time." He's been to one Marshall game since the shooting and occasionally he still speaks with Shawn. He's interested in getting rehab, but he has no health insurance and is unsure what his next move should be.

Six months after the near-execution of Satterfield, Dorothy Gaters was cornered in her office by her nephew Korbin McClain, the boys' team star who had stepped aside so Anthony Hunter could win home-coming king. McClain had seen Martin Satterfield rolling down the street on a cold morning.

"I feel so bad for Marty," the nephew told her. "All he has is a windbreaker. He doesn't even own a winter coat."

A few days later, Coach Gaters purchased a stylish insulated red Polo winter jacket for the wounded Commando, which might make Satterfield easy to spot if he ever returned to the West Side. He has decided not to. "It was a life or death situation," he says. "I had to leave for the South Side."

When Martin Satterfield was on the ground, having already taken two .40-caliber bullets in the chest, his assailant kept shooting, hitting him twice more in the face, then twice in the back when he crawled away. He recalls exactly what was going through his mind in that instant: *Stop shooting me. You got your point across.*

Today, he harbors no ill feeling for the shooter, whom he refused to identify. "I know exactly who did it, and he's in prison now," he says with a smile. That does not explain why Satterfield would not testify against the guy—it's not like he stole Satterfield's bicycle.

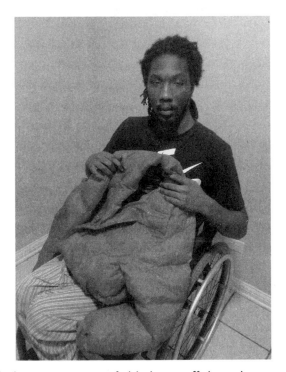

"I love that lady." Martin Satterfield shows off the Polo coat purchased by Dorothy Gaters. *Rus Bradburd*

"I'm from the streets," Satterfield says, "and that's the code. People told me let God deal with him."

Satterfield only wants to look forward although he's not working and, like Shawn, struggling to get by on $300 in monthly social security checks. "I try not to think about it," he says, "it gives me nightmares. I was twenty-one when it happened and it was the worst day of my life."

While he has deep admiration for Shawn's heroism in saving Naja, Satterfield makes no apologies for what went down in his own life. "My mind is different than Shawn's," he says. After a pause, he adds, "I still have friends who are gangbangers. They don't judge me and I try not to judge them."

Shawn needed cooperation and guidance from his health care provider, but help proved to be scarce in the profit-driven bureaucracy.

More accessible, he hoped, were the Chicago Public Schools and his union. Each of these entities would have to step forward and agree that Shawn's shooting and life stood for something important, was a powerful metaphor—and he deserved their attention, not to be abandoned.

Dorothy Gaters continued championing Shawn's cause, setting up the Shawn Harrington Recovery Fund at the local Fifth Third bank. She feared an online fundraiser would not be as effective as simply having a place to mail donations, although like so many from her generation, she didn't always recognize the potential Internet fundraising might offer.

I kept pounding away with journalists, asking them to cover Shawn's story. The more publicity we could get for Shawn, the easier the fundraising. Although his heroism was compelling, there was resistance from the Chicago media, and they put a different spin on his situation. "Shawn's story is a *good* story," I heard on two occasions. What they meant by *good* was "he lived," and that "happy ending" implied the story was less worthy of coverage.

Still, I hammered away, e-mailing and calling journalists. Dan McGrath and Dawn Turner-Trice both wrote pieces in the *Chicago Tribune*. Writers I knew on the national scene were sympathetic, but none of them bit. I began to pester Joe Nocera, the *New York Times* writer who covered both college sports and gun violence. ESPN writer Steve Dehlson had gone to the same high school as Naja Harrington's mother, so I bombarded him, too.

Chicago journalist John Conroy, who broke the massive Chicago Police Department torture scandal in the 1990s, suggested Shawn meet Alex Kotlowitz. Maybe Kotlowitz would see the potential for a great article.

Alex Kotlowitz had set the standard for writing about inner-city Chicago with his classic book *There Are No Children Here*. He'd also worked with *Hoop Dreams* director Steve James on the documentary film *The*

Interrupters, about a revenge-prevention organization that included ex-gang members. Kotlowitz, a lifelong basketball fan, was intrigued by Shawn's story. I started with a bold idea, suggesting he write a piece for a national magazine.

A few days later Kotlowitz phoned me back: "I'd like to interview you about your relationship with Shawn."

I tried to make it clear that this wasn't what I wanted. I was not interested in publicity about me, or even about me *and* Shawn. Rather, I wanted his magazine piece to keep Shawn in the public eye by focusing on his astonishing courage.

By chance Kotlowitz was writing a new book on gun violence in Chicago, examining how shootings bring people together in unpredictable ways. Maybe, he speculated, he might include something about my reunion with Shawn.

I knew that anything Kotlowitz wrote would get attention. I met with him in the summer of 2015 at the small apartment where I live each summer, in the leafy Ravenswood neighborhood on the North Side. I reminded Kotlowitz that I'd known Shawn since 1992. I detailed our past, my Chicago roots, the scouting service, seeing him play in high school, recruiting Shawn, and his brief stint at New Mexico State. Finally, seeing him get quietly forced out at NMSU.

"It's not a coincidence at all that we're in touch," I said.

But Kotlowitz kept pressing me. "Sure, but when had you spoken to him last?"

"Before the shooting? We might have talked briefly after his mother was killed."

Kotlowitz didn't know about Shawn's mother. He blanched. I gave him the ugly particulars of Frinda Harrington's murder in 2003, mentioning the mom-and-pop store at her neighbor's home, the botched burglary, the pathetic amount of cash involved.

"Your last conversation was over a decade ago," Kotlowitz pointed out, then he added, "Before Shawn got shot."

"Right."

"And before Frinda Harrington's murder, when had you last spoken to him? The last time you actually saw him?"

I was perspiring now, thinking about how I had befriended Shawn, and his subsequent dismissal from our college team. I thought about Luther Bedford and Frinda Harrington. I stretched my arms, rolled my neck. "I guess when he left New Mexico State."

"So, before Shawn got shot, you spoke to him once in the last twenty years." It wasn't a question now; it was a statement. "And you hadn't seen him since 1996. There's this coincidence of the stolen car, and Shawn getting shot because of it. That's what led to your reunion."

"I hadn't thought of it like that," I admitted. "I guess that's correct."

"And what exactly about his story caused you to reach out to him?"

"He was shot," I said stupidly.

Yes, Kotlowitz went on, but what about the story specifically pushed you to get in touch with him again?

"I knew his mother was gone. And Luther Bedford died a few years ago. I guess I figured he might need a friend." At this point I found myself tearing up. "And I have a daughter now, too," I said. "The same age as his younger one. So that really hit home for me, the way he protected the girl."

A month later, Kotlowitz called again. Shawn's story was compelling, he said, but his tragedy didn't happen in the summer of 2013. He was committed to keeping his book within those dates, and he didn't have time for a magazine project. The prospect of a story in the *New Yorker* or *Wall Street Journal* was dead.

I was about to hang up when Kotlowitz said, "Why don't you write about Shawn?"

I told him all the reasons I believed I could not. I was too close to the situation. I didn't have any kind of objective distance. I liked Shawn, was growing to love him. And besides, I was spending a lot of time try- ing to raise interest in—and money for—Shawn.

Kotlowitz said these were reasons why I should write the book. "Besides," he added, "you said you think about him all the time. If you're obsessed with Shawn and the story, why not tell it yourself?"

When Shawn and I spoke, our topics were usually his health care struggles, fundraising, and Naja's future. I came to believe finding him a rewarding job was more important. But his employer—not Marshall, but the Chicago Public Schools—was ignoring him. His union showed little interest. Plenty of schools were wheelchair accessible, but Marshall was not. If Shawn was to work for the school system again, he wanted to be at Marshall, but that did not seem possible.

In 2014, four months after Shawn was shot, I began writing to agencies, schools, not-for-profit organizations, college basketball teams, and even the Chicago Bulls, in a quest to land a better job for him. He wasn't actually ready to start work immediately. In fact, over a year later the spiraling cost of therapy meant Shawn was still at home more than at rehab, and he would still not be completely approved by doctors to return to his job at Marshall High School, a job he could not perform anyway without an elevator being installed. Regardless, I plowed ahead.

Mostly I got nowhere while Shawn sat at home without a paycheck or getting rehab.

Chicago Bulls general manager Gar Forman had been the assistant coach at New Mexico State, and I replaced him in 1994. He was sympathetic and put me in touch with the community relations crew on the Bulls staff. It was Forman who'd made sure Randy Brown attended Shawn's benefit game and brought a gift: an autographed souvenir Derrick Rose jersey. My written pitch to the Bulls, and pretty much everyone else, was this: hire Shawn as a public speaker to work within the city. He could speak at clinics, camps, luncheons, and fundraisers. He'd tell his story, push nonviolence, and, most important, ask players and coaches to be the leaders in getting young men to put their guns away.

For a time, it seemed the Bulls might come through. Forman's wife, Leslie, worked in community relations for the team and she was also genuinely taken with the story. She arranged for Shawn and Naja to be guests at a couple of games. Ultimately, though, a Bulls spokesperson said because Shawn wasn't a former Bull or NBA player, my proposal was not going to work.

I tweaked that letter on Shawn's behalf a dozen times. To DePaul University's basketball staff. Loyola University. Next I tried After School

Matters, a nonprofit that Bulls star Derrick Rose was involved with. Shawn was perfect for them. No reply. I reached out to Noah's Ark, a nonprofit founded by Bulls star Joakim Noah, who was also involved in the nonviolence movement. No luck. I tried an Illinois government organization called Project Safe Neighborhoods, run through the US Attorney's office. I wrote to PeacePlayers International, an organization that has set up shop in violent hotspots across the globe—places like Palestine, Belfast, Cypress, and South Africa.

Next, after watching the film *The Interrupters,* I pursued the crew known as CeaseFire. They were based out of the University of Illinois–Chicago, the Near West Side school. Since the film's release, the group had adopted a new name: Cure Violence. They were considering opening a branch at Marshall, a promising development. But Cure Violence relied on "soft" money, a yearly allotment from the state. Illinois voters had ousted Governor Pat Quinn, replacing him with Bruce Rauner, a man who had spent $26 million of his own money to get elected. Rauner immediately slashed funding to Cure Violence. That option was out, too.

I tried Secretary of State Jesse White, who had appeared a decade earlier in the public service announcement with Shawn to raise awareness for organ donations. White's assistant, one of only two people who took the time to meet with me in person, was visibly moved by the story. He said he would get back to us.

Susan Cochran from Gift of Hope showed promise. Gift of Hope had harvested Frinda Harrington's organs after her murder. Susan and Shawn had plenty of back-and-forth, which led to them both trying to imagine a job that might be appropriate for Shawn.

I still had an important ace up my sleeve on the job search for Shawn Harrington. It was time to play that card.

The athletics director for the entire Chicago Public School system was a forceful personality named Thomas Trotter. I had convinced New Mexico State to hire him in 1998, at a time when he had no job. In short, Trotter owed me a favor.

I figured I'd get Trotter to back my proposal—redefining Shawn's job within the schools. Insiders know the city's system was once flooded with former basketball stars, many without degrees, who had been gifted positions downtown, security jobs at the high schools, or coaching spots. If the administration could find places for a host of unqualified ex-players, surely they could create a new spot for Shawn.

It took surprisingly long for Trotter to get back to me. "I just assumed Shawn was a gangbanger," he said the day before Dorothy Gaters's benefit game. This was a common mindset in Chicago: a guy who'd been shot must have deserved it. He stayed out too late, had been at a bar past closing time, was slinging drugs, was "affiliated" with a gang. He must have been "on the street," a phrase I would hear constantly in the next two years. This would be the only time anyone suggested it about Shawn Harrington, and it was strange to hear it from a CPS administrator.

No, no, I said, Shawn had done all the right things. He was a college graduate, a good father, a productive worker at Marshall. (Trotter knew Marshall high school well from his recruiting days. He had a brief speaking part in *Hoop Dreams*.)

I drew out the details for Trotter over lunch in Greek Town one day. "I'm not petitioning you for a pay raise," I told him. "CPS just has to *reassign* him, repurpose his job." I drew out the day-to-day job description. He'd go to the high schools and talk to the athletes, coaches, and at-risk kids. Athletes, particularly basketball players, are often the most respected students at Chicago schools, and Shawn would call on the ballers to be outspoken about ending gun violence. Coaches, too, have strong cachet, both on campus and in the community, and Shawn would challenge them to take a leadership role. When he made it through the high school list, he could return to the most troubled ones or start in on the local grammar schools. We could even come up with a logo, a catchphrase that could be sewn on to every CPS uniform the following season.

Trotter asked me to rewrite the proposal, revise it until it became a pitch *from* Trotter, a memo to his bosses. He would send it upstairs.

No problem, I said. Then I pushed Trotter, indirectly bringing up his failed run as head coach at a historically black college. "Are you

going to be known as the college coach who was dumped for losing?"
I asked. "We have a chance here to make an impact and change your
legacy." I named the stats—coaches love stats—on the terrible shooting totals. Trotter, as principal at Hyde Park and now as CPS sports
boss, had been in charge during a couple of highly publicized scandals.
I knew that was a sore subject so I put it this way: "You can alter the
way people remember you."

Trotter seemed to get it. I could see his chest swell as the idea
took wings inside of him. I kept hammering away even after our Greek
chicken was just a pile of bones. "This will be a national story," I said.
"You'll be the leader of an important movement." As the highest-ranking
sports administrator at CPS, Trotter could help Shawn.

14

Wilbur Wright College coach Mike Harris was as good a fit for coaching Tim Triplett as could be hoped for, with his West Side experience and his stint in the United States Navy.

Coach Harris says Triplett was a natural leader, tough and likeable. "He had a memorable smile," Harris says, "and was always in a good mood." As he'd done at Marshall, Triplett made an impression without ever playing in a game. "Our guys responded to him quickly," Harris says, "and he gained respect."

Triplett began school at a disadvantage, Harris says, because he did not register until the last hour, when the most desirable classes were already filled. That's why he was in an 8:00 AM class, always a challenge, particularly for kids with a longer commute. Absences led to him dropping that class in mid-October. Now carrying fewer than twelve hours, he became ineligible to play in games. He continued to practice with the team, figuring on counting the year as a redshirt season. Redshirting is not an uncommon move for a freshman player who needs to adjust. It can translate into a fifth year of college, more time to accumulate credit hours needed to graduate.

Mike Harris took a roundabout journey to become the Wright coach. After years in the notorious Henry Horner housing project, his family eventually moved to the far northwest suburb of Dundee, where he was the only African American on his high school team. With the arrival of Tim Triplett on his campus, the coach began to reconsider the life of his charismatic older brother, Kenny Harris.

Kenny Harris was a stocky ball of fire who could score in a dozen ways, even in the days before the three-point line. After his family moved to the suburbs, Kenny stayed on the West Side, where he felt more comfortable.

Everyone knew him by his distinctive nickname, based on the wealthiest character on the television show *Dukes of Hazzard*—Boss Hogg.

An outstanding player at Collins High School, Boss Hogg was picked to play in the prestigious Boston Shootout as a high school senior. His dodgy grades kept him from getting a major college scholarship, and he starred briefly at Olive-Harvey, a South Side junior college, but his career ended soon thereafter. What he did right after his basketball career ended is the subject of speculation in Chicago's basketball community. "He was never really in a gang," Mike Harris says, and he doesn't know the specifics of how Boss Hogg was earning a living, except this: "He was making ends meet on the street."

Coach Harris, a thoughtful and considerate man, still thinks about his brother constantly, and he says there's a simple reason why Boss Hogg wasn't killed during his street life days. "Luck!" he says. "It had to be luck. He had his brushes, and he was shot at a couple of times."

Boss Hogg was a regular in the city's highly competitive summer tournaments, often playing two games a day, and his skills kept improving. By the time he was in his thirties, though, his own children started asking too many questions about his job. Having to answer to his kids stymied him, something that hapless defenders on the court—or, for that matter, his street rivals or the police—could not do.

"I think that Kenny wanted to answer their questions with honesty," Mike Harris says, "and also with some dignity. Eventually he was trying to avoid the perils of the street, too."

Boss Hogg took a sudden turn down a different path. A talented talker with a head for business, he started his own excavation company, the only black-owned company of its kind in the new government-mandated "empowerment zone" on the West Side. The ensuing federal grants and tax credits helped his new business soar, and KHT Trucking and Excavation did, among other projects, the groundwork in preparing two Chicago police stations. Boss Hogg's business came to the attention of top black business leaders in Chicago, and when the word got out that he had been a high school All American, he was invited to play in an elite pickup game—the one frequented by Barack Obama and then Chicago Public Schools chief Arne Duncan.

While Boss Hogg was able to defy the odds and sidestep the dangers of street life, he couldn't overcome congenital heart disease. Kenny Harris died in 2012 at age forty-four. Over two thousand well-wishers and friends attended his funeral.

Two years later, when the coach met Tim Triplett, it was impossible not to compare his new recruit to his late brother. Triplett wasn't anywhere near the shooter that Boss Hogg was—"Triplett was more *will* than skill," Harris says—but Triplett was a smart, charismatic, and brash go-getter, not unlike Boss Hogg.

———————

Ontario Brown's daughter Lykeisha recalls, "I talked to my brother a week before Christmas on speakerphone along with my mom. I told him he should come back to Chicago early, before Christmas, and we would give him his gifts when he got here. He said yes, he was going to come the next day."

Ontario Brown Jr. never made it back to Chicago. He was shot in the head during an argument among teenagers in Elkhart, Indiana, on December 19, 2014. Kept on life support after his mother decided to donate the boy's organs, he was pronounced dead the following day. He was sixteen years old and had been unarmed.

This was the only murder in Elkhart the entire calendar year. Elkhart police still had to go public in their search for Ontario Jr.'s shooter, and although there were as many as seven eyewitnesses, nobody stepped forward with information. The investigation moved ponderously slow until Ontario's friend Lenell Williams spoke up.

Williams at first lied to local police in fear of retaliation from the shooter and his friends. He claimed he wasn't with Ontario Jr. that day; he had no idea who might have pulled the trigger. Weeks later Williams returned to tell the truth. He had been an eyewitness and he named the shooter. Elkhart police arrested sixteen-year-old Keenan Mardis for the murder seven weeks after the shooting. Like Ontario Jr., Keenan Mardis was originally from Chicago.

Two busloads of friends from racially mixed Memorial High School in Elkhart made the journey to Chicago's West Side for the funeral services.

Ontario Brown Junior, whose father has been a lifelong friend of Shawn, was murdered just before Christmas in 2014. *Ontario Brown Sr.*

———————

"My supervisor," Thomas Trotter told me a month after our Greek Town lunch, "says that if we create a job for Shawn Harrington, it will be like admitting that gun violence is a Chicago Public Schools problem. They don't want to send that message."

I still believe it was the stupidest, most shortsighted response a CPS administrator could give and I could tell it was a message Trotter wasn't happy to deliver. It effectively ended my hope that the schools were interested in leading the nonviolence movement or doing their part to help slow the pace of the shootings—or help Shawn.

A few months later, in the summer of 2014, Trotter was forced out as athletics director. I'd struck out, unable to call in a marker, and with my contact gone, the window to get Shawn's job redefined was probably closed.

———————

The confusion Marshall's special education coordinator Liz Chambers felt when she first heard "Shawn got shot" seemed to have been more of a premonition almost a year later. On January 19, 2015, Shawn Holloway, who played briefly for Marshall, was sitting in the passenger seat of a friend's car when another sedan drove up and opened fire. Holloway was hit in the back and side. The driver was shot as well, but he was still able to speed off to Stroger Hospital, where he survived. Holloway had lost too much blood and died within an hour of arriving at the emergency room. He was twenty-one years old.

Just five foot six, Holloway had been a senior in 2013. He was recruited to attend Marshall for basketball as an eighth grader, but he played only his freshman season before off-the-court issues diverted him—although he attempted a hoops comeback his senior year. "He was rough around the edges," Shawn Harrington says, "a bit wild, but he had a lot of ability."

Holloway never fell off the radar of teachers and staff. At one point, Jennifer Jones, then the girls' team assistant coach, paid for his physical exam to allow him to play basketball again. Korbin McClain says, "I felt that Shawn Holloway was different than a lot of kids in trouble because he'd attempt to do better."

Longtime Marshall security supervisor Gwen Howard says, "Shawn Holloway was a different type of character. He lived that hard life. We used to talk to him to deter him from the street." Another Marshall insider takes it a step further: "Holloway represented as a gang member all day, every day."

Holloway was killed just two blocks from the United Center, where the Chicago Bulls play—and three blocks from Trotter's old office as athletics director for the Chicago Public Schools.

———————

All three of Tim Triplett's coaches at Crane had departed, so while he'd only played a single season at Marshall—half a season, really—he had to keep somebody abreast of his new college adventure. Shawn was still struggling with rehab and not involved with the team regularly. Triplett reverted to the Marshall system of texting or calling Cotton regularly, simply to ask how the Commandos were coming along.

And just because Triplett's high school days were behind him didn't mean he couldn't fall back into his over-the-top leadership role. That December he noticed his old team was playing an important game on a neutral court, at UIC. Triplett bought a ticket, and he came down from the stands to join the Commandos' bench, where he parked himself next to Coach Cotton. "Tim joined the huddle and everything," Kashanna Haggard recalls. "He was *coaching* the team."

Mike Harris estimates he had Triplett in practice well over a hundred times, including open gyms, weight training, and conditioning. Although Triplett was one of the smallest players and not the best shooter, Harris appreciated his mindset. "You never had to coach his effort," he says. "And some kids you have to train, teach them the tricks of the game and how to get an advantage. Not Triplett."

Triplett reenrolled for the spring semester. The guard was never late, never disrespectful, and was a positive influence at practice with his buzz-saw style. The coach recognized the bigger challenges Triplett faced. "You're going to have to leave the street alone," Harris would often tell him.

By that fall, Triplett's mother had moved back to Milwaukee, so he was no longer staying with her at the Adams Street apartment, the address listed on his application form. Before she moved, Jutuan Brown noticed her son was getting a slow start to Wright some mornings. "Get some rest and quit doing what you're doing at night," she told him. Later, even from Wisconsin, she fretted about Tim, wondering where he was after practice ended. "He wanted to do what he wanted to do," she says. "He wanted to be the man. *I'm grown now, you don't have to keep telling me what to do* he would say."

One day after practice, Triplett asked Harris for a lift home. Now, he told his coach, he was living on the next street over from Adams—but this was a very different address, location, and feel, not on the West Side at all. It was downtown Chicago. "Here's where I live now," Triplett announced as they turned onto LaSalle Street.

"It was right near the Willis Tower," Harris says.

A popular area for renters in their early thirties, Triplett's new residence sat within the 60606 zip code, where the residents are 94 percent white and have a college education. The value of the average one- or two-bedroom condo is about $350,000; the average salary for residents is $125,000 a year, more than twice the state's average.

In other words, Triplett didn't at all fit the demographic of the yuppie class living there. Who owned the condo was a mystery to his coach.

"You get surprised by things like that," Harris says, "or the jewelry kids are wearing. His definition of *residence* might be different than mine." All things considered, Harris was in some ways relieved that Triplett was not going home to the West Side. "I'd rather be downtown, too," he says. The coach never learned Triplett's connection to the owner.

Triplett continued to attend basketball practice every day, but without the immediate reward of playing in the games, his focus wavered. The distractions increased.

Shawn was in a rut. The $850-a-day rehab price tag was no longer covered by Shawn's insurance company. Fearful of draining his savings, he stopped going. That meant he could not get approved by doctors to return to work at a job he could no longer do.

Then, in April 2015, Shawn was nominated for free training at the Chicago Rehabilitation Institute for the ReWalk. The ReWalk is an elaborate exoskeleton that uses cutting-edge technology to get spinal cord injury patients up and walking. If Shawn could learn to use the hand controls, balance himself, and master the machine over time, he might be able to strap on the external braces and walk a little each day. Argo Medical Technologies billed the ReWalk as a miraculous breakthrough, and Shawn became one of several patients to test the new design. Although walking with the exoskeleton appeared forced and clunky, the possibility of walking was heady stuff for Shawn. Becoming a subject in the ReWalk study was doubly appealing because it involved other therapy too, which helped him make small progress. He tried not to think about the fact that the ReWalk came with a $70,000 price tag.

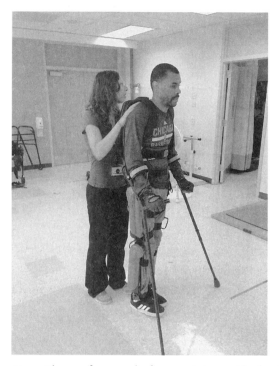

Mental preparation: Shawn focuses before training with the ReWalk.
Michael James

In February 2015, I began talking with Marvin Menzies, then New Mexico State's head basketball coach, about helping Shawn Harrington.

Menzies and his top assistant, Paul Weir, were inspired by Shawn's story. They'd brought him into the locker room before their game at Chicago State, and they got on board with my plan to fly Shawn out for a basketball game at my expense, honor him at halftime, and put on a fundraiser on his behalf.

I pushed Menzies even further, asking if NMSU would be willing to give Naja a full scholarship. It would generate great publicity if our school took care of the daughter of one of our wounded players. We might even create some kind of work-study job. Maybe she could work in sports media; after her summer internship with *True Star* magazine in Chicago, she had developed the computer, writing, and editing skills of a budding journalist.

Although Shawn often talked about walking again, I was not at all confident. I knew nothing about cures, but I was very much interested in helping Shawn *heal*. Naja getting the full scholarship—like the one I believed we took from her father in 1996—felt redemptive and fitting, and would go a long way toward healing Shawn.

Coach Menzies said he was on board. "But you've got to get the provost involved to approve it," he said. "There's only so much I can do."

I talked to Provost Dan Howard on the phone a few days later, detailing not just Shawn's recent tragedy and his daughter's story, but also our roles as NMSU coaches in cutting him loose after his knee injury. Howard got quiet when he learned the part about Shawn being pushed out the door. I pitched the idea of a scholarship for Naja as a way to somehow correct the university's—and my own—past sins. Besides the great publicity the scholarship would generate, it would be a humane gesture, the right thing to do. I said that Naja had been an honor roll student, a 3.8 GPA, but that there had been a dip since the shooting; she was hovering at a 3.4.

I even suggested that the provost make the scholarship offer to Shawn that weekend. I'd talked to a Steve Dehlson from ESPN's *Outside the Lines*. Dehlson said they would be there to film only if I could guarantee the dramatic moment would happen. The provost, however, said he could not do that. After all, Naja was not even a senior in high school. He did say he would figure out a way to bring Shawn's daughter to our school. Here's the e-mail I sent to Shawn right after that phone call.

3/2/15

The provost just told me this:

"We're going to take care of Naja, make sure she's an Aggie. But because she's just a junior, we can't offer her a scholarship just yet. It's Cart before the Horse. It'll happen in due time, but it won't happen this weekend."

His name is Dan Howard. He gave me his word: *we're going to get her down here and make things right for her.* You'll meet Dan when you get here.

Still: let's get Adrian and Provost the transcript today or tomorrow.

Rus

"You don't know how good it feels to be back in New Mexico!" Shawn said. "Look at those mountains."

It was sixty degrees and sunny, typical for winter. His friend Estell had accompanied him on the trip, and we were driving around campus with the windows down. Shawn pointed out the buildings where he had classes, the apartment where he once lived. He had not been to the Southwest since he left in the summer of 1996, but he had nothing but warm feelings for the school.

The night before the fundraiser, New Mexico State had a game against Chicago State. Shawn sat courtside in Aggie gear. When the PA announcer introduced him he received a rousing ovation. The Chicago State coach had told Shawn's story to his team, and when the players were introduced, rather than running to midcourt, they came over to shake Shawn's hand. Their coaches did the same thing moments later. As the houselights were cut and the spotlight beamed down, the home team copied that ritual.

The fundraiser the next night was at Lou and Mary Henson's understated home. Besides his success coaching the University of Illinois, Lou had served as the head coach at New Mexico State in two successful stretches before retiring, though he had not coached Shawn. This was a casual night, the only formality being Shawn addressing the gathering of forty people. "New Mexico State means so much to me," he said. "I loved my time here and I'm so blessed to be back." He thanked school administrators and boosters for coming, for their support, and he posed for photos with anyone who asked.

Provost Dan Howard came as well. It was difficult to discern how much money was raised that night because there was no collection, no basket to leave a check in, a handout flyer about the recovery fund

Lou Henson never coached Shawn, but he welcomed him back to New Mexico State. *Rus Bradburd*

at Chicago's Fifth Third Bank the only overt pitch. What was easy to tell, though, was that Dan Howard was on board with the plan to help Shawn's daughter.

"We're going to make Naja an offer," the provost said quietly to me, "that will be difficult for her to turn down."

I was delighted. I noticed him lean in close to Shawn near the end of the evening. On the drive back to Shawn's hotel, I asked what the provost had said.

"He told me they're going to make Naja an offer she'll have a hard time saying no to," he said—nearly verbatim what I'd been told. Regardless of how many checks were mailed to Chicago after the event, this news made his trip a bonanza.

A few weeks later, I got this encouraging follow-up e-mail from the New Mexico State provost:

3/29/15

Hi Rus,

Thanks for the note about Shawn and his daughter. It was an honor to spend time with him…what a wonderful man he is.

NMSU will do right by him and his daughter. Please keep me in the loop.

———————

Tevin King, the former Providence St. Mel star, signed a basketball scholarship to attend South Dakota State on April 22, 2015.

King, who had gone head-to-head against Tim Triplett so many times, was excited to begin his college career, and his South Dakota State team would go on to qualify for the NCAA tournament in his first two seasons. He had left Chicago to enroll at a prep school, worked hard at his game, kept his nose in the books, and was rewarded with the full ride. King still had to be careful about who he associated with, especially since he planned on being in Chicago all summer. "I don't get excited about being around a lot of people," he says. "I'm only social to a point and I watch how I move around." When he was in sixth grade, his paintball game had been interrupted by a Chicago cop, who handcuffed him and tossed him in the back of his squad car. Hanging out for no good reason made you more likely to get hassled by cops or gangbangers, and he was hyperaware of that fact.

Two days after signing with South Dakota State, King, back in Chicago for a brief weekend visit, was walking home from a friend's house. It was late, too late, nearly 11:00 PM, and he heard someone holler something from a group of young men on a street corner. Perhaps it was directed at him, he thought, but he ignored it—stopping to ask could be interpreted as the equivalent of "You talking to *me*?" He didn't want to invite trouble so he picked up the pace. When he was a block away, it registered whose voice had called to him.

"Before I even got home," King says, "I sent Tim a message on Facebook, just to check up on him."

King wrote to Triplett: "You good?"

"Yeah I'm good," Triplett wrote back. "Trying to finish school strong."

"You ain't got to be outside," King replied. "Stay focused and disciplined. Call me." King also sent Triplett his new phone number before he signed off.

"He never called me," King says.

15

DADDY, DO YOU KNOW THIS GUY?

On Sunday, April 26, 2015, fifteen months after he had been shot and paralyzed, Shawn Harrington's daughter Naja texted him that question, along with a game photo. The photo was an action shot of Tim Triplett in his Marshall uniform.

Tim Triplett Jr., the player predicted to change Marshall's fortunes, had been murdered on the 3500 block of West Flournoy, just four blocks from Marshall. He was nineteen years old.

Shawn Harrington texted me minutes after Naja texted him:

"I don't know how much more of this I can take."

One resident on the block had been watching a John Wayne movie when he heard shots. Outside his window he saw Triplett bleeding to death. Other than that, police had little to go on. Nobody would say who fired five bullets into Triplett's chest while he stood at the curb at noon on a sunny day.

The next day a simple tribute was set up. A single white candle. A small bunch of blue balloons. A handwritten sign nailed to a tree.

Triplett left behind three children, a girlfriend from Marshall, and his mother, Jutuan Brown. "But Tim still managed to graduate high school with honors," Jutuan Brown told the *Chicago Tribune,* "and he proceeded to go to college, had a job. He was still on point." (One Marshall administrator says that his mother's claim about graduating with honors is not quite true—"Triplett did graduate, but not with honors." None of Triplett's teammates recall him having a job.)

She couldn't muster whatever it was a mother needed to ID her eldest son's body. She was living in Milwaukee and told the *Sun-Times* that she didn't want to sully the image she had of her boy. "I refuse to see him. I can't take it. I can't take it right now," and she added, "His smile. The way he loved to play basketball and his music."

Instead, the awful task fell to Julia Triplett, Tim's grandmother. "He was in a black body bag in the emergency room," she says, "and his head was turned from me." She was able to confirm it was Tim even with that limited view. "I didn't want to see his face," she adds.

Julia Triplett returned from the morgue to the West Side apartment her grandson had walked to for his after-school visits. "Lots of kids getting killed out there," she says, "and they don't care. I'm afraid to go to the store." After a sigh she adds, "There's not enough love in the world." By the following November, she would stop watching college basketball on television. "Every time I watch it, I think about Tim," she says, "and I have to turn it off. That could have been my grandson."

A few days later, after Jutuan Brown gathered herself and found the strength to collect her eldest son's possessions at the morgue, she was perplexed. There was no wallet, no ID, just his clothes and shoes.

The funeral service was held at Pleasant Grove Baptist Church on 741 South Sacramento. The church was packed with mourners an hour before the service began, which surprised teammate Citron Miller. "I don't believe that Tim knew so many people loved him," he says.

Many people assumed Shawn Harrington would speak at the event, the wounded coach eulogizing the charismatic point guard. But Shawn figured this was Tim Triplett's day, and he didn't want to call attention to himself. Instead, Shawn wheeled himself into the back of the chapel. Upon closer examination, he noticed the dress, the markings, the colors, of a few of the mourners. "These guys were affiliated," Shawn says, using the oddly formal word that denotes gang membership. Triplett was decked out in his coffin in a three-piece suit, complete with Christian Louboutin shoes that retail at $1,400.

Funerals for young gunshot victims can be unpredictable, but nobody anticipated the wild affair that unfolded that day. Shortly into her eulogy, the pastor pulled out a pistol, waved it around, then aimed it directly at people in the crowd. "Does this make me tough?" she shouted. "Does it make me *bad*?"

The taunts continued, the pastor posing dramatically with the gun, pretending to be a gangbanger while mourners ducked or gasped. Was it loaded? Soon the woman was pacing the aisles, mocking some of the young men in attendance. Crammed into the pews at the church, everyone was trapped until the pastor had her say.

"I've never seen anything like it," Citron Miller says, "but I didn't find it offensive. If you find it offensive, you're blind to the fact of what's going on."

Tyrese Williford disagrees. "I didn't appreciate it," he says, "and neither did a lot of people. She was trying to make a statement but she should have kept to herself."

The sermon unsettled Tim's grandmother as well. "She should have let people know she was going to do that," Julia Triplett says.

Triplett's best boyhood friend from Milwaukee, Kortez Pickett, was also taken aback by the gun-waving pastor. "She wanted to prove that guns are pointless, but I didn't really like it." Even after driving two hours, Pickett declined to view the body at the front of the church, despite being prodded by some of Triplett's friends.

"I knew Tim longer than they did," Pickett says, "and I loved him. I just didn't want to see him in no casket."

The murder of Tim Triplett rocked the Marshall family. There was no announcement at Marshall this time, no gathering in the library, no calling in Dorothy Gaters for advice or leadership. The Marshall administration summoned a crisis team from the Chicago Public Schools' downtown office to talk to any of his former teammates who requested help.

Carol Brown-Robinson, the basketball team's unofficial academic advisor, remembers Triplett as "a sweet and humble kid." She says Triplett had been playful and friendly with her young son, and she had to let her boy know about Triplett's death. "You mean," her son said upon hearing the news, "the player who called me his little brother?"

Triplett's murder also radically changed the direction of this book. His mother said he was an honor roll student, but in the *Tribune* story there was this quote: "Triplett had a record of minor arrests associated with low-level drug trade over the last few years." I wanted to learn about his life, but Shawn and the Marshall people did not know him well because he had only been a Commando for nine months. Much of Triplett's background remained a mystery, and after his murder his teammates were hesitant to talk about him. They feared retribution, did not want to say anything negative about the slain guard, or, more often, simply did not know much.

Eventually, people opened up about Triplett. His friends say he was a complicated kid, and that he had another side besides the brash, tough, on-court personality. He was fun-loving, a flirt with girls, and he loved flashy clothes. Over the next two years I talked to Triplett's mother, girlfriend, family, teammates, pals, cops, and coaches—and then uncovered his Facebook page—to piece together the truth about his complicated story. That helped me to think about the arc of Shawn Harrington's life, the similarities and differences the wounded coach had with his slain player.

Tim Triplett was born on January 16, 1995. Triplett's birth pretty much ended his mother's hope of going to college. Like Frinda Harrington, Jutuan Brown (no relation to Randy Brown or Ontario Brown) was pregnant when she graduated from Farragut High School on the West Side.

The baby's father was Timothy Triplett Sr. Although they did not get married they were close, and he was more than Jutuan's high school sweetheart. They'd met in kindergarten. Jutuan was optimistic about the future of the new family.

One summer day in 1997, Tim Sr. phoned to say he was walking over to visit. He never made it. "I heard from people he was killed while being robbed," Jutuan says, "walking across Douglas Park, coming to see me. He was shot one time in the back."

Their son, Tim Jr., was eighteen months old.

"Tell me exactly what happened," the boy asked beginning at age five, and then he would pepper her with endless questions: "Why did they do it? Where was he shot? Did my father fight back?"

Jutuan and Julia Triplett, little Tim's grandmother, tried to be honest. "Some things," Jutuan sighs, "I can't answer. I told him the truth, as much as I knew, right from the start. I didn't want anyone else to tell him the wrong thing. And naturally he was hurt by the story." She would show her son photos of his father in his high school basketball uniform, which made the boy tremendously interested in the sport.

Jutuan gave birth to a second son, Tywon Jones, a year after Tim Triplett Sr. was killed.

Triplett was in third grade when things got rougher for Jutuan Brown. Her sister in Milwaukee volunteered to take Tim and his brother, Tywon, until their mother got back on her feet. Three years later, the boys moved back to Chicago's West Side, taking an apartment in Holy City, a pocket of the Lawndale neighborhood.

Holy City runs from Pulaski to Kedzie, Roosevelt to Cermak, and the designation implies a safe haven. But it was the Vice Lords street gang who named it after forming there fifty years ago, and an Old Testament–like plague of poverty and violence has a grip on the area.

Triplett attended nearby Crowne Elementary School and did well enough that his mother was infused with hope. You didn't have to be a coach to see that he was a terrific little player. It was easy to think her oldest would improve his life through basketball.

Farragut sat just four blocks away, but that did not guarantee that Triplett would attend. The Chicago Public Schools' open enrollment policy has created an ongoing battle centered on the recruitment of thirteen-year-old boys. Every high school coach knows that all eighth graders are free agents. Even after they enroll, coaches constantly re-recruit them to stay put because of the imminent threat that the best players might leave for more "exposure"—a word that sometimes means a better team, but often translates as a coach who will coddle the kid. It's a system that trashes the concept of loyalty, community, or stability. Charges of tampering or stealing kids are rampant. Nobody could expect otherwise. (The trend really took hold in the mid-1980s when a sensational sophomore named Nick Anderson was conscripted from humble Prosser High School. Prosser coach Gene Ideno quit, disgusted with the eroding integrity among coaches.)

By chance, veteran Farragut coach William "Wolf" Nelson owned the apartment building at Sixteenth Street and Hamlin Avenue that Triplett's family rented. Nelson, with his rare genius for numbers, taught math at his alma mater. He remembered Jutuan from her days as a student, and he became intensely interested in landing both Triplett and his best pal, Issaiah Hayes (no relation to Tyrone Hayes) for Farragut. Issaiah was from just south of the Eisenhower Expressway, the 290, in the violent Homan Square neighborhood where Triplett was murdered.

Coaches are hyperaware of kids whose fathers played ball because the quickness, size, and toughness it takes to succeed on the court can be genetic. Both boys had fathers who were ballers.

Farragut had gained national notoriety when six foot eleven Kevin Garnett played his final year there before skipping college to go on to instant NBA stardom. The school had its share of flameouts, too, most notably Ronnie Fields, who remains the subject of a massive mural splashed across a wall in the gymnasium. Fields, despite his thirty-four points per game in high school and his breathtaking forty-eight-inch vertical leap, was derailed by a bad car accident and messy academics. He never played a minute in college or the NBA.

Triplett did not choose Farragut, despite its proximity. Instead, he and Issaiah Hayes decided on Crane High School, twenty-two blocks from their grade school.

Crane's principal, Richard Smith, understood the recruiting pressure on young ballplayers as well as anyone. He had played at King High School when newspaper stories surfaced regularly about their coach pilfering stars from rival schools. Smith knew that the combination of recruiting and school closures meant many students don't actually live in the neighborhood where they attend school. These outsiders can be particularly vulnerable to gangs.

Richard Smith's journey to being named principal reads like an urban fairy tale, and the moral of the story is how education, hard work, and perseverance can pay off. His first position at Crane was as a custodian. He later drove a truck for the Chicago Public Schools, substitute taught at Crane, completed his master's degree, and returned as a teacher for nine years. Later, he was named dean of students, and then assistant principal. In 2007, he was tapped as Crane's principal.

Smith looks more like a superhero than an administrator. At six foot six and 235 pounds, he's chiseled muscle, and it's easy to imagine him doing something heroic for his kids. Smith still had limits to his influence. "You can control the eight hours a student is in your school somewhat," he says, "but it's impossible to control the other sixteen hours."

Smith had been Crane's principal for two months when a massive brawl erupted outside the school, just after the final bell. As many as fifty students scuffled, exchanged punches, and some swung golf clubs. In the midst of the riot, a fifteen-year-old student used a .22 caliber pistol at close range to murder a popular eighteen-year-old named Ruben Ivy.

Police said the dispute began over a baseball cap. The story got widespread media attention, and Smith grieved for years over the killing. Nobody ever suggested that the new principal could have stopped a young man with more than a dozen arrests from criminal activity, but these were *his* kids, *his* school. Already organized to the point of being overbearing, Smith turned it up a notch, became even stricter, more hands-on. This meant reining in kids like Tim Triplett.

Smith challenged Triplett from the start. One day during his freshman year, Triplett had a baseball cap on sideways, a common symbol of gang affiliation, but sometimes a wannabe fashion statement. Smith ordered Triplett to remove the hat. "I don't think he'd ever been around strong men who demanded respect," he says.

After establishing his authority Smith had trouble keeping Triplett out of his office, but not because of discipline issues. This was exactly what the principal had hoped for and he always made time for Triplett.

"They have to be around somebody who monopolizes their mind," he says. "Triplett has a beautiful mother, but he was making adult decisions on his own."

If Triplett got stuck walking home from Crane, he'd have to cross the 290 and go down Ogden, angling through Douglas Park where his father was killed. In recent years, 290 has been referred to as the "Heroin Highway" because open-market drug sales nearby are rampant. Many West Side students either live in these hotspots or travel through them to get to school. The closer to 290, the busier and more dangerous the corners can be. Crane overlooks the highway and Marshall is just a few blocks away. Sometimes drug customers, many of them from the suburbs, pay cash out the car window for marijuana, cocaine, and heroin. Often cash is taken at one location, the drugs picked up minutes later at another. In this drive-through system, somebody has to be standing on the corner selling at all hours, as Marshall player Martin Satterfield fell into doing as a boy.

An outsider might wonder why dealers are less interested in selling the marijuana in bulk for a lump sum in a well-to-do suburb. Chopping up the product into, say, "dime bags" and "jabs" of weed, causes the profit margin to rise remarkably. Provided, again, that somebody is willing to stand outside and hustle, often in terrible weather. One veteran Chicago police officer says the icy chill of a Chicago January can be a dependable litmus test for law enforcement. "That's why I love the winter," he says. "If you're out at night on the street in the cold, I know you are up to no good."

Triplett sometimes walked in the other direction from 290, hoofing it thirty minutes from Crane to his grandmother's home near the corner of Fulton and Sacramento. This meant passing through neighborhoods where gang allegiances shifted, particularly as he crossed major streets like Western Avenue.

"Aren't you scared to walk here?" Julia Triplett would ask.

"No Grandma, I'm not scared," he smiled.

"Triplett had a bit of the Napoleon syndrome," Richard Smith says, "and he didn't back down. He had that mentality, *Nobody is going to mess with me.*"

By Triplett's third year at Crane, Jutuan was confident. Her son's grades were good and basketball was going amazingly well. She was there the afternoon he exploded for fifty points in a game against Marshall, a remarkable total, especially for a smaller player. Yet his mother sensed Triplett was taking on too much responsibility—typical for a young coach, but not a high school player. At night, he'd list the team's hurdles and struggles. "He was worrying and stressing himself too much," she says, "carrying too much weight on his shoulders. He'd been that way for a long time." Jutuan became anxious about the precise personality trait that Shawn Harrington would later imagine Triplett might harness positively. Once at a game, during a timeout, she yelled down from the stands, "Tim, you can't be the coach *and* the player!" (Coach Tim Anderson heard that and called back, "He's doing fine, Mom!")

Richard Smith had another difficulty as principal. Triplett played for three different coaches in three years, although the turnover didn't bother Triplett so much. Instead, the problems right outside the school's doors tripped him up.

When the city decided to raze the Rockwell Gardens and Henry Horner projects on the West Side, the residents, whose buildings were always associated with or under the jurisdiction of a specific street gang, were dispersed in a scattershot, unpredictable way. The old alliances, structure, and stability disintegrated and new housing developments, despite their idyllic appearance, inherited generations of problems. In a complex across the street from Crane called Oakley Square (known to locals as St. Stephen's), trouble was looming.

Throughout their junior year Triplett and Issaiah Hayes got into verbal altercations with young men based in those apartments. Triplett had probably warranted suspicion because he was louder, an outsider, and possibly seen as affiliated or at least friendly with a rival gang.

"Tim talked tough and he really was a tough guy," Wolf Nelson says. "He'd say, *We street, we hard core!* And what made Tim such a good player could get him into trouble off the court."

Principal Smith had done enough outreach within the community to know exactly who the gang leaders were, who he could influence, and who he could not. "They'd occasionally come to me and say, *Smith, there's a problem.* And I'd get whoever and ask him what's going on. And it'd be over with."

One day everything changed.

Gang leaders came to Smith's office and warned him that Triplett's life was now in danger. "There's nothing you can do to save him," one man said. Triplett had crossed some line and they could no longer promise Triplett's or Hayes's safety.

A friend of Triplett's says the dispute near Crane centered on a young lady with whom Triplett was involved. "It was Tim's baby's mama, and one day these guys got into it with her and they chased her home."

A player from a rival school says, "Tim's girlfriend was threatened and these guys just grabbed her up off the streets and said to her *We can get you anytime, so tell your boyfriend to show up.*" As the basketball season went on, this friend says the pressure increased. "There were a few games Tim went out the back door afterwards. He even posted on Facebook about it."

Yet another says, "Tim was a GD [Gangster Disciple] who wasn't from the Crane neighborhood. St. Stephen's Terrace was Vice Lords. There were a lot more incidents than that [final warning]."

The principal often had to do more than his official job description. With the memory of Ruben Ivy's murder haunting him, Smith called the boys' mothers to tell them of his plan—a plan very much against the interest of his high profile basketball team.

Gangs have changed dramatically in Chicago in the last decade for myriad reasons. There has been the closing of high-rise public housing and the incarceration or death of top gang leaders. The proliferation of guns. Also, the emergence of taxpayer-funded charter schools. Privatizing public education led directly to the shuttering of dozens of Chicago public schools, the deterioration of neighborhoods, and more kids crossing lines into unfamiliar neighborhoods.

Chicago's schools had been performing poorly enough that in the 1990s the charter school movement appeared as a viable alternative. The charters came up with catchy names like Uplift Academy or Urban Prep Charter Academy and used taxpayer funding to help construct shiny new buildings. On the first day of classes in September, the charters tallied total attendance and used that number to procure more state money. Then, according to frustrated CPS teachers, the charters quickly bounced out kids with discipline problems. Those kids wound up back at public schools after student funding had been allocated.

The public schools aren't only the victim of the decline of neighborhood schools, they are also the culprits. Their open enrollment policy long ago created a tiered system with an underbelly of educational institutions.

By 2010 it became clear that the charters weren't performing any better than the public schools, but the damage had been done. Attendance at public schools had dwindled and a few of them closed. Other than unsolved murders and shootings, nothing causes a neighborhood to deteriorate more than an empty school, the hub of neighborhood activity gone.

Marshall once had a solid honors program, which police officer Sherod Dent had attended before going on to his impressive college basketball career. Declining enrollments meant that attractive feature got dissolved. Some studies today estimate that over 90 percent of West Side kids do not attend their local school, resulting in far less community involvement or social investment.

The problems on the West Side are exacerbated by an overloaded criminal justice system that targets young black men for possessing marijuana, while sending violent habitual criminals back out on the street. Factor in the declining number of cops and detectives and long waits for trials. And the mayor, in a cost-saving move, combined the five police "Areas" into three, taking veteran cops out of their familiar beats.

Another factor is the saturation of social media. "Your choices on Facebook can cost you your life," confirms Officer Dent. Social media glorifies the have/have nots, exposes young people to vast economic differences. "Instead of using it as a positive channel, it's become a *poor me* syndrome," he says. "*They have more than me, why not take from them?* kids today are more likely to think." That sometimes leads to a hardworking young gangbanger getting robbed at gunpoint by an impatient rival.

Also, Dent says, there's another big difference. "Nowadays you get more people mean mugged," meaning a menacing look that causes offense, and what young men will fight and kill for can be petty. Sometimes even the kids who don't particularly want to associate with gangs get caught up. Dent also mentions the long-gone mindset, that ballplayers were once off limits and given a sort of "Hooper's Pass."

"Yes, we were friendly with neighborhood tough guys after a playground game," Dent recalls, "but they looked at us as an investment." Gang members weren't naïve enough to think all high school stars were going to the NBA, although plenty from the West Side had done just that. Something else, what Dent calls "a *social* investment" was important. "The most influential and respected people in the neighborhood," he says, "were the ballplayers."

Those days are long gone, says Dent, for a number of reasons. "Nowadays, [gang members] want to be part of the players, but they're asking more of them, more than gear from their college."

Finally, the pervasive poverty on the West Side has gotten worse. "People with money are gods," Dent says. "That's so amplified in our society. There's only so long that a boy walks past guys slinging drugs on a busy corner before it affects him, especially if he has no money in his pocket. It takes an incredibly strong will to say, *I'm only going to play ball.*"

In April 2013, Richard Smith did the unprecedented. He pushed Triplett and Issaiah Hayes out the door at Crane and likely saved their lives. The "Emergency Transfer" papers Smith signed in the middle of the spring semester ensured the boys were immediately eligible for sports at any school within their districts as long as they were in good academic standing at Crane. The decimation of Crane's basketball team was even more painful because Triplett had proved to be a solid student. "He was over a 3.0 grade point average when he left Crane," a school administrator there says.

Smith phoned Farragut coach Wolf Nelson. "They gotta go," Smith told Nelson about his two stars, "because I'm not going to have that happen on my watch." No Chicago high school wants to lose their two star players, but the principal believed the threat to their lives constituted an emergency situation.

As much as it pained the boys to split, they couldn't settle on one school. While Triplett picked Farragut, Issaiah Hayes chose Orr, with their up-and-coming team.

Coach Nelson says that Triplett seemed fine at first. The basketball season had just concluded but the Farragut team was delighted to add the flamboyant star. The African American players there, outnumbered by Hispanic kids, form a tight unit and Triplett fit in usually.

"Occasionally I had to tell him to shut up," Nelson says.

Triplett always did, muttering "My bad, Coach."

Popular with the girls and busy with ball, Tim Triplett wasn't home much, but he was doing better than his brother, Tywon. "Tim had never been involved in gangs," Jutuan says, "but they were gangbanging hard in our neighborhood." Jutuan hoped Tim might still influence her second son in ways she could not.

Tywon, whose nickname was "Blackman," showed all the signs of being bipolar. He had been a fairly good player as a boy but he never grew. By his teenage years he turned away from one of the few outlets that West Side kids have. Soon forces that Jutuan couldn't control swept him up. "Tywon went in another direction," Jutuan says, "one that Tim didn't like, gangbanging, selling drugs, not even going to school."

One longtime friend of the family confirms this. "Tywon told everybody he didn't want to go to school. He was into the streets."

Jutuan Brown recalls that spring as a swirl of trouble. On April 17, 2013, Tywon came home from a brief stint at the Cook County Juvenile Detention Center where he had been sent after getting in a serious fight.

"Blackman had a lot of anger," says one Marshall player who knew the brothers. "He could snap."

The brothers had mostly gotten along, but seeing his mother distraught bothered Triplett, and he blamed Tywon. "You need to sit your ass down," Triplett told Tywon. "You're stressing Mom out again."

"Tywon was upset at the time," Jutuan says, "and he'd been reaching out to his dad, who didn't have time for him." All brothers are vulnerable to disagreements but this one ran deep, and Triplett's warnings would prove prescient. On May 5, 2013, a month after learning that Triplett's life was in jeopardy, she got an early afternoon call from her eldest son.

"Mom," Triplett said, "they done killed my brother."

Chicago police and eyewitnesses agreed that Tywon had opened fire from his bicycle on a gathering of people standing on the grassy area around 1300 South Independence Boulevard on the edge of Holy City. Another gunman fired back. When police tried to intervene and chased Tywon in a squad car, the teen, still on the bike, turned his gun on the driver. The police shot back. Even as he lay bleeding to death, tangled facedown in his bicycle's frame, the cops handcuffed him. He was pronounced dead less than an hour later. He was sixteen years old.

"Tim Triplett went into zombie mode after his brother got himself killed," Wolf Nelson says. "He really never came back from that."

Coaches from high schools and colleges complain that attendance and discipline slip once their season concludes. With Crane in the rearview mirror, no regular practice regime at Farragut in the late spring, no summer league schedule taped to his refrigerator, and his home life a mess, Triplett began to drift.

Jutuan Brown noticed a change in her oldest son but Triplett wouldn't admit that he was running around at night for anything besides basketball or girls. "That was the lie he told me, and now I know it wasn't the case," she says.

Tim Triplett was arrested for the first time on May 22, 2013, for "soliciting unlawful business." It was five days after Tywon's funeral.

With the season over, recently divorced Farragut coach Wolf Nelson had time to drive through Holy City regularly to check on Triplett.

Nelson often saw his new player outside Plaza Food and Liquor on the busy southeast corner of Ogden and St. Louis Avenues, just a block from Twenty-First Street. The young men there greeted each other with a little rhyme: "Twenty-first, there ain't no worse."

The coach would swing his car to the curb and give a toot, and Triplett and a couple of pals would pile into the coach's car. Nelson would hit a drive-through, load up with a feast of fast food, and bring the boys to his new South Side home, a long way from the Holy City. They'd watch NBA games or get out a deck of cards to play spades. "They'd be happy as hell," the coach says.

Wolf Nelson says he wasn't the only person to tell Triplett that the basketball/street life combination wouldn't work. He could sense Triplett slipping from his influence. "He wanted to do both," Nelson says, "play ball and run with the gangbangers on the side. Tim didn't go around with a pistol, but he'd do most of the talking and if they got into a fight, he'd fight. But he wasn't a shooter." This role mostly meant a casual affiliation with the young men outside the store on the corner, simply hanging out at night. The comradery and connections are typical for young men on the West Side and they allowed Triplett to pass safely through the neighborhood—precisely what had been disrupted by the confrontation with the young men near Crane.

When final grades came in at the end of June, Triplett had failed some classes—understandable, considering what he had been through. Nelson informed him that he'd have to go to summer school to ensure his eligibility to play for Farragut in the fall. Instead, Triplett quietly decided to leave Farragut. At one time he'd planned on playing in summer leagues like any Chicago baller. As Farragut's July basketball schedule unfolded, Triplett never appeared.

Triplett was arrested for the second time on July 16, 2013, seven weeks before fall classes commenced. This "reckless conduct" charge—running into traffic, which police figure means curbside drug sales—led to a sentence of court supervision for six months.

On July 23, before the supervision for reckless conduct was even put in place, Triplett was arrested for the third time. This "gambling" charge was the only one that led to jail time. He served two days.

By August he'd made up his mind to attend Marshall, and he showed up alone one day to enroll. According to Shawn Harrington and Henry Cotton, all this took place without their knowledge or influence. That seems a stretch to believe, considering Triplett had once scorched them for fifty points. But few kids were as distracted and isolated as Tim Triplett going into his senior year. The Marshall coaches never learned the details about Triplett's recent troubles, the death threats from just outside the door at Crane, the killing of his brother Tywon, the summer arrests. What they did know about Triplett was enough to welcome him. He was among the best guards in the city.

Somehow Triplett had gotten the idea that the transfer to Marshall meant he wouldn't have to miss any games. He believed the failing grades at Farragut would be negated and he could regain his eligibility without going to summer school. This was the same strategy New Mexico State had been using for academically deficient recruits in the 1990s. The allure of "no summer school," although a mirage, must have been enticing.

"But how could that be if you go by semester grades?" Wolf Nelson wonders now. Triplett simply was not making good decisions or thinking logically. By switching schools again, he'd put some distance between himself and Crane, and he hoped to magically erase his Fs from Farragut. He also effectively cut off any communication from Principal Richard Smith. That was his intent, to distance himself somehow from the threat at Crane, Tywon's death, and his poor grades at Farragut.

Anytime a player transfers within the Chicago Public League, an eligibility form needs to be filled out by both schools. When Wolf Nelson got to the crucial question on the form—would Triplett have been eligible to play if he'd stayed at Farragut?—he had to be honest. "No," Nelson wrote. The form required a reason, where Nelson wrote "because he flunked two classes." In September, Nelson was surprised to hear that Triplett was telling his Farragut players that he had "made those classes up." Of course, saying that didn't mean it was true, or that he would be cleared to play.

When Henry Cotton found out that Triplett had failed classes at Farragut, he cornered his new player. "Why didn't you go to summer school?" Cotton asked. Triplett claimed he was never going to stay at Farragut and did not know that his academic air-ball could follow him to Marshall. One CPS administrator believes that because Triplett never actually played a game at Farragut, he might have presumed his overall grade point average would keep him eligible. By September it was too late, unless forms could be sent back and grades changed at Farragut. Of course, any teacher would have a hard time explaining why she altered Triplett's grade months after he had transferred.

Cotton suspects that Triplett, confused by recent events, was only biding his time at Farragut before deciding on where he really wanted to be. Triplett told an entirely different story to students at Marshall when he arrived for his final year of high school. He said he'd left Crane when it was designated as a failing "turnaround school" due to low test scores and declining enrollment. (Crane once had three thousand students, but today has four hundred.) Also, he said another basketball coach was leaving. He could have remained but the students felt that this was a sinking ship.

Marshall coaches insist that the Farragut coach and principal stalled instead of completing the required paperwork in a timely manner, and that was why Triplett became snared ineligible. His solid grades at Crane added to Marshall's frustration, however much of the confusion at Marshall probably derived from Triplett's own simplistic spin.

Dorothy Gaters, acting as Marshall's athletics director, phoned Wolf Nelson at Farragut in the fall of 2013 to ask about Triplett's status after it became obvious he was not eligible.

Nelson stuck to his story. "I don't know what his situation is at Marshall," Nelson told her. "And I'm not mad at Tim for leaving. But what do you want me to do? If I change my story now, it'll look like I'm lying."

"We're trying to save a kid." Gaters said, according to Nelson.

"We're doing the same thing here at Farragut," Nelson said. "I know nothing about Marshall's program, so that's up to you."

The Marshall coaches—Dorothy Gaters, Henry Cotton, and Shawn Harrington—still blame Farragut for the delay. The Tyjuan Keith situation exacerbated this frustration. Keith was a six foot nine sophomore who announced he wanted to leave Marshall for Farragut. Marshall instantly certified him eligible and the coaches couldn't understand why Wolf Nelson would not do the same for Triplett. Nelson insists he did the right thing. "I've never stopped a kid from playing in twenty-five years, and I've never tried to keep a kid from being eligible. I liked Tim, but I wasn't about to go back and change a form I'd already signed." He believed altering his story after the fact would make him a liar and vulnerable to repercussions in the Public League, which has been rocked by grade scandals in recent years.

16

Kashanna Haggard enjoyed her freshman year at Hinsdale South High School in suburban Darien, Illinois. She felt accepted by other students and challenged academically. "I didn't get treated any different," she says. The school had a 20 percent African American student body, and average composite ACT scores for seniors was a respectable 22, slightly above the national average. In the summer before her sophomore year, Kashanna's parents told her they'd be moving to Chicago's West Side to help care for her ailing grandmother. Kashanna, her twin sister, and her older sister took the bus east to Marshall.

Kashanna was taken aback her first week. "We were just sitting around," she says. "There wasn't much real teaching going on in class." That didn't change over the next three years, she says, and she came to regret both the move to Chicago and the family's choice of Marshall. Test scores, if you believe in them, might justify her complaint. Marshall seniors average a composite ACT score of 14.6. Kashanna never bought in to the concept of a "Marshall family" like everyone else. "I was just there to graduate," she says.

Not all of her credits from classes at Hinsdale South counted toward graduation in the Chicago Public Schools. In order to complete school on time she needed a night class, which meant she only attended one boys' or girls' basketball game at Marshall.

One teacher says that Kashanna mostly kept to herself. "She was respectful," the teacher says, "and worked hard on her classes to graduate on time. She was quiet although she'd talk to me, but never about her relationship once she got a boyfriend."

The boyfriend turned out to be Tim Triplett. At night school, Kashanna sometimes crossed paths with him when he was leaving basketball practice. "I hadn't paid attention to him," she says. "I didn't even realize he was in two of my classes and I didn't like him at first."

Triplett began making inquiries and Kashanna broke down, texted him, and they started to hang out. He confessed to checking her out on the westbound CTA bus they often boarded after school. It turned out that Triplett now lived on the 4400 block of West Adams, west of Holy City and just three blocks from her home. Kashanna's mother was impressed by Triplett and that helped. "Because he played basketball," Kashanna says, "she knew he wouldn't be on the street."

Once Triplett brought over a tiny toy basket and ball for Kashanna's five-year-old brother. He got on his knees to play with the boy, laughing and teasing. Soon Triplett was anxious to get out of the apartment but Kashanna didn't want to hang out at his place because he had three younger siblings making noise. There seemed to be nowhere for the couple to go.

Despite their differences on the surface—she reticent, he animated—soon they were a couple. She recalls some of their first times together relaxing on Triplett's porch, where Jutuan made money on the side selling Sno-Balls, cones of crushed ice flavored with assorted syrups. Her favorite was green apple. Triplett liked blue raspberry.

The adults at Marshall recognized the archetype: the studious good girl with the charismatic wild boy. Even after learning that he had fathered three other kids with three separate girls—the first baby was born during his freshman year of high school—she found him difficult to resist.

Triplett felt he could trust Kashanna, although he gave her the same simplified, watered-down version of why he'd left his previous school after just two months. "Tim told me he got into a fight," she says, "and he had to leave Farragut." He talked about Crane's "turnaround" status, the constant coaching changes.

Kashanna began to feel a not-so-subtle pressure from dating the boisterous basketball star. "Everybody was always in our business," she says, which meant unsolicited advice to stay away from Triplett. Even Shawn Harrington, perhaps hypersensitive because he had a daughter nearly Kashanna's age, teased her. "Why are you with Tim?" Shawn joked when they passed in the hallways.

"I guess he knew I could do better," Kashanna says, "but nobody could tell me anything bad about Tim."

When she mentioned to her boyfriend the brief interactions with the assistant coach, Triplett said, "That's my favorite! Coach Shaky."

A month after they began dating, Triplett told Kashanna how gun violence had plagued his family, although he never told her the entire truth about Crane. She was wise enough to understand that a West Side kid with a murdered father and a gun-waving brother shot down by police had the odds stacked against him. Before Triplett had enrolled at his third high school, his dependable anchor, basketball at Crane, had been taken away from him.

Marshall's feeling of family that nearly every alum points to was already a comfort to Triplett even if Kashanna never really bought in. Succeeding as a Commando was something he *had* to do. "That's why basketball is so important to me," Triplett told her. "I gotta get out."

In Triplett's computer science class that fall, Shawn monitored a few of his own special ed kids who were in the same room. That included James King, the undersized center who was the only basketball player designated as special ed. This was where Shawn witnessed the only inkling of Triplett acting out. Triplett flirted shamelessly with the girls even after the bell had rung, until the teacher declared, "Tim, you stop bothering those young ladies and sit down!" Triplett would sheepishly return to his seat amid the laughter.

Although waiting to be declared eligible frustrated him, Triplett thrived within the rigid structure, the checks and balances in place at Marshall, which was not true for every player. "Tim loved the discipline in our program," Dorothy Gaters says, "and I remember him coming to me in the fall and saying *I wish I had gone to Marshall all four years.*"

Rather than hang around the West Side Triplett and Kashanna took the Green Line train downtown to walk the lakefront and Millennium

Park or visit the Union Station food court. Downtown Chicago is one of the world's great architectural sites and it offered the teens a very different perspective. It was impossible for them not to dream of wanting more.

Their relationship was unstable at times. Triplett was not the type to sit on the couch and rent a movie from Netflix. He wanted to go out all the time, to move. Kashanna was studious, quiet, determined, and content to stay home. "He played too much," she says. "We broke up a lot because he could be a jerk."

Triplett was arrested for the fourth time on January 2, 2014. It was two weeks before he became eligible to play for Marshall and just before 10:00 PM. With temperatures well below freezing, Triplett was picked up by police on a street corner a few blocks from his home, charged with "soliciting unlawful business" and with possession of between ten and thirty grams of marijuana, an amount probably worth between $100 and $300. Police claimed that Triplett was yelling "Weed!" at passing cars and that he had ten Ziploc bags of it in his possession.

Triplett's fourth charge (like the previous charges of "soliciting" and the "reckless conduct") was the kind the police slapped on young men they believed to be in the drug trade.

In his mug shot Triplett looks sad and lost. He's wearing a T-shirt that reads SCHNUCK's HOLIDAY CLASSIC 2013, the downstate Collinsville tournament where the Marshall boys played without him just a week earlier while he was still waiting to get his eligibility approved.

––––––––––

Tim Triplett was a prolific poster on Facebook. In fact, he had two identities there.

First, he was "Timothy K. Triplett." Posts on this page are about his basketball success at Crane and photos of his family, including his newborn son Keishawn. These posts decline, then stop after his junior year at Crane.

The second and newer Facebook page was under another name: "Danni Mob Tim." The name Danni Mob was adopted by many young men from the Twenty-First Street area, and West Siders have different takes on what it means. Some say it is simply a loose collection of friends that wanted to honor a kid named Danny Collins who was killed after an argument. Some cops who know the area suspect it's a gang name. In many of the Danni Mob photos, young men flash a single hand with one finger held back. The result is two digits, then one. Twenty-First Street. *Twenty-First, there ain't no worse.*

It is not unusual for African American teens in Chicago to use aliases or nicknames on Facebook or Instagram. Like teens everywhere, they can be obnoxious, tasteless, sexist, and threatening, and they often spell atrociously. There are dozens of young men still using the Danni Mob prefix and many of them brag about smoking powerful weed (sometimes called "loud"), of taking "molly" (the designer drug "ecstasy"), and making piles of money, although the heaps of hundred dollar bills fanned out in so many of the photos are possibly fake. On Triplett's Danni Mob Tim Facebook page, he listed his employer as True Religion Jeans, a brand he preferred that cost as much as $300 a pair. Most of Triplett's teachers, coaches, friends, and teammates were cautious in talking about him after his murder.

Days after his second arrest, Triplett posted a Danni Mob comment directed at his mother.

"I promise you want [*sic*] cry ever again."

Just after school started at Marshall in the fall of 2013, Tim Triplett posted again:

"I'm from the murder capital CHI RAQ AND SHIT HAPPENS AND SINCE IM THE SHIT IM WHO IT HAPPENS TO"

In October he posted about Tywon—"Blackman"—and the lure of the streets:

"Every night i close my eyes and Hear BlackMan talking like Tim get yo shit together so you could be rich 4ever"

His teachers thought he adjusted remarkably well, but one post on Facebook in November of his senior year reveals how troubled he was:

"life aint the same no more its to many important people missing in it like my brother my father my grandmother cousins and many more i just wanna take the time out and tell you all that i love you"

June 14, a few days before graduation from Marshall, he played a summer league game at Garfield Park, which is adorned with a gold cupola. Triplett posted on Facebook:

"Ok today is the day i can actually go perform for these college coaches at the golden dome I'm to thirsty fr [for real] I'm just try a get my ppl out this shit Lms [like my status] to wish me luck"

In the late summer of 2014, after he graduated from Marshall, he seemed aware of the complicated challenges and choices ahead:

"I'm tryna better myself as a man first that's all I have a lot of growing up to do"

———————

Triplett began taking junior college classes in the fall of 2014 and his Facebook posts included the Wright hoops schedule. He implored his friends to come out and support his new junior college team. After he was deemed ineligible, the second time in two years, his posts as Danni Mob Tim became erratic, like a confused baller who couldn't decide at which basket to shoot. In late October he posted a brief video in which he flashes a huge wad of money while mugging in front of a luxury car. In another post, he poses with stacks of money. In November, these sorts of posts continued:

> Chicago so full of fucking hate I can't wait to move from
> I'm tryna have a threesome with money and success
> Chicago fucked up

In later posts, he mentions neck tattoos, court dates, junior college enrollment, his wish to marry before the age of thirty, his desire to "make status," and his prayers to get off house arrest. He is concerned with who is "fake" and who is "real." About his oldest child, now a toddler:

"I just want to see my little man go to school be man and sign up for college boy dont be a fool be a man"

Triplett was arrested for the fifth time on January 22, 2015, three days after former Marshall player Shawn Holloway was killed.

This arrest happened just before midnight on a street near his former West Side home. Temperatures outside were below freezing and eleven inches of snow had already fallen that month. On this occasion, he was popped for "reckless conduct" and "possession of a controlled substance." The case was eventually dropped but a troubling pattern had emerged. Each of the five times Triplett had been arrested, he was not actively playing. His first three arrests happened in the summer after his brother was killed, when he'd left Farragut but still hadn't decided on Marshall, the summer when he had not played a single game with a high school team. His fourth arrest had been during the frustrating wait for his eligibility approval, two weeks before he put on a Marshall uniform for the first time. His fifth arrest took place when he had no games at Wright on his schedule. Triplett's gambling charge remained his only conviction and his court supervision sentence for "reckless conduct" still needed to be completed.

Feeling overwhelmed and depressed about the death of Tywon, Jutuan Brown lost control and hope. "I've come to know I can't do anything about it," she says. She also says the West Side was getting more menacing. "As kids, we used to fight it out if there was problem, but it's gotten extremely violent," she says. "They're straight killing people."

One longtime Chicago police officer says of Triplett, "If he was out at ten at night in that weather, he more than likely was selling drugs, either for himself or someone else. And he's trying to get money, money he's not getting at home."

———————

Tim Triplett's postings on Facebook grew more disturbing in the winter of 2015. One selfie is of him wearing a glitzy gold chain.

"Couple of hundred for the Chain Bitch. You know how I'm commin."

In another, he poses again with what appears to be a stack of hundred dollar bills.

Another post reads:

"Waiting for these house arrest ppl to come get their shit and get tf [the fuck] on. Still screaming fuck the cop [emoticons of guns being fired and police]. BLACK MAN WORLD IN A YOUNG AND FLASHY ASS NIGGA."

The posts of a conflicted teenager continued that spring:

"I'm Just Getting Money I Aint Have No Father"

"I Put On The Gang I Ain't Never Going Broke I Remember Dats I You Too [used to] Hustle By That Store I Remember Them Days when I Ain't Have Shit We'll Look At Me Now Young Nigga Living Rich"

The fifty-point outburst he had against Marshall was practically the stuff of legend among friends of Triplett, and he wrote about that game often:

"I miss high school basketball fr [for real] I remember when my moma my uncle my cuzing n everybody was at that crane vs marshall game my jr year at crane man I fuck them ppl up joe fr tho my oh was smiling so hard everytime I looked at her. she just wanna see her twin make it nbs [no bullshit]. ma I promise we ain't gone hurt for long I'm getting us out this shit hold"

Sometimes Triplett grasped the importance of basketball in his life:

> When I hoop I relieve so much stress fr tho.
> When I Do Positive Shit Such Ass School And Hooping My Life Be A Movie But When I Do Negative Shit Such Ass Ona Block And Going Out My Life Don't Be Shit But Chicago Full Of Fucking Hate I Can't Wait To Move From So God Telling Me To Keep Hooping Basically Ion [I don't] Know Why I Wanna Stop Tho

Even when feeling conflicted about his lifestyle, Triplett often mentioned Kashanna, who was doing well studying nursing at Malcolm X College after graduating from Marshall:

"Kashanna Haggard Like to argue just so i can make it up too her and tell her i love her a million times and how ion wanna loose her i finally figure her out"

Triplett's April 22, 2014, Facebook post included a photo with Kashanna and this tag:

"She Always Make Happy At The End Of The Day."

Hours before Triplett was shot, Kashanna Haggard says they argued on Facebook until he tired of the exchange and phoned her. She was supposed to go to her part-time job later at Auntie Annie's Pretzels at the airport, an unpretentious gig that required her to take the Blue Line train to O'Hare in her uniform. "He told me to come over there," she says, "to hang out until I had to go to work."

"Over there" was on the 3500 block of West Flournoy, which runs parallel to, and sits just a block south of, the Eisenhower Expressway, the 290. "I didn't like it over there," Kashanna says. "That whole block is dangerous. Too many guys outside standing around."

Triplett's final Facebook post as Danni Mob Tim was on April 25, 2015. His mother Jutuan Brown, in Milwaukee at the time, must have sensed her oldest was in trouble. She wrote:

"You need to be home with yo momma, I'm not forcing but I'm damn sure waiting."

Jutuan Brown says after her younger son Tywon was killed in 2013, she never heard from Chicago police. But why would she? There was little reason to question her after so many eyewitnesses confirmed the police's portrayal of Tywon opening fire on the crowd from his bicycle. The police have no support system in place to counsel the involved families after an event like this.

Jutuan has never heard a word from police concerning the murder of Tim Triplett, either—*Who might have wanted Tim dead? Did he have enemies? Did you speak to him the day he was shot? Can we look through his personal stuff?* Unlike with Tywon, in Triplett's case an investigation into the murder might have helped find the shooter.

Jutuan returned from Milwaukee to the Chicago area, this time to Maywood, a blue-collar suburb west of the city. She took an afternoon shift job in nearby Broadview at Principal Manufacturing, a company specializing in auto parts. She makes $8.40 an hour, fifteen cents more than minimum wage in Illinois. Jutuan had other motivations to return to the Chicago area. She says she wants to find out who killed her son, to push for justice and honor his memory. But a working woman with young kids at home has no way to even begin this quest. She also wants to keep up with Triplett's three children, two girls and a boy.

Facebook was flooded with tributes to Tim Triplett on his Danni Mob Tim page, and these continue to this day.

Chicago has countless offshoots of loosely organized young men like Danni Mob, the writer Alex Kotlowitz says. "All of Chicago's African American gangs are fractured and organized block-by-block, cliques really. There are hundreds of them in the city now, most with crazy names. And each of the cliques usually consider themselves part of a larger gang—Vice Lords, El Rukns, Disciples—but the old hierarchy is gone."

Some Chicago gang experts and West Side residents identify Danni Mob as a small faction of the Conservative Vice Lords, one of the dozens of Vice Lords spinoffs that include Traveling Vice Lords, Undertaker Vice Lords, Unknown Vice Lords, Renegade Vice Lords, and Dirty Unknown Vice Lords. All bets are off concerning who is loyal to whom, and that's part of the confusion perhaps contributing to the continuing violence.

One friend of Triplett's who will graduate from college soon says Danni Mob makes him skittish and the organization has become pervasive on the West Side. "I saw them come to the Crane games when Tim played," he says, "and you could see them walking in together, sometimes in Danni Mob hoodies. It used to give me chills. I see myself in those guys, I guess."

Triplett was also a member of a group called Young, Flashy, and Fly, mentioned constantly by his friends and teammates, although nobody volunteered names or phone numbers. Internet searches show a clothing line with the same name, and rapper Jermaine Dupri used it as a title on his CDs.

One basketball friend of Triplett says, "Young, Flashy, and Fly isn't a gang at all. It's a social group and a lot of them are cousins." The founder of the group, the friend says, owns a late model Mercedes. In one Facebook photo, Tim is sitting on that car as he gazes up at the Chicago skyline. The young men get together a few times a year in their matching "YFF" gear to socialize. They give out toys and turkeys over the holidays. (Triplett once boasted on Facebook—"Thanksgiving, YFF 'We just fed the homeless!'")

———————

When a young man in Chicago gets killed, the victim is often blamed by police, referred to as a "known gang member." Journalists report this and sometimes even parents, teachers, and friends echo the narrative. I have caught myself doing it. Perhaps it's the only way to reconcile or make sense of the escalating shootings even when a seemingly unrelated hurdle—such as Shawn's stolen car—results in tragedy.

In Triplett's case, one Marshall employee told me what several players repeated (off the record) in the ensuing months: "What made Triplett a damn good player was what got him killed. He was clever, maybe too clever for his own good. There were times when he'd charm the teacher, and he had a bit of a con man in him. That played well on the streets."

Other theories arose. Wright coach Mike Harris says the mentality of some young urban black men isn't so very different from what he was taught in the armed services. "They protect the boundaries," he says, "and people who aren't in the street in places like Chicago can't fathom that. It's like a hill in the military. *We need that hill* somebody in a position of power thinks, and that's what happens."

One man who knew Triplett has this take: "Three people were selling weed out on the different corners," he said, "and they were all working together for the same guy, and Tim Triplett was one of them. But somebody robbed two of the dealers and Tim was the only one who *didn't* get robbed. It got back to the dealer that Tim got off." He claims that Triplett's reprieve raised suspicion. Nobody else has supported that claim.

Brutal taunting on social media continued in the twenty-four hours after Triplett's death. Jutuan, Shawn, and teammate Tyrese Williford saw the posts that said, "Tim is not smiling now!" as well as images of Triplett with bullet holes in his chest, although they weren't up for long. The bragging on social media might be why another friend of

Triplett's says, "Everybody knows who killed Tim. There's already been a payback"—meaning another young man killed in retaliation. Another friend says, "It had to be somebody he knew that killed him. Close range? Lunchtime? And they were mocking him on Facebook. It had a picture of his body and it said, *How you like that hot lead, Tim?*"

One Marshall insider had a cryptic take on Triplett. "We knew some things about him," he says. However, Jutuan insists, "Tim Triplett was not a gangbanger. He had too many girlfriends."

"The millennial generation wants everything now," one coach says. "Too many young men today want to be millionaires by the time they are twenty-five. Even if it means taking a short cut—not just selling, but robbing the guy who is out there working hard on the street." A select few coaches and friends are more sympathetic, pointing out Triplett's despair over his brother's death and his poverty, the allure of fast money. It's common for young ballers to have developed relationships with other young men they can't cut off. Today, with the proliferation of handguns in Chicago, the connection has deepened. One Chicago cop at the Eleventh District station told me, "Triplett? His name has come up a couple of times in shootings. He's way more affiliated than you know."

In 2016, Marshall teammate Tyrese Williford went on to do what Triplett could have done. He became a star player at a junior college a long way from the West Side. He was surprised to learn that Triplett and his brother, Tywon, are buried side-by-side in unmarked graves in the Forest Home cemetery in Des Plaines, northwest of the city limits. "I would get him a statue if I could," Williford says.

Wright junior college coach Mike Harris only had to consider what the Marshall coaches, who'd never had trouble with Triplett, had to say about his college potential. Triplett, it seemed, kept his street life a secret because he was still the new guy, not as well known to their coaches.

One friend of Triplett's who played at a rival school has his doubts: "The coaches had to have some idea," he says. "I don't think the coaches *couldn't* know."

Officer Erick Von Kondrat, who drove Naja to the hospital and had coached football at Westinghouse, thinks the coaches' lack of awareness is entirely possible. "If a kid is handling his school business," he says, "it's likely that the coach might not hear anything. What you do outside of school might not come into play with the coach."

Had Shawn not been shot, he probably would have brokered an out-of-town basketball scholarship offer for Triplett, who was a far better player than his senior stats indicated. Shawn understood that Triplett was never really able to show what he could do at Marshall in his fragmented season. Police officer Sherod Dent had found himself in a similar situation as a Marshall senior in the 1990s. Dent suffered a season-ending injury in the fall and missed much of his final year. Coach Luther Bedford was still able to find Dent a California junior college that was willing to bite, which soon led to a Division I scholarship.

Shawn and Triplett had grown up under similar circumstances on the West Side. Battling poverty, moving from apartment to apartment, and losing a family member to gun violence. Triplett had fewer options, a narrower margin for error, and he made some unwise decisions. Of course, Shawn made what society would say were the "right choices" at every turn, and he too got shot.

———————

Triplett's case went cold quickly. Girlfriend Kashanna Haggard has never been contacted by the Chicago Police Department about the murder. Not that she'd have many clues. "It's like Tim's whole case just went away," she says wistfully. "Just like Tim."

Kashanna says her relationship with Triplett was volatile. "We were dating when he died," she says, "but it didn't seem like it." Like so many of his friends and teammates, she also learned about his death on social media, saw the graphic photos of her slain boyfriend on an anonymous and short-lived Facebook page. The photos got shared dozens of times. She uses the *wrong place at the wrong time* cliché to explain Triplett's death. "I believe it was meant for somebody else," she says, adding, "It was the people he was hanging around with." She had trouble concentrating after the killing but she had the wherewithal to know she was vulnerable. Instead of risking failing her courses at Malcolm X Junior

College, she withdrew from classes, something Triplett didn't have the option to do when his brother got killed.

Triplett's relationship with Kashanna might be viewed as his third life, one separate from both basketball and the streets. Their bond was private, except for an occasional Facebook photo of them snuggling. She has tried to move on by completing her nursing certification at Malcolm X College. Because she wasn't close with any of his friends, she doesn't really have anyone with whom to discuss the meaning of his life or death. "I talk to my twin sister some," she says, "but I really don't like thinking about it or talking about it. It's frustrating and pointless," she says before pausing. "It's pointless that he died for no reason."

18

NOLAN RICHARDSON, the Hall of Fame coach who'd lost a teenage daughter to leukemia, was taken by Shawn's heroism in saving Naja. Richardson passed the story on to the retired LSU coach, Dale Brown. In the basketball world of Goliaths, Brown is pure David. Brown began calling regularly, and Shawn was delighted to hear from Shaquille O'Neal's college coach.

Brown is a complicated man, as is reflected in his weekly mass e-mails. He will pull on your coat about something corny one week and rant about soft politicians or weakness toward radical Islam the next. Suspicious and distrustful of the Internet, he declined to donate money to Shawn via the web fundraiser. Instead, he mailed a generous check, then convinced a couple of old coaching pals to do the same. One donor was Stan Morrison, who'd been the San Jose State coach the night Shawn blew out his knee.

The concern shown by many of Shawn's friends immediately after his shooting had begun to fade. People had to go on with their own lives. On days when Shawn wasn't doing rehab, he often sat alone at his aunt Jaci's apartment with his mobile phone and the television's remote control. Despite Dale Brown's show of enthusiasm, Shawn assumed the old coach's interest would also diminish.

Shawn was dealing with a bleak financial situation. As an educational support personnel worker, he was a member of the Service Employees International Union (SEIU Local 73). When he was working, his $550 a week earnings stopped during the summers. His health insurance payments to Blue Cross/Blue Shield were reasonable, a bit less than $100 a month.

Two weeks in the emergency room and intensive care at Stroger had mostly been covered by his insurance. Blue Cross also paid for a high-grade wheelchair, his first long stints at the Rehabilitation Institute of Chicago, and later they covered his Easy Stand, a sort of standing desk that had a mechanism to lift him into a vertical position. Standing, he can watch television or talk on the phone, and being upright improves his circulation and digestion. A family member who handled the money from the benefit game and other fundraisers wound up writing checks for the $15,000 in expenses that Blue Cross declined to cover. Medicaid picked up some of the remaining costs. For the first thirty days after he was shot, Shawn received 80 percent of his pay, about $440 a week. From days thirty to sixty, while he was still staying at the Rehab Institute, he was paid 60 percent of his salary, or $330 a week. Finally, after sixty days, he was down to 50 percent of his pay. By May of 2014, just ninety days after the shooting, Shawn's paychecks had stopped entirely. His only source of income was gone and soon, because he was not working, his health insurance was cut.

Illinois's Victims of Violent Crimes program has a limit of $25,000 compensation for any one person, supposedly based on circumstances and needs. Shawn got 20 percent of that to go toward medical costs, although nobody ever explained why he would not qualify for the maximum. (Naja was awarded $250.)

Eventually Shawn applied for Social Security, which started up a year after the shooting. They pay him $300 a month.

Shawn could not get a physician's approval to return to his job without more rehabilitation that he could not afford. A doctor recommended him for Family Medical Leave Act (FMLA) coverage so that the Chicago Public Schools would be required by law to hold his job until he was fit to return. Unfortunately Marshall has no elevator and is not wheelchair accessible other than a single ramp to the building's first floor. Unless the CPS redefined his job, it was not possible for Shawn to return. Any job option sounded better than sitting in his aunt's apartment all day, but if he was to return to his old position in special ed, he'd need an elevator to be able to accompany his students from class to class. This elevator would be prohibitively expensive. The only other viable options for Shawn to stay at Marshall might be sitting at the first floor entrance metal detector, or pushing papers in the office. That was unappealing, although nobody at Marshall had made a firm offer of any new position at all.

I was warned by teachers with decades of experience that if we pushed too hard, demanded that Marshall accommodate Shawn with ramps and elevators, he would simply be reassigned to a school that was accessible, something that Shawn resisted due to his unwavering devotion to Marshall and his trepidation at taking on a new challenge. "He doesn't work for Marshall," one teacher told me. "He works for the Chicago Public Schools."

I began to push in a different direction.

An old El Paso friend named Steve Yellen proposed an online fundraiser for Shawn via RocketHub.com, but first we'd need a short film to promote Shawn's story. Yellen recycled a Chicago Comcast news program on Shawn with a voiceover by David Kaplan. Kaplan, now a major television personality in the city, was the same guy who had been my competitor in the scouting service business in the 1990s. The RocketHub fundraiser netted $15,000.

Yellen, a successful broker and delusional optimist, got serious, intending this time to raise enough money to buy Shawn a ReWalk. Yellen wanted to do another fundraiser, but he needed help. He called Greg Fleming, the CEO of Yellen's firm, to ask for advice. Fleming found the story so moving that he flew out from New York to meet Shawn. Fleming decided to spearhead the fundraiser himself in July 2015. The extravagant event took place at a swanky Michigan Avenue location. Lavish hors d'oeuvres and an open bar were available to the hundreds of friends of the investment firm. Massive tables full of sports memorabilia were auctioned off. A number of celebrities came, including some retired Chicago Bears, as well as basketball legend George Gervin. Former Tennessee congressman Harold Ford showed up, as did former Illinois governor Pat Quinn, who'd lost a close election nine months earlier.

When Rahm Emmanuel got off the elevator, his aide beelined to Shawn to ask if he'd like to meet Chicago's mayor. As cameras clicked, the mayor got so close to Shawn that their foreheads nearly touched.

Photo op: Shawn meets Mayor Rahm Emmanuel at the Michigan Avenue fundraiser. *Michael James*

"I asked him not to cut grade school athletics," Shawn says. "I told him how important they had been to me growing up. *Please don't take sports away from the kids*, I told him." Shawn had maybe two minutes with the mayor of Chicago and used the opportunity not for self-promotion, but to push for social justice.

Shawn knew that Emmanuel had lost his luster, particularly within Chicago's teaching and coaching fraternity. In 2013 the mayor shut down over fifty schools, citing their low test scores. That meant 10 percent shut their doors, the largest wave of closings in American history. Hit the hardest, of course, were the city's poorest areas and the West Side's African American and Latino children. It is impossible to prove a direct link of closing fifty schools in economically disadvantaged neighborhoods to a spike in gun violence beginning three years later, but common wisdom in the black community is that the rise in teenagers wielding pistols and the deterioration of communities is related to vacant schools.

After the silent auction, the audience was invited into the auditorium. CEO Greg Fleming showed the Comcast news program on Shawn, then interviewed him on stage. Fleming, a statesmanlike humanitarian, seemed disappointed at the end of the evening when it became apparent that he'd fallen short of the $70,000 goal he'd set for himself. Shawn, however, was ecstatic that night.

One of the stockbrokers at the event, George Cook, took a keen interest in Shawn. He invited Shawn to speak at the luncheon of an evangelical convention, where Cook spearheaded another successful fundraiser. Shawn now had nearly enough for the ReWalk, but his situation had evolved. Or devolved.

A few months later, at the conclusion of the ReWalk training, Shawn still had not mastered the technology well enough to get approved to purchase one. The truth was the ReWalk could potentially be a great danger—what if he lost his balance and fell? He began to believe a car, to be able to get out of the apartment regularly, might be more important. Even if he could finish ReWalk training and afford to buy the device, walking upright ten minutes a day was far from his most pressing need. In some ways Shawn was becoming more practical about his disability and how to best adapt, yet openly continued to say he was determined to walk on his own again.

Ever cautious, and with no foreseeable paycheck, Shawn began to stay home instead of rehabbing regularly and dipping into his savings.

Since Blue Cross/Blue Shield cut his insurance, the cost of a day's rehab—nearly $900—had become unrealistic. Shawn could pay out-of-pocket, but each time he did his nest egg dwindled. Three rehab appointments a week meant he'd be out of money in seven months. Even if he made progress after a year of therapy, was declared fit to return to work by doctors, he could not do his job at Marshall—in a wheelchair or a ReWalk.

In the end, the ReWalk experience was deflating. Shawn had dreamed of walking again with state-of-the-art medical technology, then realized he didn't have the training, balance, or ability to make it happen.

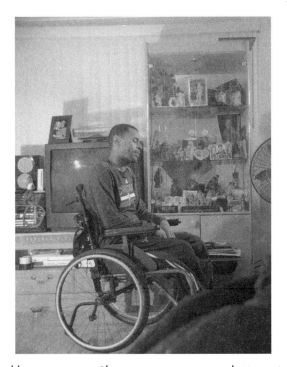

With his health care gone, Shawn spent more and more time alone in his aunt's apartment. *Michael James*

Medicare's more comprehensive coverage would begin in July 2016, more than two years after the tragedy. That covered his hydrocodone painkillers (which Shawn takes sparingly, for fear of addiction), lidocaine patches for his back, gabapentin (an anticonvulsive), suppositories, and stool softeners. His Medicare payments were $170 monthly, more than half of his income.

With his Chicago Public Schools salary cut off, Shawn used the ReWalk money over the next two years to pay down his enormous health care costs and to help his aunt make rent, buy groceries, and everything else that goes with day-to-day living. Although the heavy hitters who had helped him—Greg Fleming, George Cook, Steve Yellen—wouldn't have been upset, it still felt like Shawn had let them down.

Rahm Emmanuel soon did exactly what Shawn pleaded with him not to do—he cut elementary school sports. The mayor came up with a plan that allowed schools to have their own sports teams and coaches again if they could pay for it themselves, an impossible situation for many schools. Things would get worse for the embattled mayor. Emmanuel's handpicked choice to run the cash-strapped school system, Barbara Byrd-Bennett, pleaded guilty in 2015 to taking bribes from her former employers in exchange for awarding them no-bid contracts for over $20 million. Later she was sentenced to four and a half years in prison.

The new Chicago Public Schools boss was a lawyer named Forrest Claypool, a career politician who had run the Chicago Transit Authority, the park district, and was briefly the mayor's chief of staff. He had no background in education, but he was close friends with Rahm Emmanuel.

One of Claypool's first moves was to oust Thomas Trotter, the head of athletics who had struck out trying to help Shawn. Trotter's replacement, Randy Ernst, had been a park district administrator for years. He'd never coached in the Chicago Public Schools and had no experience in education to speak of either. But Ernst and Claypool were political insiders, part of Chicago's political machine, and their jobs paid well over $100,000 a year. These men can be most generously described as curious choices. CPS coaches and teachers grumbled.

I remained optimistic for Shawn in spite of these administrative changes. I'd played ball against Ernst in summer leagues over the years, and we'd both attended North Park College, although not at the same time. I believed I could get through to the new athletics director.

Ernst appointed Tony McCoy to oversee basketball. McCoy didn't have a background in education either, but he had lost his son to gun violence a couple of years earlier.

Dorothy Gaters held high hopes for Randy Ernst because he had a relative who had been Marshall's principal over fifty years ago. She soon grew frustrated with the new athletics director. After their initial meeting, she claims he's been a de facto no-show. "He doesn't participate at the meetings or even introduce himself," she sighs.

My subsequent attempts to reach Ernst were roundly ignored, even after I left notes at his office and tracked down his cell phone number. If administrators at CPS could not be bothered to return a phone call, e-mails, texts, a letter, and handwritten notes, it was hard to imagine Shawn getting out of limbo.

In August 2015, Keenan Mardis went on trial for the murder of Ontario Brown Jr. in Elkhart, Indiana. The only witness to step forward, Lenell Williams, testified that he and Ontario Jr. were approached on Wagner Avenue by a group of five boys, including Mardis. One of Mardis's running buddies had dated the same girl as Ontario Jr. Harsh words were exchanged, then punches. After the fight was broken up—and after Ontario Jr. and his friend walked away—Mardis ran up with a revolver to demand Ontario Jr.'s fancy belt. Ontario Jr. refused. One of Mardis's friends suggested he shoot Ontario Jr.

Mardis fired the gun, and everyone ran except Mardis, who walked away alone.

None of Mardis's group identified him as the gunman or admitted being on the scene that night. During the trial, one of those boys, who named the shooter when questioned by police, now denied knowing Mardis, saying he'd been drunk when he named the shooter.

Mardis did not testify and the defense rested without calling a single witness. Elkhart's legal system moved quickly. The trial lasted just two days, and Mardis was convicted by a jury on August 18, 2015, less than a year after the shooting.

A month later, Keenan Mardis, age sixteen, was sentenced to fifty-eight years in prison for the murder of Ontario Brown Jr.

An overt code of silence and distrust of law enforcement is often cited as a hindrance in investigations of shootings. Another factor on the West Side is fear of retribution. People keep quiet, unwilling to risk exposure as witnesses. Nothing breaks down the social order of a neighborhood like an unsolved killing, especially when many people close to the victim have at least an inkling of who did it. The biggest hindrance in solving shootings may be the shrinking number of murder detectives active on the police force in Chicago. Around the time Tim Triplett was killed, in the spring of 2015, Chicago radio station and NPR affiliate WBEZ reported the number of detectives on police payrolls had dropped by nearly 20 percent since Mayor Rahm Emanuel took office. Chicago had two hundred less detectives in 2015 than in 2010. In addition, the ranks of evidence technicians and forensic investigators have thinned by even larger proportions, with a hundred fewer investigators working than in 2010.

According to the *New York Times*, in 2015, Chicago police made arrests in less than a third of the year's 470 homicides.

Police departments strive to up their "clearance rates," but "cleared" only means *someone* has been arrested for the murder, and that person might not get convicted or have actually committed the crime. Chicago's clearance rate of 52 percent, WBEZ reported, was near its lowest level in decades, and Chicago was performing poorly compared to other major cities. Things would get worse. By 2016, according to the University of Chicago's Crime Lab, the clearance rate was closer to 25 percent. Two years after Tim Triplett's murder, for example, nobody has been charged.

Here are other statistics from the same source: Nearly 80 percent of the homicide victims in 2016 were African American. Although African American men aged fifteen to thirty-four make up just 4 percent of the city's population, they account for more than half of those murders.

The statistics on shootings that do not result in murder are even bleaker. Over the last decade about 90 percent of Chicago shootings that did not result in death went unsolved. And in 2016, the Crime Lab says that 95 percent of the shootings remain unsolved.

Distrust of the police is a hot topic these days, but in 2016, even before the start of a shocking spike in summer violence, Chicagoans phoned the emergency 911 line twenty-eight thousand times to report gunfire. Naturally, some were multiple calls regarding a single shooting and a tiny percentage turned out to be fireworks, but the statistic indicates that locals still want their police force to protect them.

———————

In the summer of 2015, former LSU coach Dale Brown nominated Shawn for national Coach of the Year honors with an organization called the National Consortium for Academics and Sports (NCAS), part of the University of Central Florida's graduate sports administration program. It was a nervy move by Brown, nominating a high school assistant who hadn't coached a game in two years.

To everyone's surprise—everyone except Dale Brown's—Shawn won. That fall, the NCAS flew Shawn to Orlando for their yearly banquet. I pushed Shawn to the stage for his acceptance speech. The award, the first-class resort hotel, the flood of well-wishers, and the interaction with other honorees all offered him a much-needed psychological boost.

Before his trip to Orlando, the wheelchair accessible ramp that Shawn used to get in and out of his aunt's apartment was stolen. That meant that in the weeks leading up to the award ceremony, the national Coach of the Year was trapped in his apartment.

19

IN THE SPRING OF 2016, University of Chicago coach Mike McGrath mentioned to me that Arne Duncan occasionally shot baskets in his gym. I got excited again, hoping that Duncan might be able to help Shawn move the stagnant Chicago Public Schools into action.

Arne Duncan grew up on the South Side and was a terrific player at Harvard. After serving as CEO of the Chicago Public Schools, he was named as Obama's secretary of education. Duncan and Obama played basketball together regularly even after the games in Chicago, which once included Boss Hogg, had moved to Washington, DC. Duncan had also been instrumental in expanding the charter school programs. While I was not a supporter of the charter movement, I knew Arne Duncan was a potential ally, a basketball man who had returned to Chicago near the end of Obama's presidency and gotten deeply involved in solving the gun violence. I believed he might also be able to help Shawn find a meaningful job within the school system.

"Please tell Arne about Shawn," I said to McGrath. I sent him online links to the Coach of the Year award, newspaper accounts of the shooting, and Dave Kaplan's television special. Nearly every media account mentioned that Shawn saved Naja, and I still couldn't watch or read any of it without getting weepy. Neither, I wagered, could Arne Duncan.

Duncan needed to know that Shawn was not asking for money. Shawn needed a new job. While Duncan hadn't been the CEO of the public schools for years, Chicago was built on clout. We invented the word. Few people had more clout than Arne Duncan.

Years before he ever enrolled at Marshall High School, Marcus Patrick moved in with his uncle. For an aspiring ten-year-old ballplayer, that was a stroke of good luck. The uncle, Lamar "Juice" Spring, worked for three decades as a CTA bus mechanic, but his passion has always been basketball. He recognized the obvious: his nephew Marcus needed to be rescued and basketball might help. "His mother was on the street," Juice says.

Juice is well known on the Chicago basketball scene for his tournaments, which take place at a church gymnasium. The gym sits just two blocks from the Marillac House, whose outdoor court was repurposed years ago. The wide-eyed young Marcus would hang out on Juice's court, the same way Shawn Harrington had done at Marillac as a boy. Marcus learned to keep score and help his uncle with the little things needed to keep the tournaments going. Growing up around the best players in the neighborhood, he developed a high "basketball I.Q." Skinny but fast, it seemed possible that Marcus could one day develop into a great point guard. By age fourteen, Marcus stood just five foot five but was recognized as one of the better young players on the West Side. Naturally, everyone hoped Marcus would grow. When he enrolled at Marshall in 2009, Shawn and the other coaches were delighted.

"Shawn Harrington was his mentor," Juice says. "He used to always tell Marcus, *You got it, you got the talent.*"

That notoriety brought a new set of problems. "Marcus got caught in a web," Juice says, "being told by some of his friends that he didn't have some of the material things that they had." Marcus thought that what Juice was giving him at home—discipline, wisdom, and security—was not always enough. "Marcus was too excited to be around guys he called his homeboys," Juice continues. "They'd take the guys shopping and they'd dress nice and hang out in certain public places. Marcus was a loveable dude, but he was socializing with the wrong people."

Occasionally, Juice would challenge his nephew's friends. "Why don't you just let Marcus be an athlete?" he'd ask. "Leave him alone and let him go on to another level. Maybe he can bring you guys along later." Juice recognized the dynamic, had seen it over and over in his gym. "Guys in the neighborhood who had power honored young guys with talent," he says. Gang members would come watch the games, bet money on the outcomes, and it was impossible for him to keep his gym gang-free. "At the big-time games," Juice says, "the older cats are recruiting the best young players to play on their summer teams."

Juice had a cautionary metaphor he would share with local young-sters. "One or two might listen but most of them don't pay attention," he says. He warned them of the dangers of the street life, stressed how they had to assume responsibility for their lives as they got older, and said to stay away from drugs and guns. "If you don't," Juice would always say, "the day will come where you're lying flat on your back on the sidewalk, looking up at the stars."

Marcus never grew much taller, and that kept him from develop-ing into a top high school player. "Marcus was a point guard who couldn't always control his speed," recalls Tyrone Hayes, his freshman coach, "although he was very unselfish. He could get on your nerves but you realized it was to get attention. Pretty soon he'd have every-body laughing."

One semester, poor grades kept Marcus on the sidelines, and a five foot six player has little hope of landing a basketball scholarship anyway. He graduated in 2013, the year before Shawn's shooting, but he stopped playing organized ball when his time at Marshall ended.

"When Shawn got shot, that really hurt Marcus," Juice says.

Marcus began getting in trouble with the police, and his nine arrests were mostly for marijuana, but twice he was arrested for heroin posses-sion and once for "criminal trespass."

In July 2015, Marcus was charged with possessing several bags of marijuana during a traffic stop. The driver, a friend named DeMorrow Stephens, was arrested for driving with a suspended license. Six months after that traffic stop, Stephens was found murdered.

Chicago police had documented both young men as Four Corner Hustlers—one of the gangs police said Deandre Thompson and Cedryck Davis were affiliated with. Juice insists that was untrue. "Marcus wasn't a gang member," he says, "but he liked to be around those guys."

On May 18, 2016, in the late afternoon, Juice was returning home, preparing to celebrate his birthday that night. He saw his nephew astride a moped on a street corner near their home. Juice waved him over and they chatted for a minute. Juice mentioned for the umpteenth time he wanted him to go back to school, enroll in a local junior college. Marcus was twenty-two years old and it was time to get serious about his life. "I'll be back to talk to you in a few," Juice told him.

Minutes later, standing outside his home, Juice heard seven gunshots. He expected to see people running or hear police sirens fast approaching. Nothing. Soon one of Marcus's friends, who everyone called "Nod," came staggering down the sidewalk.

"Nod was holding his side," Juice says, "and he couldn't speak. He was one of Marcus's friends who used to sit on the porch with us."

Nod bent over, gasping for breath, but he had not been shot. He was finally able to gather himself and say, "Remember when you used to warn us that one of these days if you're not careful you'll be looking up at the stars? Well, Marcus is down the street, looking up at the stars."

Marcus Patrick died from gunshots to the chest and wrist. He was killed at 5800 West Augusta, a couple of miles due west on the same street Shawn had been shot on—and three blocks from where he now lived with his aunt.

West Side residents believe that the city has abandoned the poor. School closings were one strong indicator. Another was Mayor Rahm Emmanuel's plans for the city to match funds with DePaul (a private university that costs $40,000 annually to attend) to build a new basketball arena.

A private university as the main tenant and beneficiary of a publicly funded sports venue is virtually unheard of. In this case, taxpayers' money would build a state-of-the-art arena in which to play eighteen games a year. DePaul was averaging a paltry three thousand fans a game for the previous decade, but the new home would seat ten thousand.

The mayor, after claiming to be confronted with unprecedented budget problems, handed out millions of public dollars to private operators for a college basketball showcase. *The Nation*'s Dave Zirin wrote, "These aren't the actions of a mayor. They're the actions of a mad king."

Rick Telander, author of the book *Heaven Is a Playground*, wrote a *Chicago Sun-Times* article and the headline said it all: With Rahm's DePaul Plan, We've Entered a New Arena of Stupidity.

———————

Shawn had been clinging to any tidbit of hope I put in his lap. A job with the Bulls, DePaul, Loyola—any of those would be great. Project Safe Neighborhoods or PeacePlayers International. Cure Violence. After School Matters. Shawn was ready, although we had hardly gotten a nibble other than Gift of Hope, the state's organ donor organization.

As the presidential campaign heated up, I even wrote to John Podesta, Bill Clinton's chief of staff and a close advisor to Hillary Clinton. Maybe the Democrats could help Shawn, find a job for him. They could point to him to dramatize the problems of our health care system and gun violence in Chicago. I never heard back from Podesta (or the Russians) and we hit yet another dead end.

Shawn still found a potential bright spot with each of my attempts, and that became the pattern. I took a long, desperate shot. He predicted it to be a game winner. In the spring of 2016, Shawn answered his phone by saying, "You are truly a miracle worker, Rus!"

Just two days after my longshot attempt to build a bridge to Arne Duncan, Shawn had gotten a call from Chicago Public Schools administrator Tony McCoy. Maybe McCoy heard from Duncan; maybe Duncan spoke to my friend, the University of Chicago coach.

"It's really going to happen," Shawn gushed, "after all this time." CPS set up a day for Shawn to come down for interviews, to fill out applications and get things started.

I hadn't yet talked to anyone with the schools since Trotter had been forced out, but I finally got Tony McCoy on the phone myself. He was impatient and a bit standoffish—understandable, I suppose, when someone he had never met rambled on about gun violence and how Shawn could be a key figure in the antigun movement. McCoy's son's murder was still fresh in his mind. He told me to back off, it was all going to happen. CPS's sports administration office would create a new position for Shawn.

Shawn was ecstatic for weeks. He had been in a rut. He feared draining the last of his savings on rehab but couldn't work without a doctor's approval. If only he had a job offer he'd risk it, pay the exorbitant fee for therapy as a career investment. The promise of a job had to come first, though. A job with a great purpose—something we had both dreamed about—was on the verge of coming through with the public schools.

20

Naja Harrington, haunted by survivor's guilt and night terrors, saw her grades slip. She would still graduate from Westinghouse with honors, just below a 3.5 GPA. Any fair observer would call that a miraculous recovery, yet it was unclear if academia would recognize her extraordinary circumstances.

In the spring of 2016, waiting patiently for a firm offer from New Mexico State, Naja began to consider other universities, just to be safe. She applied to four more: historically black Tennessee State, Marquette, Illinois State, and the University of Missouri. She was mildly skittish about traveling the distance her father did in 1995. Shawn pointed out that she wouldn't be coming home very often no matter where she enrolled. Unless she remained in Chicago as Tim Triplett had done, something Shawn refused to let happen.

Missouri, embroiled in campus controversy over racial issues, came up with a fabulous offer for Naja, a $58,000 academic stipend over four years. Shawn and Kim Jenkins calculated her total expenses to figure the remaining tab: $40,000. Her father, waiting to hear back on his job with the Chicago Public Schools and unsure when he'd get his next paycheck, advised her to sit on Missouri's offer for a while. "Let's see what New Mexico State comes up with," Shawn said.

On the morning Shawn was scheduled to meet with Chicago Public Schools athletics administrators, the friend who offered him a ride phoned at the last minute. His car's engine would not turn over. Shawn had no choice but to call CPS to reschedule. "They said they'd get back to me to set up a meeting for a later date," he says.

Shawn struggled to keep himself from slipping into depression, and the delayed meeting set him back. We had good phone conversations, usually focused on the job search, but he could disappear for a few days, not answer his phone.

In 2004, just after a teenager got killed in the Lawndale neighborhood on the West Side, a former player named Jimmy Sanders decided to do what he could to help. He bought boxes of T-shirts, spray-painted a logo on each, and started his own basketball tournament in a church parking lot. Before the games began he gathered the kids to talk about gangs, violence, and their education. The impact, if any, was impossible to measure, but Sanders kept expanding from this modest beginning. He recognized that his old friend Shawn Harrington might be a powerful speaker.

Jimmy Sanders was an interesting ally. As a senior at Westinghouse in the late 1990s, he was considered the top point guard prospect in the city, although he stood five foot seven. The *Sun-Times* wrote glowingly about his "cohesive wizardry" on the court. Sanders never played competitively after injuring his shoulder in junior college, and he's since been listed as one of the city's "Top Ten Most Disappointing High School Basketball Players." Today he sees his life as a cautionary tale about the ephemeral nature of basketball. While many Chicagoans deliberately ignore the violence around them, Sanders can't stop himself from worrying constantly about West Side kids. One of the city's top referees, he's still lean and quick on his feet. He looks like he could direct a team, although he will sneak outside for a cigarette at halftime, his only bad habit. If he has an errand to run on the West Side, where he still lives, he often yanks on his referee's jersey. A ref can be the target of verbal abuse on the court, but he figures that on the street the striped shirt will designate him as neutral, lower the odds of being accidentally targeted.

Shawn began partnering with Jimmy Sanders in the summer of 2015, putting on a weeklong summer program for kids with a "Stop the Violence" theme. Their first camp was at Orr High School, just a few blocks from where Shawn's shooting occurred. Each December, they host a huge high school tournament at Collins, their message blasted across the free T-shirts. Their camps and tournaments are unique in that participants also got a book about sports and social justice—for example, John Carlos's biography, or *Long Shot*, by former Bulls player/ activist Craig Hodges. Sanders paid for the shirts, made stencils, and spent hours spray-painting their message.

After being promised they would reschedule his meeting, Shawn would wait a year before speaking to anyone with the Chicago Public Schools again.

I had presented the idea to Shawn about repurposing his life, a new career. As a college recruiter, I got turned away constantly and often had to find a new angle, a different approach, although if a door got slammed in my face a few times I simply moved on. Shawn wanted to return home to Marshall, just as he had after the deaths of his mother and Luther Bedford, at least in his former role as assistant coach. He liked my idea of talking to at-risk kids, going from school to school, but I sensed less enthusiasm for any of my dozen longshots with nonprofits, colleges, or government entities. Ideally, he still wanted to help coach the Commandos after school no matter what his job.

With nobody returning our calls, this job was still hypothetical. I had been wasting my time with Trotter, Randy Ernst, and their staffs. Without a clear path to Arne Duncan, who everyone believed was President Obama's best pal, I continued to bang on the same doors. In the summer of 2016, I went alone to the CPS athletics administration offices, located in a building shared with an elementary school, just a few blocks from where Shawn Holloway was murdered. Their entrance in back was locked, but in the front of the building I talked my way past the principal. Both Ernst and Tony McCoy were out again, so I left them handwritten notes.

In November 2016, I stopped in yet again, this time at their new offices, in the repurposed Dodge Elementary School, seven blocks from where Martin Satterfield was shot and paralyzed. I left two more notes. Nothing.

I could understand why the Bulls, DePaul, or various social work organizations wouldn't feel obligated to hire Shawn. After all, thousands of people were being shot each year. But why wouldn't his employer accommodate a worker with a glowing reputation for his work at Marshall? They could not find the time to meet with Shawn. Every day teenagers were getting killed in Chicago, and often close to CPS administrative offices. I wondered what school the victim had attended. Was I naïve to think things might have been different if someone like Shawn could have impacted those kids, the victims or the shooters, the way he did with the autistic artist, Anthony Hunter?

I was talking to parents, coaches, and ballplayers on the West Side, just as when I was a college coach, but this time the topic was a murdered son, friend, or teammate. Each time I sought advice on Shawn's situation, Arne Duncan's name kept turning up. One friend told me that Duncan wept openly when he talked about teenagers getting killed. Yes, yes, I said, but how to get through to the person who had the most influence? I was thinking like a recruiter again, but I began to get discouraged.

Dale Brown, the retired LSU coach, became obsessed with Shawn Harrington. Brown phoned Shawn every week and sent us his weekly e-mail missives, inspiring stories of human endurance, or how our nation had lost its way.

In January 2016, Brown somehow arranged for Shawn to speak at the NCAA's coaching clinic at the Final Four in Houston. Shawn was stunned when seven-foot basketball legend Shaquille O'Neal joined Brown. The retired coach talked about gun violence and leadership to a gym full of basketball coaches and fans. Then Shaq and Dale, as a duo, presented Shawn with a check for $40,000 to buy a wheelchair accessible van.

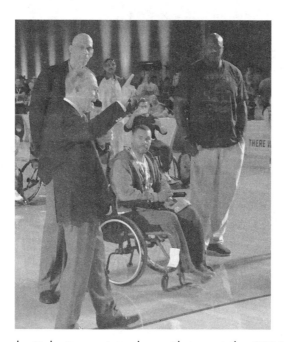

Underdog coach: Dale Brown introduces Shawn at the 2016 Final Four coaching clinic. Shaquille O'Neal, hands in his pockets, stands tall at Shawn's left. *Courtesy of Shawn Harrington*

When he returned from the Final Four, Shawn had plenty of stories about the basketball legends he met. Shaquille O'Neill was a wonderful guy, he said. Shawn had also chatted with Kareem Abdul-Jabbar, Hakeem Olajuwon, Bill Walton, Clyde Drexler, and Rick Barry. Since this was the fiftieth anniversary of the historic championship win by Texas Western (later renamed UTEP), Shawn was able to meet two of their stars, David "Big Daddy D" Lattin and Nevil Shed.

Shawn, I came to understand, was also living a double life—but one very different than Tim Triplett's. He was publicly celebrated as national Coach of the Year. He hosted his Stop the Violence tournaments and summer camps, fielded calls from celebrity coaches and NBA players, had received the mind-boggling gift from Shaq and Dale Brown. Garfield Park, where Shawn had played as a kid, created an annual youth tournament in his honor. When he showed up at any basketball game, he was surrounded by well-wishers. A feature by columnist Joe Nocera in the *New York Times* called "A Hoop Dream Sequel Written by Gun Violence" stirred up national interest in Shawn's story. A query from HBO followed, and Shawn spent a day filming Bryant Gumbel's monthly *Real Sports* program. Shawn hobnobbed with Chicago celebrities like former governor Pat Quinn, and community leaders Fathers Michael Pflegler and George Clements. It appeared Shawn had rebounded from his shooting, but behind that façade was a very different picture.

He had not been approved to work again and he had no job offer. His bank account was dwindling. Paying for Naja's college education was a worry. It would be quite a gamble to spend nearly $900 on each of his rehab sessions, not knowing when a paycheck might come. The $300 monthly social security check barely helped. He reluctantly applied for a SNAP card—food stamps. In his aunt Jaci's apartment Shawn sat, day after day, clicking the remote on a television with spotty reception.

Once, when I happened to be back in Chicago to see him, he was two hours late to a ReWalk training appointment at the RIC, where we'd agreed to meet. He was sullen when he arrived and eventually he told me why. While waiting for the taxi, a broom fell across Shawn's kitchen floor, preventing him from wheeling around in the small apartment. He bent sideways, intending to stand the broom up behind the refrigerator. He lost his balance, however, tipped out of the chair, and fell hard. The tumble knocked the wind out of him. Where the hell was his phone? He'd left it charging. He soon realized that even if he could get to it to call his aunt he'd be on the floor for at least an hour waiting for her to bail him out. He decided to scratch and scramble, claw his way back into the chair.

After he righted the wheelchair, which took twenty minutes, he heard his phone ringing in his bedroom. He still had to figure out a way to climb into the chair. The taxi, he realized, was already waiting outside. A few minutes later, his face pressed against the seat of the wheelchair, he heard a car horn sound repeatedly. He slipped, tumbled back down, banged his ribs on the kitchen floor, and knocked the air out of his lungs for the second time. Sweat was pouring off him now. He started at it again. Ninety minutes later he was back in the chair. He found the phone, rang the taxi.

Rehab that day was a dismal affair. Angry, hurt, and pessimistic for the first time since I had reconnected with him, Shawn sulked his way through the exercises, occasionally pausing to shut his eyes and gather himself.

———

Any chance to leave the apartment in his new van, what he called "the Shaq-mobile," could lift Shawn's mood now. A family reunion picnic, a burrito run, a summer league game, any chance to get out in his new wheels was appreciated. There would be no mistaken identity shootings this time because the van was the color of a new basketball.

Joe Nocera invited Shawn to speak at Columbia University's symposium for journalists on gun violence. Leo Catholic High School brought Shawn in as their featured commencement speaker. But he needed the day-to-day tasks and challenges of a job. As he struggled to keep depression at bay, the pressure of the delayed trial for his shooters, coupled with the apathy of the Chicago Public Schools, felt like a weight that might pull him beneath the surface.

He was remarkably loyal. You could see that in his devotion to his daughters, his generosity with their mother, and in his dedication to his longtime girlfriend. The starkest example was his unwavering loyalty to Marshall, his pride in having played for Luther Bedford.

It seemed clear to an outsider like me that Marshall didn't love him back, but I came to understand that if it were up to Dorothy Gaters and the staff, Shawn's job would have already been redefined. Few schools have had the turnover Marshall has had in administration. "We have a revolving door of principals at Marshall," Gaters says, estimating that she has worked for over fifteen principals, and four in the last seven years. The constant shuffle meant that Gaters's influence wavered. Shawn was beloved by the school workforce, particularly by the women who'd dedicated years of their own lives to the kids, had seen the impact Shawn had on students like Anthony Hunter. But that meant nothing to the downtown administration.

The job situation ate at Shawn. It ate at me, too.

I worried about Naja Harrington's college situation as well. If I could not help Shawn, maybe I could help her. Although other colleges made substantial bids of academic scholarships, New Mexico State couldn't get it together.

Our original contact in admissions, who had met Shawn in person when he visited, stopped returning e-mails. I kept nudging NMSU administrators, including provost Dan Howard, whose promise at Lou Henson's home after the fundraiser had led Shawn to expect an attractive offer. Eventually I got an e-mail from Dan Howard in early February 2016. Naja had fewer than five months left until her high school graduation. Our contact in admissions had taken another job, but the provost said he would look into Naja's situation himself.

The desperate waiting game—long a factor for Shawn's court case, health care, union support, and CPS job—had now carried over into his daughter's future. Two months later, Marvin Menzies, who had been on board with helping Naja get a scholarship, took a job at UNLV. Although new coach Paul Weir had become friends with Shawn, he couldn't make it happen so soon after his promotion.

Finally, on June 7—nine weeks before classes were to commence—admissions worker Brandon Fields wrote that Naja did not qualify for any nonfederal based scholarships or tuition waivers. I forwarded Fields's note to provost Dan Howard with the following e-mail:

From: rus bradburd
Date: Wednesday, June 8, 2016
To: Dan Howard
Subject: RE: Dan, on Shawn Harrington

Dan, let me know your thoughts on Brandon's note... Shawn and I were left with a very different impression when he was on campus 15 months ago.

...I'll see Shawn on Monday....thanks...

Rus Bradburd

Howard's response surprised me because it contradicted what we had heard earlier.

From: Dan Howard
To: Rus Bradburd
Subject: Re: Dan, on Shawn Harrington
Date: Wed, 8 Jun 2016

Hi Rus,

I have to believe that Brandon is providing us with an accurate picture of the situation. As you must know, it would be inappropriate for me to use my influence in this, or any other, admission or financial aid decision. All students must compete on a level playing field for admission and for our financial aid resources, regardless of the position of their parents, and even when their background stories evoke our strongest sympathies and passions. I truly would love to see Naja come to NMSU. Hopefully, she will qualify for enough federal support that attending NMSU would not be a stretch for her and her parents financially.

All the best,

Dan

I wrote and rewrote my response, then started over yet again, tempering my language. Finally I managed to write the following e-mail:

From: rus bradburd
Date: Wednesday, June 8, 2016
To: Dan Howard
Subject: RE: Dan, on Shawn Harrington

Dan, perhaps I misunderstood.

I remember you saying at Lou Henson's home, when Shawn visited in the spring of 2015, that "NMSU would make Naja a very attractive offer" and that NMSU would "take care of her." We shook hands after you said that. Maybe you were moved emotionally at the time, but putting the cart before the horse. Shawn remembers the same language.

I had a long talk with Marvin Menzies about Naja working in the Sports Information office as a scholarship/work-study student, but he finally insisted that the administration would have to spearhead this, create a position like that.

Since I'm not in admissions or aware of NMSU's minority or academic scholarships, I don't know what might happen differently here. I don't know what her Pell Grant status will be, but I suspect that with Mom a working nurse that the full Pell Grant would be a stretch.

I'm disappointed on a few levels—first, that our answer from NMSU admissions came on June 7. I thought this issue was on more people's radar at NMSU than mine, and I suspect that if I hadn't been consistently emailing NMSU people, nudging them, Naja and I would have heard nothing at all. It seems to me that we had ample time and plenty of options to make a competitive offer.

I guess I'll leave it at that for now. Thanks for responding so quickly today.

Rus Bradburd

Here is how the provost responded a few days later, ending our hopes for an affordable opportunity for Naja Harrington:

Hi Rus,

I, too, am disappointed that NMSU cannot do more for Naja. There are a number of factors that have come into play here that have impacted the university's ability to put together a more attractive package; most importantly her academic record (which was seemingly better when we spoke in the spring), and the fact that she did not apply to our Scholars Dollars Program, which would have made her eligible for scholarships controlled by the NMSU Foundation.

Perhaps we could have done more to reach out to her, but I believe Brandon contacted her personally to help her with her application and to let her know what was required in order for her to complete the application process. I do not know why it took us so long to get an offer to her after receiving her application materials. I will need to look into this further.

All the best,

Dan

In the end, I could not fault Howard for not speaking up in support of Shawn's daughter, or finding a place for her at NMSU in 2016. Not when I kept silent in the coaches meeting about Shawn's future on the other side of campus in 1996.

Naja Harrington and Tim Triplett were both African American teenagers who attended Chicago Public Schools. At least one other similarity had emerged.

In the year after Tywon's death, Triplett bounced back academically and graduated. Because of his failing grades at Farragut, he was held out of half the games his senior year at Marshall anyway, a devastating penalty for an athlete. His circumstances provided him no exception for athletic eligibility, and the blatant shortsightedness from the downtown administration affected his senior year profoundly. There is no way to measure how his life might have been different had his brother not been killed. Or if the Chicago Public Schools had granted him a waiver to play right away at Marshall because of Tywon's death. I believe that if Triplett had played the entire season, he would have garnered more offers. Even a player who had scored fifty points in a single game as a junior could not impress college scouts if he was sitting on the bench in street clothes as a senior.

It was true that Naja's grades dipped after her father was shot and paralyzed, as the NMSU provost and I had discussed at Lou Henson's home. Like Triplett, she had to bounce back from trauma and grief. Not many kids could survive an assassination attempt, see a parent paralyzed, and still finish with a grade point average right at 3.5. That dip in grades cost her dearly at a university that should have been sympathetic.

Meanwhile, Naja's wisdom in applying to other schools proved to be a good move. Illinois State offered Naja the best financial package, far better than NMSU's suggestion of letting her fill out the forms for the same Pell Grant anyone in America could apply for.

I phoned Shawn that June to tell him that there would be no scholarship for his daughter at his old school. Shawn, as usual, handled the bad news—in this case, from the college he was so proud of attending briefly—with grace and wisdom. In other words, he reacted much better than I did. "Well," Shawn said, "looks like Naja better go on to Illinois State."

Naja Harrington had a "trunk party" for family and friends to load her up with necessities before she left for college. She registered at Target for necessities like pillows, blankets, a coffeemaker, and sundries. Midway through the festivities it became apparent that Naja needed a second trunk. When somebody yelled *Speech!*, the dishes stopped clinking, the children were hushed, and everyone slowly gathered around her. This teenager had been through more than most adults could handle, yet still graduated with honors from one of Chicago's best high schools. The crowd sat up straight, smiled, and nodded in anticipation.

But Naja clammed up. She could hardly speak, and she finally said quietly, "What does everyone want me to say?" After an awkward silence, she whispered thank you and that was that.

Naja Harrington points to her solid support system when she's asked how she kept things together her final two years of high school. When pressed, she says it's simple. "I had a mom and dad to step in." Of course, Naja says, the incident with her father changed her mindset. "I know now that you could be gone at any moment," she says, "and that's made me more paranoid."

In the summer before she went off to college, she held down two jobs, one at a grocery chain, the other at a camp for young kids. "I could tell which campers come from broken homes," she says, "just being around them." All of which made her think about her father, how he negotiated his way through the West Side as a teenager not so long ago. She also thinks about the young men who tried to kill her. "Just looking at [alleged shooter] Deandre Thompson, I can tell he wasn't supported like my daddy was. You have to have someone who believes in you or you can turn down the wrong path."

She sometimes found herself weary of life in Chicago in the weeks before she left town for college. "When I'm ready to give up," she says, "I think *I could have been gone.*"

Kim Jenkins says her daughter can sink into pensive moods, and she sometimes wonders if Naja should be talking regularly to a therapist. The $250 from the Illinois Victims of Violent Crime covered just two visits to a counselor.

Naja became reticent in talking to her mother about the shooting, but Kim sees a positive side of that: "She'll say *I need to talk to my daddy.* And she'll call Shawn if she needs to share something and that's good. I know they've had long talks trying to work out everything."

"I can't change what happened," Naja says, but before anyone mistakes her point for some kind of quote on a motivational poster, she adds, "but I'm scared, too. I can't live like I'm in a shell the rest of my life. If my dad didn't believe in me as much as he did . . ." She pauses, gathers herself, then adds, "He always tells me he doesn't have any regrets. Some people might feel they risked their lives for nothing, but he believes I'm going to succeed. I think that's a good pressure."

Although Shawn had a great run at Northwest Missouri he hadn't heard much from people there. He often self-identified as a New Mexico State player. Nonetheless, I reached out to his long-retired coach. Steve Tappmeyer contributed a substantial check, pestered Shawn's teammates to help, and eventually directed me to Northwest Missouri president John Jasinski.

By chance in the mid-1990s, Jasinski was Shawn's advisor for his communications major before he was promoted to president. I was not sure whether to solicit the president's aid or to interview him for this book, so I did both. I asked him how Northwest had helped their former star in the year since the tragedy.

"Through good wishes and calls and cards," Jasinski said.

People with no connection with Shawn were helpful in more tangible ways.

Susan Cochran was an executive at the state's organ donation organization, Gift of Hope. She had a father who had been a successful college basketball coach, and she took Shawn out for lunches and organ donor events.

Charity Stripe's Mitch Saltzstein made a similar connection with Shawn. His organization put on a number of fundraisers for war veterans and their families. Shawn, of course, was not a member of the military. Nevertheless, Saltzstein helped considerably with a few of his unique fundraisers, sponsored free throw shooting contests involving local high school teams. Like Susan Cochran, Saltzstein became a trusted ally.

Former CEO Greg Fleming kept in touch and plotted new ways to assist. Two other New Yorkers read Joe Nocera's *Times* piece and, appalled by the deafness of the Chicago Public Schools, also got involved. A former prosecutor named Julian Wise rallied friends to pay a chunk of Naja's freshman tuition at Illinois State. A few months later, Wise flew Shawn to New York to be the guest speaker at the prestigious Schulte, Roth, and Zabel law firm. It was Shawn's first trip to New York City.

Another New Yorker named Madelaine Haberman donated money for Shawn's new driver's education training, and she made sure Shawn's "Shaq-mobile" was retrofitted with hand controls and a swivel seat.

Any support, small or large, lifted Shawn. Some friends feared that if he turned bitter or lost hope, Shawn might resort to drinking or smoking marijuana, but he was never much of a drinker and always disinterested in smoking weed. I pushed a "bright side" take on absolutely everything to Shawn, while cursing silently. *Maybe the Chicago Public Schools will return our calls, they must be awful busy. Maybe this is the turning point in the violence and things will get better. Maybe Naja will be happier at Illinois State. Maybe Gift of Hope will come through with a job soon. Charity Stripe might put on another event. Hey, the Bulls traded for Dwayne Wade and maybe the Chicago native could partner with us on summer camps.* Shawn was delighted by any possibility of good news. He seemed immune to bitterness.

Former Marshall player Keyon Boyd was murdered at noon on July 26, 2016.

Keyon wasn't the most skilled Marshall player and not much of a scorer. At six foot three and 150 pounds, he had wide shoulders and big hands, was wiry strong, and he rebounded with gusto. A quiet kid who worked hard on the court to prove himself, his exceptional help-side defense earned him praise from the coaches. Everyone called him "Smiley" because of his infectious grin. He ran track briefly and even played football for Marshall, earning a reputation for his fearlessness.

Keyon had an independent streak. "He was always trying to do things for himself," teammate Tyrese Williford says, "and he wouldn't ask anyone else for help." Just one season after Shawn Harrington was shot, Keyon Boyd dropped out.

"Keyon was a confused kid," says former girls' team star Jennifer Jones, who has been a gym teacher at Marshall for nearly ten years. "Marshall was like therapy for Keyon," she adds. The school was a place where he could feel safe, loved, and appreciated.

In the fall of 2015, four months after Tim Triplett was killed, Keyon returned to finish school. He was part of Marshall's Pass Program, designed for troubled students as a "credit recovery" initiative with the objective of keeping kids from dropping out or helping them gain ground if they returned. He'd been targeted early and was the only freshman in that program at one time. When Keyon Boyd reenrolled something had changed. He was always respectful, track coach Stefanie Dobrin says, "but he could get off task because of his surroundings."

Tyrone Hayes was involved with the Pass Program, and he sensed what Dobrin did. Hayes kept a close eye on Keyon. "You had a hard time *not* laughing when Keyon was laughing," Hayes says. "He was a kid who needed guidance but he accepted it." Or, accepted it up to a point. "After six hours at school," Hayes adds, "when sports are done, it was back to the reality of his life." Although Keyon wound up earning a diploma, reality hit hard in the spring of his senior year, once football and basketball seasons were complete. He had no college prospects and no job.

Marshall insiders say Keyon had a temper and he got sucked in by the streets. He had been arrested seven times, mostly during the time he'd dropped out of school. The bulk of the arrests were for small amounts of marijuana. Once he was arrested for "replica firearms," possessing a pellet gun.

Jennifer Jones had great faith in Keyon and talked with him in class daily. She understood his needs and had tried to iron out the rebellious streak that often manifested itself in his relationship with his mom. She was overwhelmed by his murder. "I just could not process it," she says. "I suppressed the whole thing. I had some good times and bad times with Keyon but he was lashing out because he wanted to be pulled in."

Keyon's murder left Tyrone Hayes groping for answers, too. "We only see kids when they're here at Marshall," Hayes says, "but when you see them away from school you might see a very different person. Kids live for today. I guess they always did but now it's even more extreme." After a pause, he sighs. "They have no plan, and after school it all goes out the window. They've put invisible handcuffs on these kids."

Somebody named Ivan posted about Keyon Boyd's murder on the *Chicago Sun-Times* Homicide Watch website:

> I didn't know him. I just manage the building over there. I was actually about to meet section 8 inspector over there and he

walked out the gangway asking me for help!....actually held this little brother in my arms as he was dying! I didn't know him. I kept telling him to fight for his life! I poured my water over his shoulder and told him to feel it against his skin, you want to live brother! And he was shot maybe 3 or 4 times. RIP brother. God bless his family.

21

IN THE SUMMER OF 2016, I rented a car to help facilitate the interviews for this book. I usually biked over an hour from Ravenswood to see Shawn at his aunt Jaci's apartment. The place was not really big enough for two, but Shawn had been living with her since the shooting. The apartment was on the dividing line between Chicago's West Side and suburban Oak Park, and the commute for me was getting exhausting.

At the Rent-a-Wreck near Midway Airport, the clerk asked me about my New Mexico driver's license. I told him I was in Chicago working on a book about a coach who'd been shot.

"You mean Shawn Harrington?" the clerk asked. I was surprised.

The clerk's name was Derrick Watt. He said Shawn wouldn't likely remember him, but they had plenty of mutual friends. Watt had lived on the West Side most of his childhood but he went to high school in Maywood, the mixed working-class suburb. He was holding down two jobs to pay the bills. Besides Rent-a-Wreck, he is a manager at a factory on the far North Side, an hour drive from the first job. Sometimes he works the overnight shift at the factory.

Watt told me the story of his son. Ramen was raised by his grandparents in a comfortable middle-class home with his own room in the basement, a huge television, and occasional access to the classy cars that his grandparents drove. He also developed into a talented artist and his painting of an angel hangs in the Maywood courthouse.

Ramen was also a track and field star at Proviso East High School until a serious ankle injury ruined his chances at a scholarship. He got discouraged. Although he graduated from high school, he moved from job to job, taking occasional college classes but never accumulating enough credits for a degree. He began hanging out on the streets of the West Side, although he was an outsider to gang life, a suburban kid.

"I remember driving through the West Side one day," his father says, "and I saw him on the street corner with no shirt on."

Ramen had a striking physique and a couple tattoos, but Derrick Watt told him the bare-chested bit was a stupid thing to do. "My son didn't understand," Watt says, "that being shirtless with tight pants was like a huge billboard that read *I don't have a gun*. He came from such a different background where the rules are very different."

On Father's Day 2012, Watt got off work at 6:00 AM, and he decided to stop by Ramen's and wake him up. He was hoping for a steak-and-eggs breakfast at his son's expense. After all, this was Father's Day. He called and texted Ramen and got no response, but he kept driving to Oak Park anyway. When he turned the corner at Austin and Chicago— less than a hundred yards from where Shawn Harrington now lives—he saw his son.

"What is Ramen doing lying in the street at seven in the morning?" Watt wondered aloud.

A week earlier, a girl Ramen hardly knew had been accosted by a young gangbanger named Tjuan English. Ramen tried to intervene, but the young man kept slapping the girl. Ramen, big, quick, and handy with his fists, beat the smaller boy off her, but he might have overdone things. Rather than making sure the girl was safe and stopping there, Ramen let his anger get the better of him. He bloodied English's nose and bruised his face.

The next week, the night before Father's Day, Ramen was at a party in Oak Park. A friend of the battered gangbanger's was there, too, and he sent a text to Tjuan English: "That dude who beat your ass is here at the party. What you gonna do?"

"I need him dead," English texted back. He arrived minutes later but didn't go inside. A quick plan was put into place. There'd be another text sent to English the instant Ramen left the party. English paced the streets for hours and worked himself into a frenzy until Ramen, a bit drunk, wobbled out the door at 6:15 AM.

Tjuan English put on a mask and fired his gun at Ramen from across the street. The first shots came from the Chicago side of Austin Boulevard from a CTA bus turnaround. Ramen was hit once and fell to the ground. English ran across the street and executed him with several shots at close range. CTA security cameras captured the entire incident.

Derrick Watt was the first person to arrive on the murder scene.

Oak Park police made an arrest days later, partly because the shooter posted information about the killing on Facebook. "I can't fight too good but I know how to shoot that thing," he wrote.

A few days later, Watt made himself view the video obtained by police. "I don't know how I was able to watch it," he says, "but I wanted to see what happened to my son."

———————

Terrell Allen was a sophomore with the Commandos when Shawn Harrington was shot and a junior when Tim Triplett was murdered. (He appears in street clothes in the photo of the anguished Triplett after the Orr game.) Like Triplett, he is from Holy City. Terrell was a solid high school player, but he had no aspirations to play in college. He'd only been a starter sporadically and besides, he stood just five foot five. A fine kid, according to Coach Cotton and the Marshall staff, Terrell decided he'd rather find a job than go to college.

I first met Terrell in Henry Cotton's office in the summer of 2016, when he did what three other players had already done—interrupted my interview to visit with his coach, though he had nothing urgent to talk about. I had come to admire Cotton, although I viewed him as a man with an umbrella in a hurricane, overwhelmed by violent forces far beyond his control.

I asked Terrell why he was wearing the white cast that covered his wrist and culminated in a curve that secured his ring and pinky finger. I nearly wisecracked, "Bet you didn't hurt it dunking." I'm glad I didn't.

"I got shot," Terrell said, "on June thirtieth."

A black truck had swerved to a stop in Holy City and opened fire on Terrell just before sunset. He ducked behind a car for cover, but not before a bullet grazed his finger. He was unfazed and matter-of-fact about his shooting.

A few months later Terrell started a job at the Walmart in Cicero, the working-class suburb to the west of Holy City. He also kept a Facebook page with the Danni Mob prefix. Before I left, he showed me the tattoo on his shoulder, commemorating his friend, Tim Triplett.

I was trying to learn who Tim Triplett stayed with overnight downtown and I was thwarted at every turn by a mysterious code of silence, until a player from one of Marshall's rivals pointed me to Instagram, which I had never used. There I found images of Aaron Hawkins, Triplett's older cousin, who lived downtown. Hawkins is also the founder of the social club Young, Flashy, and Fly.

Hawkins's Instagram photos and short videos feature a shiny black 2010 model S550 Mercedes, extravagant clothes, pricey meals, and stacks of money. Before Triplett was murdered, and in the immediate aftermath, Hawkins posted pictures of his cousin sitting on that car, gazing up longingly at the Chicago skyline, or mugging with stacks of hundred dollar bills. In one charming video, Triplett joyfully shows off his dance moves to a crew of friends while carrying a shopping bag on Michigan Ave.

I met Aaron Hawkins minutes after being interviewed for HBO by Bryant Gumbel. Both meetings took place at the Quest Multisport gym, the premier basketball facility in the city. NBA teams practice there, and so do Big East college teams that come to town to play DePaul. Jabari Parker runs his summer camp there. Quest is exclusive. You can't just walk in and start shooting baskets. Security, although informal, is tight. The place is also a generous community resource, hosting citywide events and educational camps. Shawn Harrington had volunteered, without pay, to coach a team of seventh graders once a week at Quest. Director Jerry Hardin is a former college coach who has shrewdly purposed the gym to serve two needs, accommodating prestigious teams as well as reaching out to underserved neighborhood kids.

After HBO's crew left, I invited Aaron Hawkins to join me in a private meeting room. I was put off when the other man with him stood to join us as well. He turned out to be Aaron's brother, Demonta. I didn't have the nerve to bounce Demonta out of the interview at that point, and besides, I could talk to Aaron alone later.

Unlike Triplett's coaches, teachers, friends, and teammates, Aaron and Demonta said it did not bother them a bit to talk about their cousin. "We're for real," Aaron said and stressed that Triplett and he were close. "He was like my little brother," he said.

During Triplett's senior year at Marshall, Aaron started housing his cousin from time to time in his upscale downtown condo. That happened more often when Triplett enrolled at Wright junior college and his mother moved back to Milwaukee.

"Tim was always super grateful," Aaron says. "He would always say thank you and he'd let you know how much he cared about you."

Triplett's transient nature—four schools in the previous three years—may have made him even more loyal. Despite his fractured home life, he'd stress his love of family. Aaron recognized Triplett needed a friend as well as a place to sleep. After Triplett became a regular houseguest, Aaron realized his cousin was a compulsive neat freak. After every laundry session, he neatly folded and stacked his clothes. "Y'all need to clean up around here," he announced, and he'd get to work cleaning, polishing, organizing.

I asked the Hawkins brothers what was the deal with the photos of the fancy clothes, the wads of bills, and the Mercedes 550 splashed across their Instagram feed? Why feature Triplett in those photos? What was the point? I asked Aaron about his line of work—how did guys in their early twenties accumulate that kind of wealth?

"We're party promoters," Aaron said. They served as a sort of nightclub owner without a nightclub. He said he made quite a living putting on parties, popular events that move from location to location. They have no website, office address, or publicized notices in newspapers or magazines. Their events get advertised on Facebook, Twitter, and especially by word of mouth.

I didn't see how throwing lavish parties each month could pay for a downtown condo and a Mercedes. Hawkins said the events, which might be in rented warehouses or loft spaces, charge upward of twenty dollars for admission with hundreds of guests attending. Toss in the cost of drinks or food, Hawkins said, and his take starts to add up quickly.

Why not, I wondered, show photos of the parties on Instagram, instead of the Mercedes, the fancy clothes, the stacks of bills?

"We *want* people to think we have a lot of money," Demonta said. He had kept on his pricey Canada Goose parka for the interview. "We're cultivating an image," he added. Showing off their stuff created a sort of buzz, name recognition, an allure.

I said an English teacher like me does not want publicity, does not want outsiders to know, for example, that he has saved up enough to pay for his daughter's first year of college.

"You're in a different line of work," they kept stressing. "We *do* want publicity."

I was a struggling writer on a state payroll who had no idea of a functioning business model. As I was mulling all this over, I began to consider *The Great Gatsby*. The host of gaudy parties for people he hardly knew, Jay Gatsby wanted to make everyone aware he had piles of money. Yet he was throwing galas to impress one woman, not to bring *in* money. Aaron Hawkins was putting on events as a business concern, and maybe also to gain respect, so perhaps the parties did make sense. Each year over the holidays his Young, Fly, and Flashy crew gave away turkeys or toys to the needy on the West Side. I remembered that Triplett had posted on Facebook about distributing the turkeys as charity.

Aaron stressed how close he was with Triplett, although he had no knowledge of the death threat at Crane High School, his cousin's five arrests, or his coach Shawn Harrington getting shot. He had bought the $1,400 Christian Louboutin shoes Triplett wore in his casket, but he had no idea that his cousin's grave lacked a headstone.

Although Triplett appeared on social media posing with stacks of money, Aaron does not think that endangered his cousin, and he does not believe—as I do—that Triplett leaving Chicago for college would have necessarily saved him. "He could have been home for the summer and got shot," he said.

"It's all about the way you move," Demonta added, and he explained that through common sense and good decisions, despite the 4,338 shootings in 2016, a guy could keep safe even on the West Side. Demonta said he recognized the complications in Triplett's life. "He had one foot in, one foot out."

I admitted how perplexing all this was to me. Any college freshman should be focused on his studies and basketball, have his nose in a book instead of strolling past upscale shops on Michigan Avenue. But if Triplett had nowhere to live, it was hard to find fault with him for bunking with a cousin in a high-rise condo.

A few weeks later, Bryant Gumbel's HBO program focused on the "hooper's pass," the old order that provided ballplayers a reprieve from the violence. I'd witnessed the odd alliance over the years of gangbangers and the top ballplayers. Basketball stars were the heroes of the neighborhood. Gang leaders often played pickup ball as recreation and had great influence because they had money. Shawn's shooting was a stupid case of mistaken identity, a complete breakdown of the old structure. But Tim Triplett might have been granted a hooper's pass in the past simply by being a basketball star.

Principal Richard Smith left Crane and is now in charge at Fenger, a high school in the troubled Roseland neighborhood on the far South Side. "The city of Chicago and basketball can be a beautiful combination," he says, "or it can be a terrible combination." He recalls the hooper's pass of his teenage years in Chicago. "A player *could* get a pass," he says. "I could wear my King High School jacket and go anywhere within reason, although I couldn't go to, say, Englewood and slap somebody. I grew up around the [street gang] Blackstone Rangers but they were the last thing on our minds because they weren't bothering the ballplayers. I don't think that code is alive and well any longer."

Not that the hooper's pass ever granted total immunity. Shawn and Ontario Brown Sr. were both held up at gunpoint as high school players in the early 1990s. So was Arthur Agee, an event covered near the end of *Hoop Dreams*. Agee's father was murdered years after the film was completed. Curtis Gates, whose younger brother William was the other player focused on in the documentary film, was murdered, too, and he had been a great high school player.

Tim Anderson, who coached Tim Triplett one season at Crane, concurs that whatever was left of the hooper's pass has now evaporated. "People don't understand how close basketball and the streets are with one another today," he says.

Twenty years had elapsed since I was a regular on the Chicago basketball scene, when I was often the only white guy in a jam-packed Public League gym, or taking notes at an obscure park district tournament, or observing a playground game. Most of the coaches and contacts who had helped me negotiate the city were retired or dead. With the swirl of shootings, the deafness of people with the power to change the situation, I began to realize that my "priceless education" in Chicago basketball was now obsolete.

Nobody on the Marshall team could claim immunity from the neighborhood violence, no matter how well they played or performed in the classroom.

Tyrese Williford had admired Tim Triplett since grade school days at Crowne Elementary in Holy City. In 2014, as a Marshall sophomore, he was Triplett's understudy. Two years later, Williford earned All City honors and a junior college basketball scholarship. He decided to stop attending funerals and he became withdrawn, spending more time holed up in his apartment until it was time to leave for college.

In November 2016, after playing in a half-dozen junior college games, Williford learned that his grandfather had been robbed at gunpoint for the second time back in Chicago. A few days later the grandfather died of a heart attack.

"I don't even want to know what's going on in the street," Williford said, shaking his head and naming all the Marshall players who had been shot. "We were all close," he sighed.

I reminded him of the summer of 2016's most dramatic shooting. A North Lawndale Prep and college star named Jonathon Mills was shot several times in the face in the middle of the day at a busy intersection on Roosevelt Road. That seemed to set something off in Williford and he rattled off the names of his murdered friends the way kids list the starting lineups on their favorite teams. Williford's list included Danny Collins, whom Danni Mob's name commemorates. "When Danny was shot, he was on his porch," Williford says. "Tim's brother Tywon was there, he saw it. And Danny got up and fell behind a garbage can. It's hard to see everybody just up and die."

———————

Within minutes of finishing his interview with the HBO crew, Shawn fell under a different kind of pressure—a meeting with the Illinois state's attorney.

The trial was days away and prosecution lawyers needed Shawn to see the security camera video, a twenty-second snippet. The video was of Shawn getting shot while saving his daughter's life. Shawn could not, the lawyers reasoned, see the video for the first time at the trial. He might react erratically in front of the jury, lose his focus, or even confuse Deandre Thompson with Cedryck Davis. The film might then contradict his testimony. The prosecutors wanted to jog his memory and prepare him for his day in court, so they played the video over and over. Shawn saw himself get shot and paralyzed a half-dozen times.

22

MARTIN SATTERFIELD was Marshall's first player to be hit by gunfire. Like Shawn, Satterfield remains confined to a wheelchair, paralyzed.

Soon after that, Shawn's best friend growing up, Ontario Brown, had a son murdered in Indiana.

Next, Shawn Holloway was killed.

Then Timothy Triplett.

Marcus Patrick and Keyon Boyd were murdered next. All of the Chicago shootings happened during daylight hours.

Terrell Allen was shot in the hand, although, like Satterfield, he survived.

The victims, with the exception of Ontario's son, had played basketball at Marshall while Shawn was coaching from the years 2011 to 2015. Triplett was the best player, the only one you might call a basketball star with the potential for a scholarship. That sounds like a cold judgment from an ex-college coach, but my point is that Triplett could have used the hardwood as an escape route. He didn't. The others had fewer options.

Hoop Dreams, it now seemed, was exactly that at Marshall—a dream.

Although Satterfield and some of the murdered players may have been involved, or at least friendly, with gang members, nobody ever really thought Shawn was affiliated—except perhaps for the overzealous cop who jerked Shawn out of the car on January 30, 2014.

Each subsequent shooting staggered Shawn, pushed him into despair, although he refused to pass judgment with the typical dismissals like, "He should have known better than to . . ." or "What was he doing out on that corner?" Shawn, like Williford, couldn't bring himself to attend the memorials for the other players after Tim Triplett's wild funeral service.

It was difficult for me to see God's hand in any of this, but I kept quiet when Shawn talked openly about God's will, being prayed for, and his general reliance on Christian faith. Between his degree in communications and coaching at one of the highest profile programs in the city, he had plenty of experience with the media, but I occasionally found his responses perplexing. "Rus usually calls me every day," he told one reporter, "and sometimes he'll say *What's wrong, Shawn? I can hear in your voice that something is not right.*"

I had never said anything remotely like that to him, but I let it pass. I thought it might just be his reflexive way of saying something kind about his old coach. Later it dawned on me. Maybe Shawn wanted me to ask him more direct questions about his mental health and wished I was more inquisitive about his mental state. I resolved to be more intrusive, however if Shawn was in a bad place emotionally he became much harder to reach on the phone. This didn't matter so much in the summers when I was in Chicago because I could text him and tell him I was outside his apartment. Open up! But during my school year in New Mexico his unresponsiveness, especially in the winter months, made me anxious.

He told one friend that I was like a father to him. "He means that he ignores my advice and calls," I responded, "and gets testy when I bug him."

Most baffling to me was his allegiance to Marshall. Shawn phoned me minutes before columnist Joe Nocera arrived at his apartment. "I don't want anything printed that might hurt Marshall," he said, as if I might have a chance to look over the shoulders of the *New York Times* editors and insist on some changes. "I just don't want to make things harder for the school to attract students," he added. Enrollment at his alma mater had plummeted. Shawn was still more worried about Marshall than himself. I reminded him that none of the kids had been killed while attending the school or inside the building. Their shootings were not something that rivals, parents, or prospective students could blame on Marshall.

Shawn was intensely proud not just of Marshall's history of great basketball teams, but also of how well even the benchwarmers had done after graduating, something he attributed to the coaches' discipline and hands-on approach to kids. He had introduced me to countless former Commandos—this guy an accountant, another a teacher, this one in the armed services, another in graduate school. Marshall's Patrick Beverly had gone on to a lucrative NBA career. Keifer Sykes and Al McKinnie were on the verge of signing NBA contracts. Shawn was happy about that, but he was prouder of the less glamorous success stories.

I continued to challenge Shawn about his dedication to the school that had no elevator, that could not accommodate his wheelchair. He had no reason to wait around. *Let's move on* I told him, quit holding out hope that Marshall could find a place for him. Not that any of my letters, calls, or e-mails had presented a more tangible option. Loyalty was deeply ingrained in Shawn, who often tagged his texts to players with "C4L"—*Commandos for Life.*

As the shootings increased in number I really *could* hear it in Shawn's voice. "Seems like there's no end in sight," he told me one morning.

He was correct.

The homecoming dance at Marshall in 2016 was ruined when a student named Jamel Thomas was killed after leaving his job at the Portillos hot dog chain to get to the event. Jamel Thomas was not a ballplayer. "But there had been a cloud hanging around Marshall since Shawn Harrington was shot," says phys ed teacher Jennifer Jones, "and there it was again."

Then, on October 30, 2016, a six foot five Marshall basketball player named Edward Bryant was murdered in Old Town. Edward Bryant's twin brother, Edwin, who played football at Marshall, was murdered at the same time. The twins had begun their career at Lincoln Park High School, in an affluent area a mile from where they were killed. They had switched to Marshall as "Safety Transfers," a decision made in conjunction with the downtown administration echoing Tim Triplett's transfer three years earlier. "There were threats made against them," one Public League coach says.

The murder of the Bryant brothers broke the pattern in a few ways. It was not broad daylight. It was not an impoverished neighborhood. And, most important, the twins were still in school. The drive-by shooting happened at 3:15 AM in the 1300 block of North Hudson, a rare occurrence in the mostly well-to-do neighborhood just north of downtown. A junior at the time, Edward Bryant was already gaining attention from college coaches. His size, long arms, and fluid style made him the best college prospect of Marshall's murdered players.

Vince Carter, the Von Steuben coach who is deeply involved in social justice issues, had mentored Edward on summer league teams. Carter also helped found a Chicago coaches-against-violence initiative that included Shawn. The Bryant twins had been students in Carter's summer and after-school tutoring programs from the time they were

Edward Bryant and his twin brother, Edwin, were both actively playing sports at Marshall when they were murdered in the autumn of 2016.
Courtesy of Vince Carter

sixth-graders. When Carter's players asked him about the killings, he did something he'd never done—he lied to them. The coach told me virtually the same thing he told *Tribune* reporters. "I said that everything is going to be all right, but the truth is that I did not have any more answers. I didn't know why or how, so I just told my kids that it's going to be all right." Carter has closely followed the Chicago shootings and the links to basketball. "The stories are starting to get blurry," he sighs. When I mentioned to a different coach that I feared another teammate of Triplett's could be murdered next, the coach said "Next? If you're on the street, you are always *next!*"

In November 2016, the Bryant twins were commemorated at a Marshall basketball game. Over a ten-hour day I interviewed teachers, security guards, and coaches who knew Shawn Harrington and the murdered players.

While waiting for my first appointment that day, I was sitting at the entrance near the metal detector used for security. Suddenly, a Chicago police officer and a hefty student burst out of a door, wrestling and shouting. The cop kept telling the teenaged student to stop resisting and an instant later pulled out what I thought was a gun. It wasn't—it was a Taser gun that the cop used to a quick and effective conclusion. The student walked like Frankenstein for a moment before he collapsed, shaking and drooling on the tiled floor. After a few minutes, the boy started to mumble and must have said something the cop didn't like, because the cop challenged him to get back up and get Tasered again. At that point, an administrator asked me to clear the hallway, although it was already empty. I waited in the main office, more than a bit rattled, wondering why anyone would send their kid to Marshall.

By the end of the day I had an answer.

Although Marshall changes principals as frequently as players change sneakers, the school has a core of employees who are stubbornly loyal—not just to the school, but to each other and to their underdog kids. One employee after another told me a similar story. They'd worked there for years, with no plans to pursue a more upscale school or job. All confessed an obsessive love of the school, a commitment to their students. Every worker knew every kid by name and made reference to "the Marshall family."

I interviewed track coach Stefanie Dobrin in a third-floor classroom during her free period. She had known Tim Triplett and Keyon Boyd well, and she'd been teaching at Marshall for over a dozen years, ever since she graduated from college. Not everyone has the endurance or measurable success of Dorothy Gaters, but Dobrin was yet another employee with singular devotion to the school. She had grown up in a well-to-do suburb, and she stressed to me that Shawn's return to the West Side after getting his college degree was honorable. When the final bell rang it was time for practice, but she still had a few minutes so I hung around. She did not have to go far. Track at Marshall takes place in the hallways in the winter. Stretching, sprints, distance work, interval training, it all happens for the boys and girls in the long corridors and stairways. Her classroom instantly became a locker room as a dozen athletes streamed in. Some peppered her with questions. Most changed right there on the spot.

One girl came in looking distraught.

"I want to practice today," she told the coach, "but I don't have any shoes to run in anymore."

Dobrin hollered for the rest of the team to start warming up. Then she turned back to the student in her street shoes. They were both quiet for a few seconds until the coach kicked off her new Nikes and handed them to the girl.

"Here," Dobrin said. "We're about the same size. Now you give me your shoes." That was how track practice began at Marshall.

23

DEFENSE ATTORNEY DONNA ROTUNNO is known in legal circles for her fearlessness, her willingness to take on controversial cases. Now she was representing Cedryck Davis for the attempted murder of Shawn Harrington. Rotunno's client had a much longer rap sheet than the other accused shooter, Deandre Thompson, but Davis might have been harder to convict because over a hundred days had passed before Shawn and Naja picked him out of a police lineup. There was an odd detail about Davis and his hoodie in the lineup that she planned to hammer away at. Maybe she could cast doubt or poke holes in the police work. She did not have a good feeling, however, about her client's chances. "I knew walking in how this one could end," Rotunno says.

Police, prosecutors, Shawn, and his daughter all believed that Cedryck Davis was the man up ahead in front of Shawn's rental car. Shawn's bullet wound in his spine indicated that Davis was probably not the shooter who did the damage—the devastating shot had more than likely come from the side or the rear, from Deandre Thompson. Rotunno knew that meant nothing under the letter of the law. Both young men were being tried for the same crime, and attempted murder was still an attempt. Due to Illinois gun laws, both Davis and Thompson were looking at a minimum of fifty-two years if convicted. That's why, when the state's attorney's office offered a plea bargain deal a few days before the trial, Rotunno paid attention. The prosecutors wanted Davis to plead guilty and implicate Thompson. In exchange, the state would agree to a twenty-five-year sentence for Rotunno's client, but Davis would have to testify against Thompson in court.

Rotunno cornered Davis the next day and told him of the twenty-five-year offer. "Truth in sentencing" laws in the state meant he'd have to serve 85 percent of that, meaning twenty-two years. He'd already been sitting in Cook County Jail for nearly three years, and that would count as time served. He could be out of prison in nineteen years, when he was in his mid-forties. But nineteen years to Davis seemed like a lifetime. In addition, there was the code that young men on the street sometimes live by. You don't snitch, you don't plead guilty. "I tried in every way I knew to get [Davis] to take that deal," Rotunno says, "but going to trial and taking your medicine is somehow seen as more honorable." That mentality sometimes confounds her. "You're going to be honorable now?" she asked Davis. "Nobody else is being honorable."

Rotunno had an odd connection to Shawn. They were the same age, and she had been a good high school basketball player at Immaculate Heart of Mary, the sister school to Saint Joseph's—the second school featured in *Hoop Dreams*. Rotunno and her teammates were friendly with the film's protagonist, Arthur Agee. After Agee left St. Joe's to attend Marshall, the girls occasionally made a point to go see Marshall games. Rotunno attended boys' games at both St. Joe's and Marshall, was in the bleachers a few times over the course of the documentary film.

Rotunno's own IHM team had once played at Marshall. She remembered riding the team bus the twelve miles from the suburbs to the West Side on the 290 expressway. Her team was escorted inside by security guards, which had never happened before.

Rotunno could not have known that a team of boys sat in the stands that afternoon to support the Marshall girls against her Catholic school. This was in keeping with Luther Bedford and Dorothy Gaters's policy of sending one team to support the other. A nonleague game like Immaculate Heart of Mary meant the Commando boys did not have their own contest that day. It was an odd coincidence that Shawn Harrington and Donna Rotunno had seen each other play high school basketball.

The Sunday before the trial began, Shawn and the Marshall family were rocked yet again by awful news. Courtney Hargrays, Shawn's high school teammate who had coached the Commandos to a state championship, was involved in a terrible car accident on the Eisenhower Expressway. Hargrays, the driver, was in a coma. All three of his passengers died at the scene. The passengers included security guard Tyrone Hayes's niece, as well as Henry Brooks, who had served as the basketball team manager when Shawn was in high school.

Shawn went to visit Hargrays in the hospital, with no inkling of how responsive his friend might be. Shawn found him in a coma with countless tubes keeping him alive. "What's up, Slow Motion?" Shawn asked while holding his hand. Hargrays squeezed a couple times. The trio of stars from the 1993 Marshall Commandos had been stricken with devastating tragedies, all within a three-year period. First, Shawn's shooting. Next, Ontario Brown's son was killed. Now Courtney Hargrays was fighting for his life.

———————————

Jury selection in the trial for the attempted murder of Shawn and Naja Harrington began on January 17, 2017. The trial began the next day. The jury was made up of four men (none African American) and eight women (four of whom were African American). Nearly three years had elapsed since the shooting.

The trial took place in one of the newer Cook County courtrooms known to attorneys as "the fishbowls." The gallery is separated from the proceedings by a Plexiglas partition. Observers sit in a semicircle behind the glass and listen via speakers. Friends and family of the accused tend to sit on one side of the aisle, the victim's supporters on the other.

Judge Thomas Byrne, with his round glasses and long, serious face, was a model of efficiency running through the morning call. He set bond for defendants, scheduled hearings, and punished parole violations. Silence fell over the courtroom when he called accused shooters Deandre Thompson and Cedryck Davis into the courtroom. Observers leaned forward in their seats, straining to hear what would happen in the fishbowl.

Although the *New York Times* had published a long piece about Shawn's situation two days before Christmas, only a single reporter, from the Chicago ABC television affiliate, attended the trial. When the PA system in the courtroom malfunctioned, like the police POD cameras at the corner of Augusta and Hamlin three years earlier, the lone reporter complained about the volume. A bailiff propped open the double doors leading into the courtroom proper but the proceedings still felt oddly distant.

Deandre Thompson wore a crisp maroon dress shirt and black-rimmed glasses. His nickname was "Stay High," something the state's attorneys would frequently remind jurors, but on this day he looked as though he was on his way to a college dance.

Cedryck Davis, known on the street as "Lil' Ced," is the taller of the two and appeared less comfortable. He had been in court quite a bit more than Deandre Thompson in the last few years, and he seemed hyperaware of the stakes. Davis was also clean-cut in a blue suit and tie. The dreadlocks he was known to wear had been cut off before the police arrested him.

The prosecution was not allowed to bring up either man's previous arrests, and they were being tried at the same time for the same crime. In his opening statement, a prosecutor described how Davis moved ahead of Shawn's vehicle to the intersection of Augusta and Hamlin while Thompson stood on the sidewalk a short distance from the rental car. Both men, he said, pointed guns at the Impala and fired "a hailstorm of bullets" before they fled. He did not say that the city's POD cameras had failed, but he mentioned that the surveillance video taken from the corner store showed these events plainly. He mentioned Charles Molette (although not his nickname, "Bang Bang"), who volunteered to police that he could identify the defendants as the same men who had shot another victim nearby two days earlier. Molette had not been an eyewitness to Shawn's shooting, but he had seen the first one. Police and the prosecuting attorneys would try to link Shawn's shooting with the matching bullets from the previous attempted murder. Molette's identification the day of the shooting "sent the police investigation into overdrive," the prosecutor said.

Thompson's attorney, Marc Gottreich, began the defense's opening statement. Gottreich is short, with close-cropped hair and an ingratiating manner that implies he'd like nothing better than to dispense with the necktie and talk over coffee in the second-floor cafeteria. He emphasized, as Davis's attorney Donna Rotunno would later, that this shooting was a tragic event and that Shawn Harrington was a good man. No one disputed that but sympathy was not at issue. "This is about identification," he said. "It wasn't Deandre Thompson or his codefendant who shot Shawn Harrington." He said that the only real evidence against his client was a glance by Naja Harrington in a moment of chaos. Davis's defense also focused on identification, claiming that there was not a single credible witness in the case.

The state's first witness was Charles "Bang Bang" Molette, who was now serving five years on a drug offense. A burly, recalcitrant twenty-year-old in prison garb, he took the witness stand with all the enthusiasm of someone being lowered into a well.

Eugene Wood, the lead assistant state's attorney, is a genial African American man with graying hair and a moustache. He questioned Molette while holding a printed version of his signed statement, which he kept waving at the witness. Wood repeated what Molette had allegedly said in his statement, that he saw the defendants shoot another man on January 28, and he said the same duo had also shot the basketball coach by mistake. After running into a police officer he knew canvassing the area the afternoon of the shooting, Molette had decided to tell his story.

But on the witness stand, Molette denied not only that he knew the first victim or the two defendants, but also that he'd ever talked to police or given a statement.

The questioning by Eugene Wood that followed was awkward.

"Were you in the area of Lawndale and Thomas, 1100 North Lawndale, on January 28, 2014?"

"No, sir."

"Did you know Darren Deer [the shooting victim from two days prior]?"

"No, sir."

"Did you tell Officer Jaglarski on January 30, 2014, that you had information about the Shawn Harrington shooting?"

"No, sir."

Laboriously, Wood questioned Molette almost line-by-line on the statement he now denied giving, with the witness answering "No, sir" every time. Molette now claimed he had never even been to the Area North police station.

Deftly, Wood flipped his glasses onto his head, lowered them to his nose, then flipped them up again as he switched from reading parts of the statement to scrutinizing Molette. He found a page in the statement and flipped his glasses up yet again with a flourish.

"Who is pictured in this photo?" he asked and held it up to the witness's face.

Molette hesitated. "Me," he admitted.

It was a photograph of Molette at the police station, taken on the day he denied being there.

"Bang Bang" Molette's recanting was a tough break for the prosecution, and it spurred the defense to argue that the witness's testimony shouldn't be allowed. Judge Byrne ruled that this evidence was not unduly prejudicial and the jury could weigh both the old statement and the recantation, deciding what value to give Molette's contributions. The fact that Molette claimed he'd never been to Area North while Wood held photographic evidence of him at the police station clearly registered with the jury.

The defense tried to chip away at Molette's credibility, pointing out that his alleged statement had not been videotaped. Molette signs his name in cursive, while his signature on this typed statement was printed. Why didn't he handwrite the entire statement himself? (Jurors later learned the assistant state's attorney who took the statement spoke to Molette alone, did not take notes, did not videotape him, and typed the statement up since Bang Bang did not want to have to write it himself by hand.)

Molette's photo from the police station could have persuaded the jury that he was lying on the stand, but honest with the cops three years earlier. Or it could have meant that the defense had succeeded in getting jurors to discount Molette entirely.

After a lunch break, state's attorney Eugene Wood escorted the afternoon's first witness into the courtroom. The gallery went silent as Shawn Harrington wheeled down the center aisle, between the defendants' families and his own. Because he was in a wheelchair, he sat next to the witness stand, meaning he did not face the jury. Rather, he was positioned to face Thompson and Davis.

Under questioning by Wood, Shawn calmly told his story: the morning ritual with Naja to Westinghouse, the two men on Hamlin Street, one on the corner in a hoodie pointing at his car. Shots ringing out, glass flying, the windows gone. "I heard at least ten shots," he said. "But when I first heard the shots, I turned and saw two people." He recounted pushing Naja down, down. He raised his head momentarily when the shooting stopped to see the bullet hole in her headrest.

He instructed Naja to dial 911. Police arrived quickly. He'd been hit in the back and his right shoulder, though he did not realize at that instant that he'd been shot. Yes, he answered Wood, those were the injuries that left him paralyzed from the waist down. Wood asked if Shawn could identify in the courtroom today the man who had pointed at him from the corner before firing at his car.

"He's right there in the blue suit," Shawn said, pointing at Cedryck Davis. Wood showed Shawn a photo of the police lineup from which he'd identified Davis in April 2014, and he pointed to Davis again as the second man from the right.

Next, the state's attorneys tried to play the surveillance video recovered from the small grocery store at the corner of Augusta and Wood. As if by design to build tension, they couldn't get the video to work on the giant display monitor—as though the faulty police POD cameras had somehow infected the grocery store security video. The judge dismissed the jury and after a short break the state resolved its technical problems.

The silence is the eeriest thing about the video. Hamlin Street is snowy and calm. A car passes through the frame. A moment later, the white Impala rental car appears. Two men walk casually toward it, one from in front of the car on the street corner to the south, one from the adjacent sidewalk. They raise their hands and appear to shoot at the car. Their faces are not clear, and neither are the guns in their hands.

The car rolls forward, and the two men quickly move out of the frame. The whole film clip lasts seconds. No loud pops. No screams. No sirens. No human faces. No blood. It would be a leap for anyone to connect the fleeting image on the screen with the human tragedy it reflected.

After watching himself get shot and paralyzed, Shawn sought out a familiar face in the gallery. He made eye contact with his aunt Jaci and took a deep breath. At that instant, an African American woman with a blonde dye job sitting next to Jaci jumped to her feet and hurried out of the courtroom. Shawn knew another round of questions were coming. He remained composed, but now his answers to the defense lawyers came haltingly and he seemed a little unsteady under cross-examination, as if he were back on the court and facing a gimmicky zone defense he did not recognize. Two decades earlier, Luther Bedford would have signaled for a timeout to help Shawn.

Thompson's attorney, Marc Gottreich, asked Shawn if he'd initially told police that he could identify both of his assailants.

"I'm not sure. I might have," Shawn said.

Was he able to identify anyone from the photos the police had showed him at the hospital? Gottreich wondered.

"Not initially," Harrington said.

"And you couldn't identify the second guy, the one behind the car?"

Harrington corrected him. "It was more to the side," he said, but no, he never identified the second shooter. Only Davis, who stood at the intersection past the front end of the car.

The defense strategy was tricky because while the defendants were charged with the same crimes, they had different counsel and faced different odds. The jury could return a mixed verdict, for example, convicting Davis, who'd been identified by both Shawn and Naja, but not Thompson, whom only Naja identified. Gottreich understood this. He shared strategy with Davis's attorneys, but he also left a little space between his client, Thompson, and the codefendant.

Davis's attorney, Donna Rotunno, has a soft voice but cuts an imposing figure with her long brown hair and striking features. She is tall even without the high heels. She needed to cast doubt on Shawn's identification of her client but obviously didn't want to be seen as harassing the shooting victim in the wheelchair. She unloaded a series of questions she already knew the answers to in order to undermine the identification of the shooters.

On the day of the shooting, Shawn said he'd been shot by two black males and he described their jackets and hoodies to police. You didn't mention eye color? Rotunno asked. Skin tone? Weight? Facial hair? The type of pants? The brand of shoes?

The answer to every question was no.

"And you weren't looking up as you were shielding your daughter?"

"No," Shawn said.

Rotunno asked Shawn to confirm two other facts that she returned to again and again. In the lineup Shawn was shown, only one person wore a black hoodie—Davis. And the first lineup Shawn saw with him was three and a half months after the shooting.

State's attorney Eugene Wood's response to Rotunno's cross-examination was swift and impatient.

"Before the shooting happened, you saw the individual you identified, you focused on him while you were slowing down because he was pointing at your car?" Wood asked.

Yes, Shawn said, he'd had a clear look at the person on the corner. He had noticed Davis as the rental car slowed, was absolutely certain Davis was the man he'd identified.

Wood escorted Shawn out of the courtroom.

The state called its next witness, Naja Harrington.

Naja was in her first year at Illinois State University. The burden on her was enormous. Her father, whose thinking, instincts, and composure had saved her life, had forged his steady cool playing and coaching in the pressurized Red West conference. A basketball star, communications major, and coach, he was used to an intense level of stress, being in the spotlight, and answering difficult questions. Naja had grown up differently, and on this day she looked young and vulnerable enough that at a glance she might be mistaken for the high school sophomore she was on the day of the shooting. Six months earlier, at her off-to-college trunk party, she had been tongue-tied and embarrassed when it came time to speak up and thank family and friends. Now she had to hold up under the sharp questioning of seasoned attorneys with everything at stake.

Naja put any doubts to rest as soon as she began speaking. Poised and methodical, she detailed what happened that morning. She saw two men on the right side of Hamlin Street, one on the side of the car, another up ahead at the Augusta intersection, perhaps twenty-five feet away. The man at the intersection wore a black hoodie with gray sleeves and the one on the sidewalk, to the side of the car, wore an orange Chicago Bears jacket.

"I had no trouble seeing them," Naja said. "The guy in orange was about fifteen feet away. I saw him first."

She knew that the sounds she heard next were gunshots, but initially she didn't know where they came from. The first hit the back passenger door, and her father pushed her down as bullets hit the rear window. She heard ten to fifteen shots total. The car rolled into a snowbank, and she didn't know at first that her father had been wounded. A white man appeared at the car, asked if she was all right, and he offered to call 911.

The state took her off the witness stand briefly to have her pick out the defendants in various lineup photos, printed and displayed on the TV monitor. She didn't hesitate once, stretching to point at the monitor over her head. When asked if she recognized in court the man she'd previously identified in the black hoodie, she pointed at Davis. "He's wearing a blue blazer, closest to the corner," she said. Next she identified Thompson, saying, "He's the one farthest from the corner, wearing maroon." The more Naja spoke, the more she emanated confidence.

Rotunno emphasized that Naja was upset when looking at the lineup, that the man in the hoodie had had his hood up, his face turned away part of the time. Like her father, Naja had given police few specifics about the shooters beyond clothing—two young black males, average height. Rotunno ran through the same list of features she'd questioned Shawn on. No mention of skin tone? Eye color, facial hair, or weight?

No, Naja said. She had offered no details about any of that.

Shawn saw just one lineup with Davis in it, the one in which only Davis wore a dark hoodie. Naja had seen another in which all the participants wore hoodies and had the hoods up.

"In the lineup where they all wore hoodies," Rotunno asked, "how could you recognize people?"

"By their face," Naja said, as if it was the most obvious answer in the world.

———————————

The second day of the trial was dominated by a string of expert and police witnesses, patrol officers, detectives, an evidence technician, and a forensic scientist. (Surprisingly, Jason Edwards, the former high school basketball star who subdued Thompson at the Barber Shop, was not called.)

The evidence presented seemed more real than the pantomime-like video footage. Five bullet holes in the car door, three bullets retrieved from inside the car, one that fell out of Shawn's clothes in the ambulance. There were the recovered .40-caliber expended rounds in and around the rental car, the one live .380-caliber round, the recovered .380-caliber cartridge case from in front of the grocery store. The matching bullets from the crime two days earlier. And, of course, the hole in Naja's headrest.

Detective Mark Leavitt testified that Charles Molette's interview lasted an hour, and that Molette said he had witnessed Stay High and Lil' Ced shoot a young man named Darren Deer two days before Shawn was shot. Molette, the police officer said, provided information that implicated them in Shawn's shooting.

The defense attorneys hammered at the police for not releasing the typical "Investigative Alert" (IA) after getting all this information from Molette. It was only after matching the ballistics from the two shootings that an IA was released. Someone could infer from this that the cops had no faith in Molette's information.

The defense also pressed hard on the fact that only Naja Harrington could ID both shooters from lineups. Although Shawn had told police he could spot both shooters if given the chance, he could only pick out Davis and was never shown a lineup with Thompson.

Although there was no chance they might testify, a dozen policemen sat in the gallery on the final day of the trial. The reason for their attendance was obvious—they believed they had nabbed the right guys, they supported the prosecution, they wanted two guilty verdicts.

In closing arguments, the state went first, followed by the defense. The state was allowed time for a final response. Assistant state's attorney Michael O'Malley spoke in fairly formal language.

"Three years ago, Shawn Harrington lost the use of his legs and nearly his life because of the violence of these two men," O'Malley said. "Acts such as the ones they committed are hard to comprehend. Such brazen malice directed at another human being is almost beyond the pale of reason."

O'Malley put definitions and portions of the jury instructions on the TV monitor for the jury as he made his argument. The jury was instructed to determine if each defendant "or one for whose conduct he is responsible" was guilty or innocent. The phrase, which O'Malley used multiple times, meant that Davis and Thompson were in it together, each responsible under the law for the damage the other did. Each man could be called equally guilty whatever his level of involvement.

Of course the defense tried to cast doubt on everything. Why hadn't the prosecution proven that Charles Molette actually knew the two accused men? Why didn't the prosecution prove that Thompson and Davis knew each other? Why hadn't Thompson been put in a lineup for Shawn? Why was Davis the only man in his lineup wearing a hoodie when Shawn identified him? Why weren't more cops in the room with Naja when she identified the shooters? How come police never searched for the orange Chicago Bears jacket? Where were the guns used in the shooting?

Eugene Wood delivered the state's response. Calm and collected through most of the trial, now he was highly animated.

"Naja Harrington absolutely *nails* them in the lineup," Wood said. "She knows who is who. Deandre Thompson was a little north of the intersection, right by the car. Cedryck Davis was on the corner and had the other gun."

Jury deliberations began Friday. The entire trial had lasted less than a week. Neither Davis nor Thompson had taken the stand to testify or provided an alibi. Neither had a witness who could attest that they were not at the 7:45 AM scene of the crime. Defense attorneys had left the burden of proof to the prosecution, whose case hinged on three things. First, Shawn picking out Davis three months after the shooting. Second, the wobbly witness Charles Molette, who had recanted and was serving a five-year prison term—jurors had to decide if and *when* was he telling the truth. Finally, the prosecution's case rested mostly on the testimony of a cool and self-assured teenaged honor roll student, Naja Harrington.

The next day, Shawn returned to New Mexico State for a halftime fundraiser. He was in such a good mood that it gave me pause. This was the second time NMSU's athletics department honored him, and on this occasion they created a local Shawn Harrington Recovery Fund. New head coach Paul Weir gave Shawn the hero treatment, bringing him into the locker room to wish the Aggies well. At the halftime ceremony, Shawn was presented with a framed Aggie jersey. He didn't seem to notice the logo for the Aggies on our team's warmup gear—"Pistol Pete" waving a pistol. I didn't bring it up.

Shawn and I always viewed his single season at New Mexico State very differently. Although he'd played exceptionally well before getting hurt, the team had a subpar record. I always believed he was cast off. His version is that he decided to leave of his own volition after leading the team in scoring, assists, and steals. I did not know how he stayed so resolutely positive about his time in New Mexico. We'd yanked his scholarship—subtly, yes, but deliberately. Nobody tried to talk him into staying when he mentioned transferring to Northwest Missouri. Perhaps I had misremembered the circumstances. In any case, I was relieved that Shawn didn't blame me for his departure from New Mexico State. He clearly had a different way of thinking about obstacles and bad news.

"That's just the way business is done in the basketball world," he said to me once, and in many ways his take was accurate. I stopped bringing it up. I wish I could say today that I believe I am wrong, that Shawn was correct, but I still can't, and I have nobody else to ask. I've long been estranged from the old head coach, and I see him as less reliable than me. Our other assistants either were not in meetings about Shawn's status or do not remember. It is also possible I am guilty of some kind of clouded thinking, believing the NMSU provost had made verbal promise of a scholarship to Shawn's daughter Naja, or that I completely misunderstood that conversation. But Shawn said he heard precisely what I heard. Did the provost make the academic equivalent of a campaign promise—or, worse, some kind of goodwill "recruiting talk," a friendly con that I knew all too well? Nobody at NMSU ever explained to us the decision, other than the brief e-mailed mention of Naja's grades being "seemingly better when we spoke in the spring."

———————

The jury deliberated as we drove around Las Cruces with the windows down, Shawn marveling at the mountains and the sunshine. At the end of this drive, state's attorney Eugene Wood called with the verdict. Both Deandre Thompson and Cedryck Davis were found guilty on all counts.

Wood said the obvious, that this time Naja Harrington was the hero. Her unwavering testimony sealed the case. The shooters were looking at a minimum of fifty years of prison time.

"You don't know what a relief this is," Shawn told me.

———————

Ten days after the verdict, former Marshall player and coach Courtney Hargrays died of complications from his car crash.

24

THE COMBINED WEST SIDE NEIGHBORHOODS OF GARFIELD PARK, Austin, Lawndale, and West Humboldt Park—where Shawn Harrington was reared, educated, employed, and shot—have the highest incidence of gun violence in the city.

Chicago, like other large cities in America, has actually experienced a steady decline in killings over the last twenty-five years. While Chicago's murder rate is alarming, it is actually lower than during the mid-1990s, when homicides peaked at more than nine hundred a year. But shootings are up. And most experts concede that the declining murder rates are a result of the technologically advanced trauma units that now dot the city landscape.

The year Shawn was shot, the City of Chicago released the police camera records of the execution of Laquan McDonald, thirteen months after Mayor Rahm Emmanuel's office signed off on a $5 million payout to McDonald's family. The persistence of freelance journalist Brandon Smith kept the story alive. Smith, using the Freedom of Information Act, finally forced the city to release the police cam video, which revealed a disturbingly needless assassination of a seventeen-year-old. In the video, a host of police and squad cars gathered around McDonald, who is clearly carrying a knife. As he strode away from the police, an officer named Jason Van Dyke opened fire, shooting over a dozen times.

In 2014, the year Shawn was shot, there were twenty-six hundred shootings in Chicago. That was up from 2,272 in the previous year. About 70 percent of those were of teenagers or young black men shooting each other, a number that remains consistent over the past decade.

In 2015, shooting victims, those who lived, numbered 2,964. Homicides that year totaled 480. By 2016, shooting victims totaled 4,367. The vast majority of the 762 murders that year were gun related.

"There's a lot of hatred going around," says Citron Miller. The former Marshall player came home to Chicago after one year of junior college. He now works for the Chicago Park District. "There's no guidance," he says. "Everyone is just running wild."

Even in the aftermath of the Marshall players' shootings, Dorothy Gaters insists on keeping things in perspective. "People have asked me how I deal with the violence on the West Side of Chicago, and my answer is this. Gun violence is a *national* problem, not a West Side or Chicago problem." She pauses here before pointing out, "Columbine High School isn't on the West Side, and neither is Sandy Hook Elementary School. San Bernadino isn't, either."

Neither, it should be noted, is Las Vegas. Or Aurora or Colorado Springs. Or Charleston, South Carolina. Or Virginia Tech. Or, for that

A new purpose: T-shirts at the admissions table for the first Stop the Violence tournament put on by Shawn and Jimmy Sanders. *Michael James*

matter, Elkhart, Indiana. Saint Louis, New Orleans, Albuquerque, and Newark all have a higher per-capita murder rate.

"We've all got to push," Gaters says, "and teach nonviolence."

"Most defendants act fearful and abashed at a sentencing hearing," veteran *Sun-Times* court reporter Andy Grimm says. Not Cedryck Davis and Deandre Thompson.

Grimm says just before they were sentenced, the young men were surprisingly nonchalant and wore "bemused and amused smirks."

Shawn and his family had declined to attend, but the shooters had an unusually high number of family and friends there. While many of Chicago's accused rely on public defenders, both Thompson and Davis had retained relatively high profile lawyers.

All in all, it was an unusual day in court. Often the convicted make a general apology, if only because acceptance of guilt, even a hint of culpability, is considered by the judges before sentencing. Making a claim of outright innocence at sentencing can damage a defendant's chance at a lighter sentence. A small percentage of people do assert their innocence, and Davis had done exactly that in a prepared statement. Davis took the liberty of signing Thompson's name to it as well. Thompson's lawyer insisted that his client's name be removed.

The shooters sat together, whispered back and forth, then peered over their shoulders to family members in the gallery. "I think they had low expectations," Grimm says.

Thompson seemed to focus, however, when Naja Harrington and her mother's victim's impact statements were read aloud.

Both shooters were sentenced to fifty-nine years in prison.

Truth-in-sentencing laws for gun crimes in the state mean Cedrick Davis and Deandre Thompson will spend fifty-two years behind bars before they can apply for parole—both young men will be at least in their mid-seventies when they are released. The ordeal was over, but it did not feel like anything you might call a "conclusion."

On May 15, 2017, a few weeks before the final manuscript for this book was due, former Marshall player James King was shot to death with a single bullet.

James King was Marshall's undersized senior center in 2013–2014, the year Shawn got shot. Like all Commandos, King was known for relentlessly battling bigger opponents. His murder, like the other five, was a kick in the gut for Shawn, but this one was different. King was one of Shawn's special education students, and they had spent hours together in the classrooms. King rarely got a lift from Shawn because he lived so close to Marshall, but they were close.

King had been visiting relatives in Englewood, a violence-plagued area on the South Side, nine miles from Marshall. At nearly midnight, and moments after saying his good-byes, he was murdered in front of his car. He had no documented history of gang involvement. He had been arrested for marijuana once, and another time for "simple battery" (a fistfight). In other words, he was a typical American teenager in many

An old soul: James King, Marshall's undersized center in 2013–2014, became the sixth Commando killed by gunfire in 2017. *Worsom Robinson*

ways. King was twenty-one years old. This appeared to be a mistaken identity shooting, like Shawn's.

King's friends and teammates all describe him as laid-back. He loved his hats, particularly his Chicago White Sox baseball model, and his "Buck 50" hat, a stylish retro design from the 1990s that featured the face of a clock on top of the snakeskin-lined brim. King was an old soul, happy to lounge around on the couch, sip a beer or two, and occasionally even smoke a fat cigar. He did not go out much, had no urge to run around at night.

On an early season road trip in 2013, Coach Henry Cotton polled the team. Who did the Commandos want as team captain?

Tyrese Williford, just a sophomore then, suggested James King. He got shouted down. King was too quiet, everyone else said. That was exactly what made James King different. "He never got mad at anyone, never talked trash, and he kept to himself, minding his own business," Williford recalls. "I thought of him as a leader for those reasons."

James King was not picked as captain but he played his best basketball of the season in the following week, registering a triple double in the next two games. The reason for his energy and motivation was obvious. Somebody, a lowly sophomore, had publicly recognized his value.

POSTSCRIPT

THE SEARCH FOR ARNE DUNCAN'S cell phone number kept stalling, as if he were an elite basketball recruit beyond my grasp. Two weeks after the trial, I finally tracked it down. As was often the case in my advocating for Shawn, I had been pounding on the wrong doors. Plenty of Chicago coaches still had Arne's number from the days when he was CEO of the school system. While I was going after attorneys, business bigwigs, and philanthropists who might know Duncan, the answer waited for me in the Chicago basketball community that I used to know so well. In the spring of 2017, I got through. He told me he had read the *New York Times* piece on Shawn and was surprised to learn that he was still in a rut. His tone was compassionate. He was genuine and said he would make some calls. I learned later that Duncan occasionally visited the grieving families of teenagers who were killed. He did not seem like a typical administrator.

Within a week of my first conversation with Duncan, and three years after the shooting, Shawn got his second call from the Chicago Public Schools. A few days later, they offered him a new position at his old school as a "restorative justice counselor." He would counsel students, like Tim Triplett, who had families and friends damaged by gun violence.

Shawn got a second job offer soon after that, this one from the office of Illinois secretary of state Jesse White. He suddenly had two good options to consider, but I knew which one he would choose. By June, Arne Duncan and I reversed rolls. He began bugging me to make sure that Shawn was set to return to work at Marshall.

That summer, Shawn's legs began to occasionally twitch involuntarily. It was impossible to say what that meant exactly, a bit mysterious, but his nerves had somehow changed at some level.

Shawn started his new position at Marshall in the fall of 2017 at twice the hourly wage of his old job. The new role might evolve into traveling from school to school to speak with at-risk kids, athletes, and coaches. While he no longer had the big Expedition to give a kid a lift home, he did have the orange Shaq-mobile. His real office was now on the first floor at Marshall, so an elevator was not imperative.

Before anyone commends me for my perseverance, let me confess. I occasionally get calls from former players. They want help getting back into school, finding a team overseas, landing a post-basketball job, or paying a delinquent bill. Most of these guys I cannot or do not support. There are more than a few ex-players who I have no interest in ever seeing again. Anyone who has coached at a high level for very long will understand this. The truth is that if Shawn had not been shot, I likely would have never seen him again.

The new window opened to me by Shawn's shooting offered a very different view of the city, one with some insight, limited as it might be. I used that window to reconnect with Shawn, think about the bloodshed and how it has affected the people at Marshall. If there is any redemption in this book, it abides in Shawn's unique courage, mindset, and endurance. My role as a white person who became determined to help an African American man in need is one I struggled with, since it fits with a common but problematic narrative. A dozen other people have quietly worked to make Shawn's life better, but this story is the one from my point of view.

As the number of Marshall ballplayers murdered grew, this book nearly veered out of control. Shawn Holloway, Tim Triplett, Marcus Patrick, Keyon Boyd, Edward Bryant, James King—all murdered. Shawn Harrington, Martin Satterfield, Terrell Allen all wounded by gunfire. Shawn's case was the only one that led to an arrest. Nothing devastates a neighborhood more completely than an unsolved murder or shooting. As I connected with people on the West Side, I learned that everyone— players, coaches, teachers, parents—had a connection to the carnage.

Three codes of silence exist in Chicago. The first within the police force, and the second among victims of gang-related crimes, have been well documented. The third has not. That code of silence is the inability or unwillingness of people affected by gun violence to tell their stories to young people, to each other, and to Chicagoans not directly affected.

People I interviewed often resisted opening up, but I was guilty of that myself. During my eight years coaching at UTEP in the 1980s, I had a great stress-reliever, an outdoor El Paso boxing gym directed by Rocky Galarza. The boxing workout was a therapy that transported me far away from college hoops. I rarely missed a day and because of my own pathetic and aborted playing career in basketball, Rocky became my coach more than anyone else had. Rocky Galarza was murdered in his sleep by a girlfriend in 1997. Just before Shawn returned to work at Marshall, I finally told him Rocky's story.

Tim Triplett never revealed to Shawn that his father had been murdered or that his brother died months before he enrolled at Marshall. Shawn did not tell Triplett or the Commandos about Frinda Harrington's murder. Coach Henry Cotton never showed his team or Shawn the scar where the bullet hit his leg. This code of silence seems nearly as crippling as the first two. My hope is that this book might push others, particularly Chicago Public School students, to write or tell their stories of how gun violence has affected their lives.

In July 2017, Shawn attended a stepping picnic at Garfield Park. "Steppin' in the Park" is a regular drug-and-alcohol-free dance event created for people in recovery. As word spread, the afternoon dance attracted all kinds, although the music is considered outdated by the younger crowd. There was no dance floor on the sunny July afternoon that Shawn attended; without any recent rainfall, the dancers' busy feet lifted a vague haze from the patchy grass. While Shawn was marveling at the dancers and talking to friends, he felt a warm hand on his back. He turned to see an African American woman with blonde hair.

"You don't know me," she said, "but I hope that God will continue to bless you in your life." She bent at her waist to give Shawn a long embrace.

Shawn thanked her and acknowledged his many blessings, all the while trying to place this lady's face. He knew her from somewhere. They looked at each other for a long moment.

"My son," the woman finally said, "was one of the young men who shot you." She gave Shawn a sad smile and moved away.

Many Chicagoans ignore the situation or tune it out, as I once did, in order to simply move forward and not spend their days weeping in a closet. On the West Side, that's impossible. There, violence can't be contained in the morning paper or the nightly news. To most of those in "safe" neighborhoods, the epidemic happens "over there," and to "them," and is an acceptable level of violence. Arne Duncan, a much wiser man than me, must agree. One day, he sent me three texts that, combined, said this:

"Black lives don't matter. We can say they do, but our collective actions don't match the words. In fact, quite the opposite. If these were white folks being killed in Chicago, everything would change."

Shawn displayed astonishing courage when the bullets started flying, something that I first attributed to his love of his daughter. Later, I factored in his playing for Luther Bedford. A third aspect in his background has to be considered, and that is his long association with gun violence on the West Side. Shawn reacted like a loving father and an unselfish point guard, yes, but he also responded like a combat veteran.

Shawn continues to be a great father, and to think like a point guard, too, though he has plenty of his own problems to worry about. For example, he connected former Marshall student Anthony Hunter to a nonprofit art collective called Project Onward, which works with talented artists overcoming challenges such as autism. Hunter had been languishing at home after finding Chicago's Art Institute unaffordable. And Shawn helped Dorothy Gaters organize a benefit game to raise money for the Courtney Hargrays Memorial Scholarship Fund, using his own savings to pay for a memorial banner.

———————

Of course there's no way Luther Bedford could know that I belatedly tried to keep my flimsy word, finally honored my commitment to his player. I immersed myself in helping Shawn with the vague hope that my dishonesty (in recruiting him while pretending to be his friend) and faithlessness (in watching him forced out at New Mexico State) was not the final buzzer. I used to be a college recruiter but I was also a coach, and like any coach who has done poorly, I was anxious for another season to begin. Naja making good grades at Illinois State was a first step. Shawn's new job was another. Everything after his shooting is the final quarter of a hard-fought game.

I recently sat down with the Chicago journalist John Conroy and told him Shawn's entire story. I thought Conroy would comment on the shootings, the trial, our health care system, or the role of the police. Instead he said, "I hope that you and Shawn can get to be real friends now."

I hope so, too.

"My Daddy has had a lot of happy times," Naja Harrington says, "since it all happened. He has his down times, but he's been uplifted." *Michael James*

ACKNOWLEDGMENTS

I WOULD LIKE TO THANK several friends for their sage advice on this book during the writing and editing process. First, Barry Pearce, whose sharp eye, sense of story, working knowledge of Chicago, and steadfast friendship have been invaluable.

Thanks also to Michael Austin, whose wisdom and suggestions were of great help.

Robert Boswell, as always, helped with shrewd critical advice. Could any writer have a better friend or mentor? Boswell and his wife, the great short-story writer Antonya Nelson, have enriched my life in countless ways for over two decades.

Hillary Billman, Jerry Hardin, Tom Spieczny, Susan Hammond, and Kitty Spalding were perceptive early readers whose comments were important.

My wife, Connie Voisine, is usually my last reader because of her insight and fearlessness. Thanks, Connie. Thanks to Alma, and my parents, Arnold and Julia Bradburd.

Veteran Chicago journalist John Conroy has changed the world with his brilliant investigative reporting. He has been an inspiration to me since 1982.

Conroy introduced me to Alex Kotlowitz, whose books about race and Chicago have been a big influence.

Officers Sherod Dent, Erick Von Kondrat, Miguel Flores, and Jason Edwards of the Chicago Police Department were perceptive, engaging, and fully human. Other police officers were helpful as well.

Thanks to New Mexico State employees Mario Moccia and Chet Savage. Also Marvin Menzies, Paul Weir, and Dan Howard.

Thanks to the journalists who took a strong interest in the Shawn Harrington story, especially Dan McGrath. Also, David Zirin, Ben

Osborne, Dawn Turner-Trice, Rick Telander, David Kaplan and Sarah Lauch, and Alexander Wolff, who provided key insights.

Big thanks to Joe Nocera, who did a terrific piece for the *New York Times* that changed the discussion and Shawn's profile. That led to HBO featuring Shawn on *Real Sports*. Thanks to Bryant Gumbel, Katie Melone, and Maggie Burbank at HBO.

Nocera's piece also connected Shawn to a former New York prosecutor, Julian Wise, who has become a close friend to Shawn. Wise brought Shawn out to speak at the prestigious law firm of Schulte, Zabel, and Roth in Manhattan.

Special thanks to Dwight Anderson.

Another New Yorker, Madelaine Haberman, led the charge in helping Shawn get his driver's license and "Shaq-mobile" in order.

Three brokers took an intense interest in Shawn and were moved by his courage. Big thanks to all of them: Greg Fleming, George Cook, and Steve Yellen. Any time I hear Wall Street get bashed, I make sure to bring up this remarkable trio of great humanitarians.

Thanks to two of the top photographers in Chicago, Michael Gaylord James and Worthem Robinson.

Gift of Hope worker Susan Cochran has become a caring friend and advisor for both Shawn and me.

Charity Stripe and Mitch Saltzstein have continued to help Shawn and have proven invaluable.

Richard Lapchick and Suzi Katz at the National Consortium for Academics and Sport recognized Shawn and his courage by making him Coach of the Year in 2015.

Former LSU coach Dale Brown has been relentless in his interest, care, and concern about Shawn. Dale led Shawn to the pinnacle for any player or coach, the NCAA Final Four, although they did not take the usual route. That led to Shawn meeting Shaquille O'Neal and a new independence.

David Druker and Illinois Secretary of State Jesse White have been great.

Arne Duncan changed the course of Shawn's life and the arc of this book. Thanks so much, Arne.

Attorneys Eugene Woods and Donna Rotunno squared off in court, but both are smart, kind, and offered interesting observations.

Thanks to Bobby, Lee, and John Byrd.

Thanks to Jon Billman, who helps keep me focused. Same deal with Tony Hoagland and Kathleen Lee.

Thanks also to Jordan Wankoff, Paul Tyler, Matthew Muhammad, Tracy Dildy, Jelani Boline, Sean Pryor, Ernest Obedele Starks, Mark Medoff, Mat Johnson, John Keane, Joe Scapellato, Rory Fanning at Haymarket Books, Tony Barone, Jack Fitzgerald, Patty Nolan, Dick Versace, Billy Knox, Brendan Bulger and his wife Caroline, poet Jeff Thompson, Vince Carter, Bobbito "Kool Bob Love" Garcia, Katy Hogan, Paige James, Dana Kroos, Chris Bracey and Matt Maloney at Oak Park-River Forest High School, David Brower, Keith Johnson, Johnny Smooth Melvin, Charles Redmond, Thomas Trotter, David Bachman, George Demos, Bob Ociepka, Lorenzo Davis, Camille Acker, Peter Gilbert, Tony Judge, Jon Ferguson, Lewis Thorpe, Casey Gray, Lily Hoang, Father Michael Pfleger, Steve "Snow" Sanderson, Lou Adams, Issaiah Hayes, Jack Nixon, Marlon "Pookie" Jones, Jason Groves, Dan Crosby, Leo Catholic High School, Richard Coltharp, John and Pat Quinn, Michael Haywood, Lydia Apodaca, Al McKinnie, Nick Nurse, Clay Billman, Chris Burnham, Phil Hurst, Chris Darnell, Judge Wendell Griffen, Sean Ryan, Richard Greenfield, Gar and Leslie Forman, Rhys Jones, Mark Rudd, Jim Tracey, Lillie Robertson, Ken Cochran, Charles Redmond, Tom and Sylvia Bennet, Casey Owens, Liz Schirmer, and Rob Wilder.

Thanks to Kashanna Haggard and Jutuan Brown for their endurance and courage.

Thanks to Barry Thatcher, who kept pushing me in the right direction.

Thanks to the *Chicago Tribune, New York Times,* the *Sun-Times* and Andy Grimm, *Las Cruces Sun-News, Las Cruces Bulletin,* the *Elkhart Truth,* and the University of Chicago Crime Lab, an independent research center founded in 2008.

Special thanks to Jimmy Sanders, who has partnered with Shawn with his camps and tournaments.

Special thanks to Darrell Brown, who passed away while I was working on this book.

Thanks to Lou and Mary Henson for treating Shawn like one of their own.

Special thanks to my great friend Dennis Daily, who dug deep to uncover his old photos of Shawn playing at New Mexico State.

Thanks to the people who harness the power of sport to push for social justice and racial progress: David Meggyesy, Doug Harris, Phillip Shinnick, Steve Yellen, Gordon Thompson, Michael James, and the crew at Athletes United for Peace. Also Tracy Yellen, Dave Cullen, George Quinlan, Toni Smith, Rory Fanning and Craig Hodges, Barbara Horne, and John Carlos. Thanks to PeacePlayers International and Sean Touhey, Brendan Touhey, Gareth Harper, Casey Tryon, Rochelle Coleman, and Ryan Hage.

Thanks to Gary Broadnax and Jerry Hardin at Quest Multisport for helping Shawn.

Thanks to Mark Jackson at Project Onward and the Bridgeport Art Center for their help with Anthony Hunter.

Thanks to everyone at Marshall High School, including Dorothy Gaters, Gwen Howard, Tyrone Hayes, Murph, Stephanie Dobrin, Jennifer Jones, and Henry Cotton. Special thanks to Arthur Agee for his insight and wisdom. Thanks to other Commandos as well: Citron Miller, Terrell Allen, Martin Satterfield, Ontario Brown, and Tyrese Williford. Thanks to the Marshall Alumni Association. Maurice Ali Copeland has been a great friend to Shawn and may soon qualify for status as an Honorary Marshall Commando.

Special thanks to Estell Harper for her kindness, grace, and dignity.

Thanks to Glen Heffernan, Tevin King, and Teadric Anderson for their insight into the city and the world of basketball.

Thanks to Gabrielle Giffords and Peter Ambler.

I lived in Belfast, my second favorite city, for ten months while writing this book. I learned a lot about how people wrecked by gun violence can move forward. Thanks to Belfast friends Mickey Burns, Brendan McCourt, John T. Davis, Kathleen McCracken, Bernie Stocks, Hazlett Keers, David and Claudia at No Alibis Bookstore, David Cullen, Katie Radford, Brendan O'Hare, Stevie Porter, Gerry McCartney, Shane McAleer, Máirtín Ó Muilleoir, Muriel Moore, and David Williams. Also thanks to Larry Nugent, Shane McAleer, Ciaran Dalton, Sile Boylan-O'Connor, and Clodagh Ryan for their insight into the violence in the north of Ireland.

Thanks to Jutuan Brown and Kashanna Haggard.

Thanks to Bonnie Nadell.

Thanks to Lee K. Abbott and Craig Holden for their sage advice and friendship.

I scored just thirteen points in my college career, but I scored big with the Chicago Review Press and Lawrence Hill Books. Editor supreme Yuval Taylor was the only one who saw the pitch for this book, and he recognized the power of the story and a writer who needed a lot of help. Thanks also to team members Michelle Williams, Caitlin Eck, and Mary Kravenas.

Thanks to young hotshot photographer Adam Jason Cohen for the photo on the cover of this book.

Special thanks to Kim Jenkins, Claretha Jenkins, Naja Harrington and Malia Harrington, and Jaci Harrington, five of the greatest women in Chicago.

I would like to acknowledge the gunshot victims mentioned in this book and their families. Four of them survived: Shawn Harrington, Terrell Allen, Martin Satterfield, and Henry Cotton. Seven of them did not survive: Frinda Harrington, Shawn Holloway, Tim Triplett, Marcus Patrick, Keyon Boyd, Edward Bryant, and James King.

Finally, a million thanks to Shawn Harrington, who has done more for me than I ever could for him. C4L.

INDEX

Page numbers in italics refer to images. The abbreviation S.H. refers to Shawn Harrington.